WORKING OF MUTUAL FUND ORGANISATIONS IN INDIA

Working of Mutual Fund Organisations in India

P. MOHANA RAO

KANISHKA PUBLISHERS, DISTRIBUTORS
NEW DELHI 110002

KANISHKA PUBLISHERS, DISTRIBUTORS
4697/5-21A, Ansari Road, Daryaganj
New Delhi -110 002
Phones : 2327 0497, 2328 8285
Fax : 011-2328 8285
E-mail : kanishka_publishing@yahoo.co.in

First Published 1998
Second Edition 2013

ISBN: 978-81-7391-263-7

PRINTED IN INDIA

Published by Madan Sachdeva for Kanishka Publishers, Distributors, 4697/5-21A, Ansari Road, Daryaganj, New Delhi-110 002, Typeset by Sunshine Graphics, Delhi, and Printed at Rajdhani Printers, Delhi.

Preface

Metamorphic changes took place in Indian Financial System during eighties and nineties consequent upon deregulation and liberalisation of economic policies of the Government. A lot of structural changes and innovations have occurred both in International and National Financial System. Consequently, a sea change in money and capital markets undergone for furtherance in financial activities. Simultaneously, household savings and investment attitude and preference have increased. Emergence of new financial institutions and instruments came into existence to cater to the needs of public.

As household sector's share is much large in the country's savings, it is all more important to show a nice and right path for their savings. The way for the household sector's investment in Mutual Funds in India made a beginning in the second half of the eighties although UTI doing business since 1964 as a premier institution in the Mutual Fund Industry. Till 1986, it continued as a Mutual Fund monark in India.

To meet the needs of vast household and middle class category of Indian population, new financial instruments and institutions are aimed at increasing the range of investment avenues. Such instruments are Units and institutions are Mutual Funds.

A Mutual Fund is a company, corporation, trust, partnership that combines the assets of all of its shareholders or partners into one common investment account for the purpose of providing diversification and professional management. This pooling allows thousands of investors to share, according to their amount of investment, the performance of the fund that is managed with what is presumed to be expertise. By means of a variety of stocks, shares, bonds, debentures, money market instruments, novel, innovative financial instruments in the funds portfolio the investing masses gain access to a wide range of securities. Mutual Funds provide a wide range of services to investors not otherwise available to the small investors. Thus, Mutual Funds are companies or corporate entities which pool the investments of a number of investors by way of investment funds of equal size. They collect funds from investors and invest in a variety of securities on behalf of investors. They distribute income among investors on an equitable manner. Thus, they act as intermediaries.

The present work is structured around latest developments in Mutual Fund Organisations which consists of 8 Chapters. First Chapter deals in Mutual Funds—An Indian Panorama. The Second Chapter highlights on Methodology. Third Chapter focuses on Working of Mutual Funds. Fourth Chapter emphasises on Investment Procedure of Mutual Funds. Fifth Chapter analysis Accounting and Reporting Standards for Mutual Funds. Sixth Chapter critically deals in perceptions of many sections of society. Seventh Chapter deals in Financial System and Institutional Services and Eighth Chapter deals in Conclusions.

In undertaking this project the author had to refer to national as well as international journals and reports. To the writers, he expresses his gratitude. He owes special thanks to his family members particularly to his wife and kids for their patience and tolerance throughout the project.

The research expresses his gratitude to the Mutual Fund managers for their timely supply of materials and reports and help they extended.

The author is grateful to University Grants Commission, New Delhi for funding the present study under minor research project scheme.

P. Mohana Rao

Contents

	Preface	v
1.	Mutual Funds—An Indian Panorama	1
2.	Methodology	32
3.	Working of Mutual Funds	44
4.	Investment Procedure of Mutual Funds	99
5.	Accounting and Reporting Practices in Mutual Funds	119
6.	Investors' Perceptions on Mutual Funds	146
7.	Financial System and Institutional Services	161
8.	Conclusions	239
	Questionnaire	245
	Bibliography	249
	Index	256

CHAPTER ONE

Mutual Funds—An Indian Panorama

Introduction

Basically Mutual Funds (MFs) are institutions who mobilise resources from the small investors. The savings of small investors are, thereafter, utilised to purchase the securities of companies and corporations. It is, thus, an institutional arrangement for resource mobilisation from small, marginal and household sector investors. Such accumulated funds are utilised to acquire shares and securities of reputed companies. Mutual Funds become a major vehicle for mobilisation of savings, particularly from small and household sectors, for the investment in stock-market. The importance of mutual funds has been increasing in the capital market by expanding the investors base. In the 1992-93 budget, the Finance Minister's proposal to allow to set up mutual funds in joint and private sectors has further gained the momentum and significance for the mutual funds. A mutual fund is an institutional device or an investment vehicle through which, the investors pool their funds under the direction of an investment manager. These funds are invested in a wide variety of portfolios of securities in such a way as to minimise risk, while ensuring safety and steady return. MF is an institutional device to bridge the gap between the supply and demand of capital in the market. A Mutual Fund is an investment company or a trust that pools the resources of thousands of its shareholders or unit-holders and invests on behalf of them in diversified securities and a cross-section of companies to attain the objectives of the investors, which in return achieve income or growth or both.

Mutual Funds are the major types of investment companies. Investment Companies are financial intermediaries (middlemen) that pool the funds of investors who are seeking some general investment objective and invest them in a number of frequently traded different types of securities (e.g., Common Stock, bonds, money market securities). These pooled funds provide thousands of investors with proportional ownership of diversified portfolios which are operated by professional investment managers.[1] According to the author, Mutual Fund is an investment company. Investment Company is a financial intermediary (middleman) which pools the funds of investors. Investors are contributing their moneys or savings into the company. Such investable funds are invested in the frequently traded securities in stock-markets. The funds are invested in different types securities, e.g., common stock, bonds, money market securities. These pooled funds provide thousands of investors with proportional ownership of diversified portfolios. The management of funds and investment policy is entrusted to an experienced professional named "Portfolio Manager".

According to Frank K. Reilly,[2] "An Investment Company is a pool of funds belonging to many individuals that is used to acquire a collection of individual investments such as stocks, bonds, other publicly traded securities." Investment Company is a company which collects funds from many individuals. These individuals are treated as investors. The funds are used to acquire stocks, bonds, other publicly traded securities.

Features

Mutual Fund Offers :

(a) Professional Management,
(b) Portfolio Management,
(c) To Common Investing Group, diversified investment opportunities are available,
(d) Collective sharing of burden out of Fund Management,

(*e*) Collective Sharing of Profit Earned,
(*f*) Less Transaction Cost, and
(*g*) Port-Folio Contraction as per the objectives of individual mutual fund scheme.

"Mutual Funds exist to give small investors an alternative way to invest in capital markets and to provide an alternative source of money to finance industries by buying their securities. Mutual Funds also allow small investors to have a measure of self-defense when investing in markets which have become increasingly dominated by giant financial institutions. By buying shares in a mutual fund, the individual becomes part of an institution and so can stand on more even terms....Mutual Funds are organised, operated, and managed by companies that do the Practical Administrative things that allow the fund to function. They select the funds strategy, hire the managers, market the shares to potential investors, and do the paper work (keeping records of shareholders' holdings, sending statements, proxies, and other materials to the investors; redeeming shares of share owners who decide to cash out etc.)."[3] From the very definition, the function of a Mutual Fund can be highlighted as:

(*a*) Mutual Fund collects nominees from small investors or unit holders;
(*b*) The nominees so collected are inverted in buying shares of companies. Thus, MFs provide funds to companies for business purposes;
(*c*) They act as indicators between investors and companies;
(*d*) By buying shares (or units) in a mutual fund, the individual investor becomes part of our institution and so can stand on more even terms.......;
(*e*) Mutual Funds are organised, operated, and managed by companies that do the practical administrative things that allow the fund to function; and
(*f*) They select the fund's strategy, hire managers, market the shares to potential investors, and do the paper work.

In the words of Joel Ross[4], Mutual Fund is "taking the 'pool' of money and investing it in the securities of wide range of companies, managers of mutual funds decide when to buy, sell, or held in order to achieve the objective of the fund..... policy removes the risk associated with putting all your eggs in one basket, as the typical small investor tends to do." According to him, Mutual Funds are collecting or pooling money from small investors. The movies are invested in a variety of securities. The Mutual Funds decide when to buy, sell or hold securities.

"A Mutual Fund means pooling the investments of a member of inventory by way of investment in units of equal size."

"Mutual Funds are Corporations which pool funds and reduce risk by diversification."

"Mutual Funds are financial intermediaries which bring a wide varieties within the reach of the most modest of investors."[5]

Mutual Fund

"A Corporation that provides an investment service for its stockholders. Organised under state laws and subject to SEC as well as state regulation wherever its shares are sold, its operations are carried on through an affiliated management company whose officers are usually officers of the fund. Known also as an open-end company, its shares are continuously marketed by the management company. Redemptions may be made at any time.[6]

According to Regulation 2 (m), "Mutual Fund means a fund established in the form of a Trust by a sponsor to raise monies by the Trustees through the sale of units to the public under one or more schemes for investing in securities in accordance with these regulations."

The features are :

1. MF is established as a fund in the form of Trust;
2. It is established by a Sponsor;
3. It is created to raise monies through sale of units;
4. It sells one or more schemes; and
5. The funds raises so are invested in securities in accordance with the regulations.

"Units" means the interest of the investors in a Mutual Fund Scheme, which consists of each unit representing one undivided share in the assets of a scheme. For instance, the amount of a particular scheme is Rs. 60 crores of which each unit is Rs. 10/- and therefore total units are 6 lakhs. Sponsor means any body corporate who, acting alone, or in combination with another body corporate, establishes mutual fund after completing formalities. Thus, sponsor can be either a single body corporate or a concern or in combination of with another body corporate. It has power to create mutual fund.

Now, hereafter, the money collected under any scheme of a Mutual Fund shall be invested only in transferable securities whether in the money market or in the capital market or in privately placed debentures or securitised debts {Reg 40(1)}.

Mutual Funds in India, are known by different names in different countries. In the United Kingdom, they are known as "Investment Trusts" while in the USA and most other countries, they are called "Investment Companies".

Phase—I (Up to 1986)

The idea of Mutual Fund took shape in India in 1963 with the set up and enactment of Unit Trust of India (UTI) by framing an Act titled UTI Act, 1963, to operate both as a financial institution and an Investment Trust. The then Finance Minister Mr. T. T. Krishnamachari, told the Parliament that "UTI would provide an opportunity for the middle and lower income groups to acquire without much difficulty, property in the form of shares....This institution is intended to cater mainly to needs of individual investors whose means are small." In 1964, the Board of Trustees formulated an open-end scheme and launched in July 1964 with sale of units being open in the month of July 1964 at the nominal value of Rs. 10 each. Thus, the UTI came out with its first open-ended scheme in 1964. Till 1987, the UTI with a very few schemes was holding the key of the entire mutual fund industry. The UTI was set up, on the lines of 'Unit Trusts' in Britain, with objective of affording small savers a means of acquiring a share in the prosperity of a number of industries through facilities for investment, incorporations the benefits of diversification, safety and reasonable return. It was, initially, subsidiary of RBI. It is managed by trustees. It was accorded a monopoly status. It was combined with management and trustees in body viz., "the board of trustees". The Unit scheme was prescribed under Section 21 of the UTI Act, 1963 following more or less on the lines of the trust deed by the UTI in UK or a prospections by mutual funds in the USA. The first scheme was titled "The Unit Scheme—1964". It was a growth cum income scheme. Till 1986-87, it launched 20 schemes and had mobilised investible funds amounting to Rs. 45,640 millions.

Phase—II (1987-1993)

The middle of 1986, there was only one Mutual Fund (MF), namely Unit Trust of India (UTI) operating in India. UTI is a public sector financial institution. As a public sector institution, UTI had a complete monopoly of the unit trust business. The scene has changed since 1986, although it still retains a near monopoly. Government of India amended the Banking Regulations Act to permit commercial banks in the public sector to set up mutual funds. The State Bank of India was the first bank to promote a mutual fund called 'SBI Mutual Fund' in July 1987. In December, 1987, Canara Bank established its subsidiary, Can-bank Mutual Fund to enter mutual fund business.

The Government permitted insurance corporations in the public sector to join the Mutual Funds bandwagon which was till then being dominated by the commercial banks. LIC of India set up LIC Mutual Fund in June, 1989, with a view to targeting small investors particularly from the rural and semi-urban areas. The General Insurance Corporation of India (GIC) set up GIC Mutual Fund in 1991.

Period 1987-1991

During this period of 1987-1991, five public sector banks and two public sector insurance corporations entered and commercial Mutual Fund business in India. Two decades later, thus, in 1986-87, Government allowed SBI to set up a Mutual Fund which was established in 1987 in the form of a Trust in accordance with the Indian Trust Act of 1882.

Reserve Bank of India Guidelines

The Reserve Bank of India (RBI) monitors the operations of nationalised banks, interalia, issued a set of guidelines in 1987. This set of guidelines were to be expected to be followed by the bank sponsored mutual funds. There are :

- *(a)* Mutual Fund should be constituted as a trust under the India Trust Act. At least two outside trustees should be in the Trust.
- *(b)* Mutual Fund should have a full time executive for the day-to-day management.

(c) Mutual Fund is separate from the sponsor bank. These should be an arm's length relationship between the mutual fund and the sponsor bank.

(d) Every sponsor bank should contribute at least Rs. 25 lakhs.

(e) A Mutual Fund should have a clear statement of objectives and policies for the fund. It should publish.

(f) Operations must be restricted to Capital Market Investments. Mutual Funds are not to undertake direct or indirect lending, underwriting, bill discounting and money market operations (subsequently Mutual Funds were allowed to undertake money market operations).

(g) Restrictions must be placed on the cost of managing any scheme.

(h) A Management Information System (MIS) should be evolved to maintain date and to submit various reports.

Ministry of Finance Guidelines

The Ministry of Finance issued guidelines in June, 1990 which are:

1. All Mutual Funds, except the Statutory ones will now require the approval of the Controller of Capital Issues. Thereafter be registered with the Securities and Exchange Board of India (SEBI). The existing mutual funds must themselves registered with SEBI with 90 days.
2. Sponsoring Institutions will have to contribute a minimum of Rs. 2 crores to the corpus of the funds. The contribution can be converted later into a subscription.
3. Such funds except those established with the declared objective of undertaking investment in immovable property shall not undertake any activity relating to acquisition of immovable property except for their own use. The fund may, however, subscribe to the bonds and debentures issued by institutions dealing in housing finance.
4. A Mutual Fund shall not invest more than 5 per cent of its assets in the shares of any company. It shall not also invest more than 5 per cent of the shares of any company under any one scheme.
5. A Mutual Fund should not normally invest in another

Mutual Fund. A Mutual Fund should not normally keep deposits with companies and other bodies corporate.

6. A Mutual Fund should maintain separate accounts in respect of each scheme.

It is to be noted that these guidelines are not applicable to Country Funds established abroad as India Fund, Indian Growth Fund which are governed by their own schemes. They get approval from Finance Ministry of Government of India.

Role of SEBI

In March, 1991, the Government, in principle handed over the function of Regulating Mutual Funds to SEBI. From March 31, 1991 the SEBI directed all the existing Mutual Funds by its guidelines.

In October 1991, SEBI issued guidelines.

SEBI is an autonomous body. The Government has accorded statutory status to SEBI as an autonomous body on January 31, 1992 for the promotion and regulation of the Capital Market.

In the interest of Investor protection, SEBI has been given wide ranging powers to oversee the constitution as well as operations of Mutual Funds. It is also empowered to impose penalty on Mutual Funds should they fail to compel with its guidelines.

Role of Private Sector

In 1992-93, the Mutual Funds industry was thrown open to private sector

In 1991-92 Budget speech, the Finance Minister announced that the private sector would soon be allowed to enter the Mutual Fund industry. Thereafter, 10 member study group headed by Dr. S.A. Dave, Chairman of the UTI, was entrusted the task of evolving a framework for legislation for the regulation of Mutual Funds may be permitted in the joint/private sector. The study group was also asked to review the existing regulatory framework for the established funds. The Dave panel submitted the following recommendations in September, 1991.

The monopoly of the Big Eight (UTI, SBI MF, Canara Bank MF, Indian Bank MF, Bank of India MF, Punjab National Bank MF, LIC MF and GIC MF) was ended by new economic policy spearheaded by Dr. Man Mohan Singh from 1991.

In October 1991, SEBI issued guidelines for the formation of Asset Management Companies (AMCs) for Mutual Funds.

The Ministry of Finance, Department of Economic Affairs, issued a comprehensive set of guidelines on February 14, 1992.

The Government issued comprehensive regulations in January 20, 1993 which have largely on the pattern of the guidelines for Mutual Funds notified by the Government on February 14, 1992.

Private Sector Mutual Funds

The existing Mutual Funds, it was felt, had failed to live upto the expectations of common investors in view of :

(i) Poor servicing.
(ii) Inordinate delays in the receipt of unit certificates.
(iii) Inordinate delays in the receipt of dividend warrants.
(iv) Indifferent performance of the most of the Mutual Fund schemes which under-performed the market thus denying the investors a reasonable return.
(v) Absence of adequate discourse return.
(vi) Lack of an investor-friendly approach in general.

These above causes have encouraged the Government to give permission to private sector to open MFs. The monopoly of the Big Eight (i.e., UTI, SBI MF, Canara Bank MF, BOI MF, Indian Bank MF, Punjab National Bank MF, LIC MF and GIC MF) was ended by the new economic policy spearheaded by Dr. Man Mohan Singh from 1991. The process of economic liberalisation threw the doors open to players in the private sector to provide the much-needed competitive edge and a wider scope of options to the investors.

Features of Private Sector Mutual Funds

Private sector MFs are allowed to take advantage of collaboration with foreign investment and fund managers.

The Finance Minister, in his Budget speech disclosed the Governments intention of allowing the private sector to launch mutual funds. Thereafter a 10 member study group headed by Dr. S.A. Dave, Chairman of the UTI, was entrusted the task of evolving a framework for legislation for the regulation of mutual funds that may be permitted in the joint/private sector. The study group was also asked to review the existing regulatory framework for the established funds. The Dave Panel Recommendations were submitted in September, 1991.

Types of Mutual Funds

1. *According to SEBI*
   - (*a*) Money Market Mutual Funds (MMMF)
   - (*b*) Off-shore Mutual Funds
   - (*c*) Asset Management Mutual Funds (AMC)
2. *Yield and Investment Pattern*
   - (*a*) Income Funds
   - (*b*) Growth Funds
   - (*c*) Balance Funds
   - (*d*) Specialised Funds
   - (*e*) Area Funds
3. *Specialised Funds*
   - (*a*) Global Funds
   - (*b*) Regional or Country Funds
   - (*c*) Sector (Industry) Funds
   - (*d*) Taxation Funds
   - (*e*) Real Estate Funds
   - (*f*) Junk Bond Funds
4. *Load and No-load Open-end Funds*
   - (*a*) Front-end load
   - (*b*) Back-end Load
5. *Stock Funds*
   - (*a*) Growth Funds
   - (*b*) Income Funds
6. *Bond Funds*
7. *Index Funds*
8. *Dual Funds*
9. *Leverage Funds*
10. *Money Market Mutual Funds*
    - (*a*) Commercial Papers (CP)
    - (*b*) Certificates of Deposits (CD)
    - (*c*) Bills Discounting
    - (*d*) Treasury Bills.

Chart 1.1
Mutual Fund Organisations in India

- TRUSTS (i.e., UTI)
- Public Sector
  - Financial Institutions (FIs)
    1. ICICI MF
    2. IDBI MF
  - Public Sector Banks (Commercial Banks)
    1. SBI MF
    2. Canara Bank
    3. Indian Bank
    4. BOI MF
    5. BOB MF
    6. PNB MF
  - Insurance Sector
    1. GIC MF
    2. LIC MF
- Private Sector
  1. Alliance Capital MF
  2. Apple MF
  3. Birla MF
  4. CRB MF
  5. JM MF
  6. Kothari Pioneer MF
  7. Kotak Mahindra MF
  8. Morgan Stanley MF
  9. Sri Ram MF
  10. Sundaram MF
  11. Tata MF
  12. Tauras MF
  13. 20th Century MF

Chart 1.2
Regulatory Framework of Mutual Funds

MUTUAL FUNDS

- MFs approved by as per SEBI
- UTI as per UTI Act, 1963
- MMMFs as per RBI
- Off-share Mutual Funds as in the form of FIIs as per SEBI and RBI guidelines
  - *(a)* Mutual Funds
  - *(b)* Pension Funds
  - *(c)* Investment Trusts
  - *(d)* Asset Management Companies (AMCs)
  - *(e)* Nominee Companies
  - *(f)* Institutional/ Incorporated Port Folio Managers

FII = Foreign Institutional Investors
SEBI = Guidelines — January 20, 1993.

Prior to SEBI Regulations, Mutual Funds were governed by guidelines laid down by the Ministry of Finance and RBI.

Mutual Fund Schemes

Mutual Funds float various varieties of schemes to cater to the requirements of different classes of people. Essentially schemes floated by Mutual Funds are of two types, namely (1) Open-ended, and (2) Close-ended. Basic characteristics of these two types of mutual fund schemes are given in Chart - 1.3

1. Open-ended Schemes
2. Close-ended Schemes
3. Income-Schemes
4. Growth Schemes
5. Equity-Linked Savings Schemes (ELSS)
6. Value Added Schemes
7. Miscellaneous Schemes
   - *(i)* Unit-linked insurance scheme
   - *(ii)* Children's Gift Growth Plan
   - *(iii)* UTI's Senior Citizen's Unit Plan
   - *(iv)* Children's College and Career Fund
   - *(v)* LIC Mutual Fund's Dhanvidya, etc.

Open-Ended Schemes

1. These are available for subscription all the year round excluding the period of book-closing.
2. Open-ended schemes may or may not have a specified redemption period.
3. Sale and purchase prices are fixed by the mutual fund concerned from time to time.
4. Repurchases are generally allowed at specified rates.
5. Each open-ended scheme must have a minimum corpus of Rs. 50 crore. In case the fund manager is unable to raise this amount at the time of issue or 60 per cent of the targetted amount whichever is higher, the entire subscription must be returned to the investors.

Close-ended Schemes

1. Close-ended schemes are open for subscription only during a specified period.
2. Usually the redemption period is also specified.
3. The duration of the scheme varies. Usually, it is 5 to 7 years.

Chart 1.3
Mutual Fund Schemes

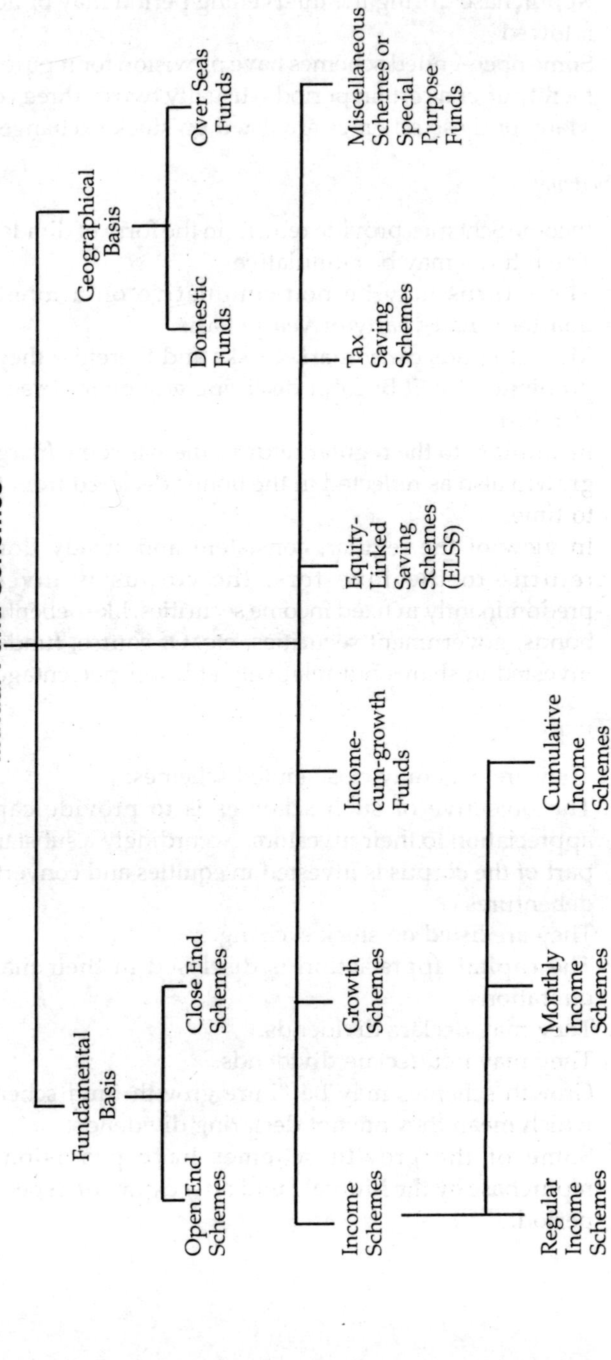

4. Repurchase during the intervening period may or not be allowed.
5. Some open-ended schemes have provision for repurchase facility after a certain period—usually two or three years.
4. Many of these schemes are listed on stock exchanges.

Income Schemes

1. Income Schemes provide returns in the form of dividends.
2. The returns may be cumulative.
3. The returns may be non-cumulative on a monthly, quarterly, half-yearly or yearly basis.
4. Mutual Funds carry market risks and therefore they are prohibited by SEBI from declaring any guaranteed rate of returns.
5. In addition to the regular returns, there is some marginal growth also as reflected in the bonus declared from time to time.
6. In view of the regular, consistent and steady flow of returns to the investors, the corpus is invested predominantly in fixed income securities, like debentures, bonds, government securities, etc. Of course, funds are invested in shares but relatively at lower percentage.

Growth Funds

1. They are generally close-ended schemes.
2. The objective of such schemes is to provide capital appreciation to their investors. Accordingly a substantial part of the corpus is invested in equities and convertible debentures.
3. They are listed on stock exchanges.
4. The capital appreciation is disclosed in their market quotations.
5. They may declare dividends.
6. They may not declare dividends.
7. Growth schemes may be "Pure growth fund schemes' which mean they are not declaring dividends.
8. Some of the growth schemes have provision for repurchase by the Mutual Fund after expiry of a specified period.

Equity-Linked Savings Schemes (ELSS)

1. They are popularly known as tax-planning schemes.
2. They are essentially close-ended schemes.
3. They are floated by almost all public sector mutual funds in the last quarter of each financial year.
4. Investment upto a ceiling of Rs. 10,000 provide tax rebate to the extent of 20 per cent (25% in case of artists, writers, dramatists, etc.) under Section 88 of the Income Tax Act, 1961.
5. The duration of the scheme is 10 years.
6. Repurchases are allowed after a specified period usually 3 years.
7. They are listed on stock exchanges.
8. During the stock-in-period of 3 years their units can not be traded, pledged or transferred.

Value Added Schemes

1. In addition to income/growth schemes, some of the mutual funds schemes have the provision for 'value addition'. This is usually in the nature of personal insurance cover for accidents, etc.

Miscellaneous Schemes

1. They are designed to serve specific purpose like children's education, hospitalisation expenses, schemes for senior citizens, insurance cover, etc.
2. Usually, they are open-ended schemes.
3. Investment matures after specified period or on fulfilment of the objective of the scheme.
4. Dividend accrued each year is usually re-invested.
5. These are neither traded nor transferrable.
6. They are not listed on Stock Exchanges.

Participants

1. Sponsor
2. Mutual Fund established in the form of a Trust
3. The Asset Management Company (AMC)
4. Custodians

Asset Management Company (AMC)

According to Regulation 2 (d) of SEBI (Mutual Funds) Regulations, 1993, an "Asset Management Company" means a company formed and registered under the Companies Act, 1956 (1 of 1956) and approved by the Board Under /Regulation 20.

1. An Asset Management Company is a Joint Stock Company.
2. It is promoted and sponsored by financial institution or bank or LIC, GIC or any other.
3. Such AMC should be approved by the SEBI under Regulation 20.
4. The application for the approval of the AMC shall be made in Form A.
5. Memorandum and Articles of Association of the AMC should be submitted to the Board for approval.

Appointment of AMC

Sponsor shall appoint AMC. It is approved by the Board. It is created to manage the affairs of the MF and operate the schemes of such Fund [(Reg. 19 (1)].

According to Reg. 19(2), the appointment of an AMC can be terminated by majority of the Trustees or by 75 per cent of the limit of the unit-holders of the scheme.

According to Reg. 19(3), any change in the appointment of the AMC shall be subject to prior approval of the Board.

Approval of AMC

Regulation 20 of SEBI, 1993, grants approval of AMC, the Board may take into account the following :

1. Sound Track Record of AMC, if it is already existing;
2. Directors of AMC are persons professional experience in the relevant fields, such as, port folio management, investment analysis, financial administration.
3. At 50 per cent of Board of Directors are not affiliated of, or associated in any manner with the Sponsor Company or any of its subsidiaries or the Trustees.
4. The Chairman of the AMC should not be director of a Trustee Company or Trustee of Board of Trustees.

5. AMC should have a minimum net worth of Rupees 5 Crores. Net worth means paid-up capital of the company and free reserves.

According to Regulation 21 of the SEBI, the grant of approval of AMC, the following terms and conditions are followed:

(a) The AMC has professionals with adequate experience in the management of MFs.
(b) Any Director of AMC shall not hold the position of a Director in another AMC or of Trustee in any MF.
(c) Any material changes in AMC should be informed the Board.
(d) Any change in Board of AMC should be informed and approval is obtained.

Business Activities

Under Regulation 23, (1) No AMC shall act as a Trustee of any MF; (2) It can undertake to activities like Financial Services constancy, exchange of research on commercial basis.

Obligations

1. Investment of funds pertaining to each scheme must be invested according to the provisions of that scheme.
2. The AMC should submit to the Trustee, quarterly reports on March 31, June 30, September 30 and December 31 on its activities.
3. The AMC shall be expected to meet all its expenses of Office, Personnel and Administration, etc.
4. Reporting Services.
5. Annual Reports.
6. Advertising.
7. Accounting.
8. Tax Returns.
9. Insurance.
10. Pensions and Research.

Objectives of AMC

To manage the assets of the MF and Other activities it can carry out, such as, financial services consultancy which do not conflict with the fund management activity and are only secondary and incidental.

Chart 1.4
Mutual Funds with their Objectives

Name/Type of the Mutual Fund	*Objectives*
1. Income Funds	1. Maximise Yield
2. Growth Funds	2. Maximise Capital appreciation
3. Balanced Funds	3. Growth-cum-Income Approach
4. Specialised Funds	4. Investment in Specific Industries
5. Area Funds	5. Investment in Specific Geographical areas, usually a country
6. Money Market Mutual Funds (MMMFs)	6. Short-term investment to realise interest and redemption of short term notice
7. Stock Funds	7. Investment Commonstock or equity shares *(a)* Income or dividend *(b)* Growth
8. Bond Funds	8. Income in the name of Interest or/and Premium on redemption. Risk is Less.
9. Balanced Funds	9. Security and Income
10. Index Funds	10. Income Varies on Indices of Stock Market
11. MMMFs	11. Short Term Investment Interest
12. Dual Funds'	12. Investment in equity and preference shares
13. Leverage Funds	13. Maximise capital appreciation
14. International Funds	14. Investment in Foreign Securities.
15. Global Funds	15. Investment in Foreign Companies
16. Regional or Country Funds	16. Investment in Specific Country or Countries
17. Sector (Industry) Funds	17. Investment in Particular Sector
18. Taxation Funds	18. Tax exemption benefits to investors
19. Real Estate Funds	19. Investment in Real Estate Institutions.

Chart 1.5
Distinction between Open-ended and Close-ended Funds

Open-end Funds	*Close-end Funds*
Constitution: Usually Constituted by agreement selling out the relationship between the various prescribed and participations parties, and governed by legislation distinguishable from commercial law.	A closed-end investment Company has an authorised capital end issued capital, and is subject to companies Act.
Responsibilities: Responsibilities are laid through a formal contract between management company and trustee companies are custodians, for an operation of unit-holders fund.	*Responsibilities:* Responsibilities are laid down through a formal agreement between management company and trustees to operate unit-holders funds.
Trading : The Sale and Purchase prices are fixed by the Mutual Fund concerned from time to time. No listing is done.	*Trading:* They operate their shares in stock market by listing
Price Determination: NAV	Price determination is done by demand and supply.
Perpetual Succession: Present	*Perpetual Succession* : Not present.
Subscription: They are available for subscription on all the year round excluding the period of book closing.	These are open for subscription during a specific period.

(*Contd.*)

Open-end Funds	Close-end Funds
Redemption Period :	
They may or may not have a specified redemption period	Redemption time is specified
Sale and Repurchase Prices:	*Sale and Repurchase Prices:*
They are fixed by the mutual fund concerned from time to time.	Through stock exchanges and stock-markets.
Repurchase Price:	
These are generally allowed at specified rates.	Repurchasing during the intervening period may or may not be allowed. Some schemes have repurchase provision facility after a certain period.
Minimum Corpus :	*Corpus:*
Each scheme must have a minimum corpus of Rs. 50 Crore. In the case the fund manager is not able to raise this amount at the time of issue, or 60 per cent of the targetted amount whichever is higher, the entire subscription must be returned to the Investors.	Each scheme is needed to raise atleast Rs. 20 Crores as its corpus fund. If the minimum amount of Rs. 20 Crore or 60 per cent of the targetted amount, whichever is higher, is not raised for a closed-end scheme, then the entire subscription is refunded to the investors.
Duration:	
Through out the period of operation	Duration of the schemes varies. Normally it is five to seven years.
Listing: No done	*Listing:*
	Many of these schemes are listed on the stock exchanges.

(Contd.)

Open-end Funds	*Close-end Funds*
SEBI: SEBI's approval is essential	*SEBI:* The closed-end schemes shall be considered for approval of SEBI as per procedures applicable to capital issues by companies.
Opening for Subscription: First 45 days of the subscription period shall be considered for determining the target figure or minimum size of the scheme.	The closed-end schemes of MFs are not permitted to be kept open for subscription for more than 45 days.
Liquidity: In order to provide continuous liquidity of the schemes to its investors, the MFs shall sell and repurchase units at predetermined prices based NAV and such prices should be published atleast once in a week.	*Liquidity:* In order to provide continuous liquidity for close-end schemes, such schemes are listed on the stock exchanges.
Corpus Size: It is never determined.	*Corpus Size:* Corpus size is determined in advance
Opening and Closing Dates: These are not fixed and never announced to public.	These are fixed and announced to the public
Meaning: It means that the fund continuously has units available for sale. Normally it stands ready to redeem outstanding units upon request.	*Meaning:* Open and close for subscriptions only on particular dates; terminated at specified periods.

Chart 1.6A
Structure of a Mutual Fund

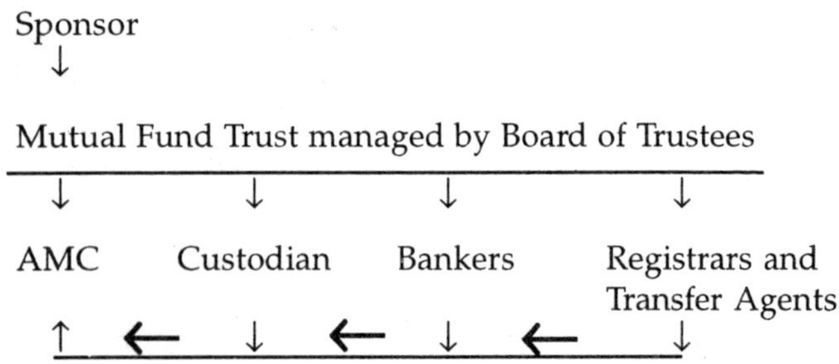

Chart 1.6.B
Structure of a Mutual Fund

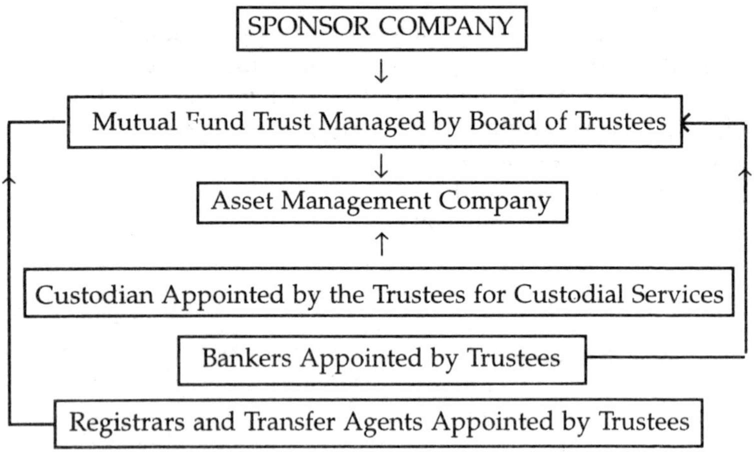

Trustee

According to Regulation 2(0), "trustee" means a person who holds the property of the mutual fund in trust for the benefit of the unit holders.

Unit-holder mean a participant in a scheme of a Mutual Fund.

A MF is established in the form of a trust by the sponsor. It is managed by a Board of Trustees in whole favour trust deed is executed by the sponsor. Trust deed lays down guidelines for the management of funds. The trust appoints and establishes AMC. It is the job of the trustees to ensure that the schemes floated and managed by AMC as per the Trust Deed. There is an arms length relationship between Trustees and AMC. Trustees are the principal control of the Capital Property of the Mutual Fund schemes. They are required to act in their interest.

Rights

1. Trustees have the right to obtain from AMC relevant information as well as a quarterly report on its activities.
2. Trustees are vested with powers to dismiss the AMC under specific conditions as per SEBI regulations and with its approval.
3. Trustees are required to appoint a custodian and supervise its activities.
4. Trustees are required to get auditor's report of AMC.
5. Trustees have the right to appoint bankers.
6. Trustees have the right to appoint Registrars and Transfer Agents.

Obligations

1. Trustees are required to submit a six monthly report to SEBI on the activities of Mutual Fund.

Custodian

A Custodian is appointed by the trustees of Mutual Fund to provide necessary custodial services.

A custodian should have :

1. a should track record,
2. necessary infrastructure,
3. office space,
4. during the tenure of office, custodian should act as sponsor, trustee, and associate with AMC, and
5. He should get permission from SEBI.

Mutual Fund Industry—Indian Panorama

The foundation for mutual fund industry in India was laid by the Parliament in 1963. Unit Trust of India was founded in 1963 with the enactment of UTI Act. This was the brain-child of Mr. T. T. Krishnamachari, the then Minister of Finance of India. He made it clear to the Parliament that Unit Trust of India would provide an opportunity for the middle and lower income groups to acquire without difficulty, property in the form of shares,....This institution is intended to cater mainly to needs of individual investors whose means are small with this objective, UTI came out with its maiden scheme, an open-ended one, in 1964 which is popularly known as US-64. Till 1987, UTI was holding a key position in India Mutual Fund industry. Till 1987, it had a very few schemes.

Followed by the Government decision to permit nationalised banks to set up Mutual Funds, State Bank of India set up SBI Mutual Fund, Canara Bank set up Canara Bank Mutual Fund, respectively subsequently other public sector banks and insurance companies viz., Indian Bank, Bank of India and Insurance Corporation of India joined the race by the end of 1990. In 1992-93, the Mutual Fund industry was thrown open to private sector too.

Table 1.1
Mutual Fund Institutions—Big Eight

Name of Institution	*Name of Mutual Fund*	*Year of Establishment*
1. Unit Trust of India	UTI	1967
2. SBI	SBI Mutual Fund	1987
3. Canara Bank	Canbank Mutual Fund	1987
4. Indian Bank	Ind bank Mutual Fund	1989
5. Bank of India	BOI Mutual Fund	1989
6. Punjab National Bank	PNB Mutual Fund	1989-90
7. L I C	LIC Mutual Fund	1989
8. G I C	GIC Mutual Fund	1990

Indian Financial System—A View

In general, the Indian Financial system has taken a turn-around during the first half of 1990s. Simultaneously, Mutual Fund industry has taken a turn-around during the said period. The new Government assumed office in 1991. It initiated a number of policy measures willing to make the financial sector more efficient and viable. The Government's intention was to bring the country's financial sector more close to international standards. The Government has accorded statutory status to SEBI as an autonomous body on January 31, 1992 for the promotion of an regulation of the Capital Market. Though an ordinance, later, SEBI was amended on 25th January, 1995 endowed with more powers. It was done for the orderly development of the capital market and protect the investors. Over the past four years the Indian economy could attain remarkable improvement. Consequently, Indian economy reached to back on the path of sustainable growth.

Savings have been maintained at a relatively high level during the period of reforms. At the same time, investment have been maintained at a relatively high level during the period of reform. The Gross Domestic Savings (GDS) as a percentage of Gross Domestic Product (GPD) has grown significantly. The household savings increased considerably. There has been a change in the profile of the savings of Indian households. The asset preference of the households have been shifted from physical assets to financial assets.

From Table—'Mobilisation of resources........' Mutual Funds in India comprise of various sectors such as, public sector banks, public sector financial institutions, MF sponsored by UTI and private sector. All these are playing an important role in mobilising resources. The entry of private sector mutual funds imparted competitive officiating in the Mutual Fund industry. It helped the investors to choose from schemes with different maturity periods and various risk-return trade-offs. As far as mobilisation of resources concerned, UTI reins the majority share by mobilising more than 80 per cent of the total funds raised. Total subscriptions to the schemes of mutual funds amounted to Rs. 2017.9 crores in 1987-88 has increased to Rs. 13017.8 crores in 1992-93. Later, due to overall dullness in capital market conditions, the resources mobilised by private as well as public sector mutual funds has fallen to Rs. 11405.9 crores in 1993-94. Private sector MF entered in the MF industry in 1993-94 by mobilising Rs. 1551.4 crores compared to Rs. 396.5 crores collected by both public sector banks and public sector financial institutions excluding UTI. On the very fast year of it is entry, private sector could raise a deal funds.

Table 1.2
Mobilisation of Savings by Mutual Funds

(Rs. Crore)

Year	Public Sector Banks	Public Sector FIs	Mutual Funds Sub-Total	Sponsored by UTI	Total	Private Mutual Funds	Grand Total
1987-88	250.3	—	250.3	1767.6	2017.9	—	2017.9
			(12.40)	(87.60)	(100)		(100)
1988-89	319.7	—	319.7	3464.0	3783.7	—	3783.7
			(8.45)	(91.55)	(100)		(100)
1989-90	899.1	315.2	1214.3	5490.9	6705.2	—	6705.2
	(13.41)	(4.70)	(18.11)	(81.89)	(100)		(100)
1990-91	2176.0	603.5	2779.5	3198.8	5978.3	—	5978.3
	(36.39)	(10.10)	(46.49)	(53.51)	(100)		(100)
1991-92	2304.4	427.1	2731.5	8685.4	11416.9	—	11416.9
	(20.18)	(3.74)	(23.92)	(76.08)	(100)		(100)
1992-93	1204.0	756.8	1960.8	11057.0	13017.8	—	13017.8
	(9.25)	(5.81)	(15.06)	(84.94)	(100)		(100)
1993-94	147.5	249.0	396.5	9458.0	9854.5	1551.4	11405.9
	(1.29)	(2.19)	(2.99)	(82.92)	(86.40)	(13.60)	(100)
1994-95	194.4	37.6	232.0	6961.0	7193.0	557.3	7750.3
(April -Sept.)	(2.50)	(0.49)	(2.99)	(89.81)	(92.80)	(7.20)	(100)

Source : RBI, Mumbai; Report on Currency and Finance, Vol. 1 1993-94.
UTI data incorporated for the last two years.
Figures in brackets indicate percentages.

Mutual Fund Industry—Growth

Unit Trust of India (UTI) was created in 1963. The first mutual fund was launched in 1964 by UTI. In the very first year of its launch, UTI has mobilised total amount of Rs. 24.67 crores. Slowly and gradually, the fund had grown in its size. In 1971, the second fund known as "Unit Linked Insurance Plan—1971" (ULIP—1971) was launched. Till 1986, there was no competition to UTI. It collected Rs. 24.67 crores in 1964-65 raise up and up to Rs. 6738.81 crores in 1987-88 showing a growth of 47.66 over the previous year 1986-87. In 1987, the Government of India permitted two public sector banks to commence mutual funds. Latter some more public sector banks were added. Two insurance corporations, viz. LIC and GIC started MF business. The MF industry was thrown open to private sector in 1993 slowly, element of competition took place in the industry. The first private sector fund was set up by the asset management company viz. the Kothari Pioneer Mutual Fund. By the end of 1994-95, 21 oganisations managing 172 funds have been set up.

The investible funds of the UTI and the rest of MF from 1964-65 to 1993-94 increased enormously from mere Rs. 24.67 crores in 1964-65 to Rs. 61028.51 crores in 1993-94. UTI alone collected Rs. 24.67 crores in 1964-65 to Rs. 516708.88 crores in 1993-94. Despite the competition from other Mutual Funds, UTI continues to be the pioneer in MF industry.

The data in Table—"Investible Funds" shows investible funds of Mutual Fund Industry ever since the start of new Mutual Funds in 1987. The share of rest of the industry increased from 12 per cent in 1988-89 to about 15 per cent in 1993-94.

Significance of Mutual Funds

(i) The MFs have been functioning like financial intermediaries to mobilise savings of public, invest them in a variety of securities and in those avenues where there is a demand of funds.

(ii) These institutions employ experts who possess professional knowledge and expertise for the selection and supervision of their investment portfolios.

(iii) The diversification and expert investment knowledge ensure steady and regular earnings to the funds and a

share in the general property to the investor.

(iv) The Mutual Funds will relieve the investors from the problem of investing their savings and dealing with them effectively. Further, these will ensure a low risk, steady return, liquidity and capital appreciation.

(v) These funds make available relatively bigger lots of funds to needy industrial concerns and thereby reduce their burden and botheration involved in raising finance directly from individual savers.

(vi) The MFs have been opening off-shore funds in various foreign countries, in order to attract foreign capital flow into the country and to secure profitable investment avenues abroad for domestic savings.

(vii) The income levels of urban and rural middle class people are increasing and these people are saving part of their income to invest in profitable and safe avenues, since they are aware of the time benefits if they invest their money in capital market. The MFs are channelising such savings to the needy industrial undertakings.

(viii) In this context the Mutual Funds have tremendous scope for growth in the country in nineties and thereafter.

(ix) In view of recent liberalised economic and industrial policies and concessions such as excise and customs given in recent budget for the growth of industrial sector, the capital market—both primary issue market and secondary—have been witnessing unprecedented booming trends. Hence, MFs have been able to speed their wings by spreading their funds in various industrial sectors.

(x) *Investors' Confidence :* MFs are playing significant role in mobilising savings from public and in the process, it has provided stability to the Indian Capital Market. They have proved to be the mainstay in the market in times of high degree of volatility. They have garnered investors' confidence as a large section of savers are willing to put their savings in the MFs.

(xi) *Savers' attitude :* Savers are more interested in the MFs and willing to put their savings into MFs because of low-risk, reasonable returns, guarantee to get back their investments with adequate appreciation.

(xii) *Income Tax Relief (U/s 88) :* There are several Mutual Fund

Table 1.3
Investible Funds

(Rs. Crore)

Year	Mutual Funds (Other Than UTI)		UTI		Total (2+3)	
1	2	Growth	3	Growth	4	Growth
1988-89	1621.00 (12.05)	100.00	11835.00 (87.95)	100.00	13456.00 (100)	100.00
1989-90	1480.00 (9.52)	91.30	15892.00 (91.48)	134.28	17372.00 (100)	129.10
1990-91	1188.89 (5.27)	80.33	21377.00 (94.73)	134.51	22565.89 (100)	129.89
1991-92	5672.08 (15.14)	477.09	31806.00 (84.86)	148.79	37479.08 (100)	166.09
1992-93	8011.21 (17.05)	141.23	38977.00 (82.95)	122.55	46988.21 (100)	125.37
1993-94	9323.92 (15.28)	116.39	51709.00 (84.72)	132.66	61032.92 (100)	129.89

Note : Figures in Brackets indicate percentages.
Growth in Percentages.

Source : Mutual Funds Fact Book, UTI-CM, Mumbai, p. 13.
Results Computed.

schemes to tax-paying class who get rebate on investment in these schemes. They get a high relief due to these schemes.

(xiii) *Highly Liquidity :* Wherever investor feels like withdraw the scheme can get immediately on repurchase price or NAV price.

(xiv) *Government Control* : There is a great deal of control by the Government through SEBI on Mutual Fund industry for there is a vast corpus invested by household sector of India.

(xv) *Good Portfolio Management :* There is every possibility of expert and specialised professional managers appointed by Mutual Fund organisations, good portfolio management is possible which results high benefits to Mutual Fund holders.

(xvi) Risk of loss due to ill informed and misinformed purchase/sales is reduced as the managers of MFs have better access to information. Many an investor has to come to grief by falling prey to misleading and motivated "headline" leads and lips. Risk is reduced due to diversification of portfolio in terms of companies and industries. Even a small investor of Rs. 1,000 in MF gets the benefit of diversification. As the savings and investments are pooled, there are advantages of economies of scale. Even a small investor of Rs. 1,000 can reap the benefits of large size fund of Rs. 50—100 crores. The funds are handled by professional experts who are specially trained and have considerable experience. The returns are automatically reinvested. The investor need not be bothered about paper work and the trauma associated with frequent switch over of stocks. Near iron clad safety from the wily operations.

(xvii) Returns and capital appreciation are higher than that from bank deposits. Investors in MFs enjoy tax benefits Under Section 80 C and in some cases, 80 L, 88 of the Income-Tax Act of 1961.

(xviii) MFs are ideally suited to a developing economy like India. This is because there is a large number of small investors, who have the ability to save and recently, they have also shown their willingness to enter the capital market. MFs are more useful kind helpful to the investors who are shy of capital market. The claim to offer professional management of funds to diversify and thus reduce the unsystematic risk, while offering good returns. Thus, MFs can serve the investors at large in a better way by providing them good returns. A MF is also an effective agency for the mobilisation of resources for the economy. It is also contended the MFs may also prove to be helpful to avert the crisis of in the Capital Market.

Definitions

"Mutual Fund is a non-depositing, non-banking financial intermediary."

"Mutual Fund is a Corporation which accepts money from savers and uses the same to buy stocks, long-term bonds, short-term debt instruments issued by business or Government units."

"Mutual Funds are corporations which pool funds and reduce risk by diversification."

"Mutual Fund is an American concept and it implies investment trust, investment company, Mutual Fund, money fund, etc.

A Mutual Fund is an institutional device or an investment vehicle through which, the investors pool their funds under the direction of an investment manager. These funds are invested in wide variety of portfolios of securities in such a way as to minimise risk, while ensuring safety and steady return.

Notes and References

1. Halin, John A., *Investors Guide to Mutual Funds*, Prentice Hall, UK, p. 3.
2. Reilly, Frank K., *Investments*, The Dryden Press, USA, 1982, pp. 525-526.
3. Killer Howard and Sontag, Harvey, *The Right Mix : How to Pick Mutual Funds for Your Portfolio*, McGraw Hill, New York, 1993, pp. 80-81.
4. Ross, Joel, *Mutual Funds — Taking the Worry of Out of Investing*, Prentice Hall, 1988, p. 8.
5. Reilly, Frank K., *Investments*, CBS College Publishing, 1982, pp. 526-528.
6. *Kohler's Dictionary for Accountants*, PHI, New Delhi, 1993, p. 339.
   Mutual Corporation : A form of Corporation permitted under state laws, limited mostly to savings banks and insurance companies.

CHAPTER TWO

Methodology

Chapter two deals with Methodology on "Working of Mutual Fund Organisations in India" which covers objectives, hypothesis, design and Methodology, sample, statistical tools used, period of study, tools for /collection of data, limitations, terminology, broad-sheet on big eight Mutual Funds and table showing growth of Mutual Fund Organisations in India.

Objectives

The objectives of working of Mutual Fund organisations in India are bifurcated into *(i)* Main Objectives, and *(ii)* Subsidiary Objectives.

Main objectives of the study comprises of *(a)* Resource Mobilisation by Mutual Funds from small and marginal investors, *(b)* Resource Mobilisation activities of Mutual Funds in India under different schemes offered to public at large to suit their requirements and social and economic conditions and back-grounds, *(c)* Investment policy of Mutual Funds and deployment of funds (i.e., investable funds) in various segments in investments keeping in mind the risk, income, profits, etc.

Secondary objectives consist of *(i)* Organisation structure of Mutual Fund, *(ii)* Working of Unit Trust of India, Life Insurance Corporation of India, General Insurance Corporation of India and other five public sector Mutual Fund organisations in the field and *(iii)* Perceptions of investors in Mutual Funds.

Hypothesis

For a researcher hypothesis is a formal question that he intends to solve. Thus a hypothesis may be defined as a proposition or a set of propositions set forth as an explanation for the occurrence of some specified group of phenomena either assorted merely as a provisions conjecture to guide some investigation of accepted as highly probable in the light of established facts

In the present study, the hypothesis outline 'mutual Fund Organisations in India mobilize and pool large sums of savings of small and marginal investors for the industrial capital and act as catalysts for economic and industrial growth of India' and 'mutual Fund Organisations are better than the financial intermediaries such as UTI, GIC, LIC, ICICI, IDBI, SFCs in the activity of financial resource mobilisation.

Design

A research design is the arrangement of conditions for collection and analysis of data in a manner that aims to combine relevance to the research purpose with economy in procedure. It comprises of:

- *(i)* sample design,
- *(ii)* the observational design,
- *(iii)* the statistical design, and
- *(iv)* the operational design.

The sample design which deals with the method of selecting items to be observed for the proposed research study. An emphasis needs here that universe is too small and is not reporting sample survey. All the eight Mutual Fund organisations are taken purposely. They are:

- *(i)* SBI Mutual Fund,
- *(ii)* Can Bank Mutual Fund,
- *(iii)* Indian Bank Mutual Fund,
- *(iv)* BOI Mutual Fund,
- *(v)* PNB Mutual Fund;
- *(vi)* LIC Mutual Fund,
- *(vii)* GIC Mutual Fund and UTI.

All these are taken into consideration for study for they are the 'Big Eight' public sector Mutual Funds. All these are taken for study because the number of organisations are less. They are not large in number.

Sample Unit

The sample unit in the study covers the whole nation geographically since these are established by the public sector organisations and national commercial banks of India. Resource mobilisation and fund rising is made through total branch network of sponsor organisations. The coverage is broad and nation wide.

Source List

Source list is otherwise is known as sampling frame. It includes all the items of a universe (i.e., in case of finite universe). The sample comprise of all 'Big Eight' Mutual Fund Organizations.

Size of Sample

At this stage, all eight public sector mutual fund organisations are considered for study and data processing and analysis.

Non-Probability Sample

Non-Probability sampling procedure which does not afford any basis for estimating the probability that each item in the population has been included in the sample. It is otherwise called by different names as 'deliberate sampling', 'purposive sampling', or 'judgment sampling' Since units are selected deliberately, our choice concerning the items remains supreme.

Statistical Design

It covers the question of how many items are to be observed and how the information and data gathered are to be analysed. The data was collected through the questionnaire by considering a lot of relevant points. Wherever necessary direct interview and direct contact is to be used to make the survey. Primary source and secondary source are used to gather data. In order to analyse the data, a number of statistical techniques are to be used to compute the results of the proposed study.

Period of Study

Period of study covered comprised of 1964-65 to 1993-94 in

regard to Unit Trust of India since it has been founded in 1963 and commenced its commercial operations in 1964. In regard to public mutual funds, the period covered was 1986-87 to 1993-94.

Collection of Data

Tools used in collection of data are comprising of

(i) Primary tools, and
(ii) Secondary tools.

Primary Tools in collection of data are

(i) Direct interview method, and
(ii) Questionnaire method.

Direct contact with the prospective and present investors was made for analysis of 'perceptions of investors' for which a comprehensive questionnaire was prepared by consulting experts in the field. The questionnaire was printed and served to different investors across the country to elicit answers for the research questions.

Secondary tools used in collection of data are:

(i) Annual Reports of UTI;
(ii) Annual Reports of different public sector Mutual Funds;
(iii) Reserve Bank of Bulletins—various issues;
(iv) Offer documents issued by different schemes by Mutual Funds;
(v) Chartered Analyst—Various Issues; and
(vi) Financial dailies like Business Line, Financial Express, Economic Times, etc.

Limitation

The limitation in the present study is that the study has not considered private sector mutual funds. Only 'Big Eight' Mutual Fund organisations are considered. A broad-sheet on big-eight mutual funds was depicted to highlight summarised and total picture.

Terms Used

Adviser

Also called 'investment adviser'. The Organization employed by a Mutual Fund to give professional advice on the fund's investments and asset management practices.

Table 2.1
Broad Sheet on Big Eight

Sl. No.	Mutual Fund	Asset Management Co.	Year of Incorporation	Sponsor	Unit Capital 1993—94 (Rs. Crore)	Investors Base (Crore)
1.	SBI Mutual Fund	SBI Funds Management Ltd., 191, Makar Towers "E", Caffe Parade, Mumbai - 400 005.	July, 1987	State Bank of India	2,474.66	0.32
2.	Can Bank Mutual Fund	Can Bank Investment Management Services Ltd., Orient House, Adi Marrban Path, Ballard Estate, Mumbai - 400 038.	Dec., 1987	Canara Bank	2,992.29	0.18
3.	Indian Bank MF	IND Fund Management Ltd., Ist Floor, D.G. Chambers, 100/104 Nanak Motwani Marg, Fort, Mumbai - 400 023.	6th Nov., 1989	Indian Bank	513.47	0.05
4.	Bank of India MF or BOI Mutual Fund	BOI Asset Management Co. Ltd., 24th Floor, Jeejeebhoy Towers, Dalal Street, Mumbai - 400 023.	1989	Bank of India	6665.08	0.06

5.	PNB Mutual Fund	PNB Asset Management Co. Ltd., Jeevan Bharati, Tower II, Level III, Cannaught Circus, New Delhi - 110 001.	1989-90	Punjab National Bank	249.05	0.02
6.	LIC MF	Jeevan Bhima Sahayog Asset Management Co. Ltd., Industrial Assurance Building, 4th Floor, Opp. Church Gate Station, Mumbai - 400 020.	June 1989	Life Insurance Corporation of India	1643.26	0.13
7.	GIC MF	GIC Asset Management Co., Universal Insurance Building, 2nd Floor,Sir P.M. Road, Fort, Mumbai - 400 001.	1990	General Insurance Corporation of India	781.81	0.07
8.	Unit Trust of India	Unit Trust of India 13, Sir Vithaldas Thackersey Marg, Post Box No. 11410, (New Marine Lines), Mumbai - 400 020	1963	—	38,981.93	3.64

Table 2.2

Break-up of Big Eight—Yearwise

Year	*No. of Institutions*	*%*
1963	1	12.50
1987	2	25.00
1989	4	50.00
1990	1	12.50
Total	8	100.00

Table 2.3

Break-up of Big Eight—Regionwise

Name	*No. of Institutions*	*%*
Mumbai	7	87.50
New Delhi	1	12.50
Total	8	100.00

Table 2.4

Break-up of Big Eight—Nature of Institution

Institution	*Number*	*%*
Special Parliament Act	1	12.50
Public Sector Banks	5	62.50
Insurance Sector	2	25.00
Total	8	100.00

Table 2.5
Break-up of Capital of Big Eight
Year Ended 1993-94

(Rs. in Crore)

Name of Institution	*Capital Rs.*	*%*	*Investor Base*	*%*
SBI Mutual Fund	2,474.66	5.12	0.32	7.16
Can Bank Mutual Fund	2,992.29	6.19	0.18	4.02
Indbank MF	513.47	1.06	0.05	1.12
BOI MF	665.08	1.38	0.06	1.34
PNB MF	249.05	0.52	0.02	0.45
LIC MF	1,643.26	3.40	0.13	2.90
GIC MF	781.81	1.62	0.07	1.56
UTI MF	38,981.93	80.71	3.64	81.45
Total	48,301.55	(100)	4.47	(100)

Note : Results Computed.
R indicates ranking amount wise.
Figures in brackets indicate percentages.

Source : Mutual Fund in India — Fact Book; UTI-ICM, New Mumbai, 1995, p. 13

Automatic Reinvestment

An option available to Mutual Fund unit holders in which fund dividends and capital gains distribution are automatically ploughed back into the fund to buy new shares and thereby increase holdings.

Accumulation Plan

An agreement provided by the fund management whereby regular purchases of small or large numbers of shares may be made. The Plan normally provides for automatic reinvestment of income dividends and capital gains distribution.

Bid Price

The price which the management company would pay for Units sold back to it. It is also called "Redemption Price".

Balance Fund

It indicates the investment policy of "balancing" its portfolio, generally by including bonds, preference shares and equity shares.

Book Shares

A modern share recording system that eliminates the need for mutual fund share certificates but gives the fund share owner a record of his holdings.

Book-End Load Fund

A fund that imposes a contingent deferred sales charge upon share redemption.

Cum Distribution

Unit trust prices are assumed to be cum distribution (i.e., the buyer is entitled to the next income distribution and seller is not) unless they are expressly stated to be ex-distribution.

CAGR

Compound Annual Growth Rate

Custodian

The Organisation that keeps custody of securities and other assets of a Mutual Fund.

Close-End Investment Company

A Mutual Fund whose amount of capital is relatively fixed. No new shares are normally issued except for reinvestment purposes. Fund shares are traded on a national stock exchange or OTC market in the same manner as do operating corporations.

Distribution

Payments of income from a Unit Trust of India.

Diversification

Spreading the risk; Mutual Funds spread investments among a number of different securities to reduce the risk inherent in investing.

Ex-distribution

Seller is entitled to the next income distribution.

Ex-dividend

The process whereby a stock price is reduced when a dividend is paid.

Expense Ratio

The ratio of annual expenses to the average net asset value of the fund's shares during the year. Fund expenses reduce the unit holder's investment.

Front-End Local Fund

A fund that charges an upfront sales charge.

Load

The amount added to the asset value of shares in open end fund in computing the offer price. This added amount covers commissions and other costs and is usually stated as percentage of the offering price. Thus, there are load funds, low-load funds and no-load funds.

Income Distribution

Income of a trust/fund is distributed, usually half-yearly on fixed dates, to unit holders in strict proportion to the number of units held. Virtually all the income or 95 per cent of the income of Mutual Fund is distributed after deducting the annual management charge. Distributions are paid net of tax. But for income tax purposes they need to "grossed up" at the basic rate.

Management Fee

The amount paid by mutual funds to their investment advisers. The average annual fee industrywide is about one-half of one per cent of fund assets.

Net Asset Value Per Share

The market worth of a mutual funds total assets—securities, cash, and any accrued earnings—after deducting liabilities, divided by the number of shares outstanding.

No Load Mutual Fund

One which charges no fee or commission to sell or buy back its share.

Offer Price

The price at which units can be purchased. It consists of the value at lowest offer prices on the stock exchange of the underlying securities, equalisation and initial costs.

Open-end Fund

A fund whose shares are redeemable at any time at asset value. Except for funds that no longer accept new shareholder, new shares are offered continuously.

Peps

Personal Equity Plans.

Portfolio

A Portfolio refers to a group of securities managed collectively.

Portfolio Management

Review of the Portfolio selected as needed to "best" meet investor's objectives.

Portfolio Turnover

A measure of the average percentage sales/purchase activity of a fund's portfolio.

Spread

It is also called "Bid spread" or "offer spread". The percentage difference between the bid and offer prices, usually 5 per cent—6 per cent. The spread on a trust may vary from day-to-day, depending on market conditions.

Up Front Load

Initial Issue Expenses.

Trust Dead

The legal document drawn up between the trustees and the managers for regulating the operation of the trust.

Trustees

Institutions such banks and insurance companies which as custodians of a Unit Trust/Mutual Fund's assets on behalf of Unit holders and watch their interests generally.

Turnover

The amount of change in the trust port folio during a specified period. Twenty per cent turnover would indicate that a fifth of the securities held by the trust/MF had changed.

CHAPTER THREE

Working of Mutual Funds

Chapter three deals with Working of Mutual Funds. It comprises of SBI Mutual Fund, Can bank Mutual Fund, Ind bank Mutual Fund, BOI Mutual Fund, PNB Mutual Fund, LIC Mutual Fund, GIC Mutual Fund and Unit Trust of India.

Table 3.1. shows the break-up of 'big-eight' Mutual Funds as on August, 1994. The table records 133 Mutual Fund schemes in aggregate.

Out of 133 schemes, 28 were growth schemes, 54 were income schemes, 21 were income and growth schemes and 30 were tax saving schemes in operation. Highest position went to income schemes while the lowest position gone to income and growth schemes. Out of eight MFs, UTI has 54 schemes. Second position has taken by LIC Mutual Fund operating 18 schemes.

SBI Mutual Fund

The Imperial Bank of India was established in 1921 by amalgamation of the three Presidency Banks of India. Until 1935, it undertook central banking functions besides normal commercial banking activities. In 1935, Reserve Bank of India was formulated and Central Bank activities were looked after by it. Imperial Bank of India was reconstituted as State Bank of India under the State Bank of India Act, 1955. It has seven subsidiary banks, viz., State Bank of Bikaner & Jaipur, Hyderabad, Indore, Mysore, Patiala, Saurastra and Travancore and these were joined under the State

Table 3.1
Total Schemes Introduced by all Mutual Funds (August 1994)

Sl. No.	Name of Fund	Total Schemes	Growth	Income	Income and Growth	Tax Savings
1.	SBI Mutual Fund	17 (100)	3 (17.65)	2 (11.75)	6 (35.30)	6(35.30)
2.	Can bank Mutual Fund	17 (100)	4 (23.53)	– (0.00)	7 (41.17)	6 (35.30)
3.	Indian Bank Mutual Fund	9 (100)	3 (33.33)	2 (22.23)	1 (11.11)	3 (33.33)
4.	Bank of India Mutual Fund	5 (100)	2 (40.00)	1(20.00)	– (0.00)	2 (40.00)
5.	PNB Mutual Fund	5 (100)	– (0.00)	1 (20.00)	1 (20.00)	3 (60.00)
6.	LIC Mutual Fund	18 (100)	1 (5.56)	8 (44.44)	5 (27.78)	4 (22.22)
7.	GIC Mutual Fund	8 (100)	1 (12.50)	4 (50.00)	1(12.50)	2(25.00)
8.	U T I	54 (100)	14 (25.93)	36 (66.67)	– (0.00)	4 (7.40)
	Total	133 (100)	28 (21)	54 (40.60)	21 (15.84)	30 (22.56)

Note : Figures in brackets indicate percentages.
Results Computed.

Source : Securities and Exchange Board of India, Mumbai.

Bank of India (subsidiary banks) Act 1959. The State Bank of India has 8,691 branches as on March 1993 and 47 offices abroad in 31 countries. Besides the Bank has established its European subsidiary, the SBI European Bank Ltd., in London in 1992 to exploit emerging opportunities arising out of integration of markets in European countries. Nearly a quarter of banking business in the country is with SBI. Besides commercial banking business, SBI has diversified significantly to merchant banking, home finance, factoring, and mutual fund, for which subsidiaries have been created. The SBI is functioning as the flagship of Indian banking.

SBI Mutual Fund has been constituted as a trust with the State Bank of India as the principal trustee. It has made an initial contribution of Rs. 5 lakhs towards the trust. It appointed a Board of Trustees to supervise the activities of the fund. The Board of Trustees have entrusted the work of management of the fund to SBI Funds Management Ltd., which is a subsidiary formed by the SBI with a capital of Rs. 5 crores. SBI, the sponsor and the principal trustee is not responsible or liable for any loss or shortfall resulting from the operations of any scheme of the Mutual Fund beyond the initial contribution made by the bank of any scheme of the amount of Rs. 5 lakhs towards setting up of the Mutual Fund. The trust is administered by the Boad of Trustees comprised of the following eminent people viz.,

(*i*) Sri R. N. Malhotra, Chairman, Board of Trustees,
(*ii*) Prof. A. M. Khusro, Editor, Financial Express,
(*iii*) Sri K. P. Rao, Trustee, Chartered Accountant, and
(*iv*) Dr. M. K. Sinha, Trustee, Managing Director, SBI.

In terms of the investment management agreement, SBI Funds Management Ltd., the asset management company is a wholly owned subsidiary of SBI. It has assumed the day-to-day investment management of the fund and in that capacity makes investment decisions and manages the mutual fund in accordance with the scheme objectives, deed of trust and provisions of the investment management agreement. The Board of Directors of the SBI Funds Management Ltd. (AMC) comprises of the followisng eminent people:

Shri P. G. Kakodkar, Chairman,
Prof. S. L. Rao, Director,

Shri Atul Munim, Director,
Prof. B. Nag, Director,
Shri R. G. Kare, Director,
Shri R. Viswanathan, Director, and
Shri M.P. Radhakrishnan, Managing Director.

Organisation

The day-to-day operations of the AMC are looked after by experienced and qualified professionals, consisting of senior officials on deputations from the State Bank Group, as well as directly recruited officials of the AMC.

The collection of savings is been carried out with the help of designated branches of SBI and associated banks of SBI and its subsidiaries.

Keeping the individual objectives of the various schemes and the economic environment, the investment is being made.

Fund maintains the books of accounts on accrual basis. Investment in securities transactions are accounted for on a trade date basis. Dividend income is accounted on an accrual basis. Interest income is recorded on an accrual basis. Gains and losses on sale of investments are accounted for in the year in which the sale contracts are entered into. The cost being computed on the basis of average cost of investments for which payments have been made and does not include purchase contracts awaiting completion.

Products of SBI Mutual Funds

Till 31st December, 1995, the Mutual Fund has launched a total of 20 schemes which can be broadly categorised under six heads, viz., (A) Regular income schemes; (B) Monthly income schemes; (C) 80 CC schemes; (D) 80 CCB schemes; (E) Growth schemes and (E) Cumulative income schemes.

(A) Regular Income Schemes

Magnum Regular Income Scheme (MRIS 87) was the first scheme launched by the SBI Mutual Fund. It commenced from 1st January, 1988. This was followed by two others, MRIS 89 and MRIS 90. MRIS 89 commenced from 1st April, 1989. MRIS 90 started from 1st August, 1990. The investment objective of the regular income schemes is to achieve a combination of income and growth and to provide regular income to the investor. The targetted return specified is a minimum of 12 per cent p.a. along with some capital appreciation.

(B) Monthly Income Schemes

SBI Mutual Fund issued two schemes, viz. Magnum Monthly Income Scheme (MMIS 89). It commenced from 1st September, 1989. Magnum Monthly Income Scheme (MMIS 91) started from 1st July, 1991. The investment objective is to provide a monthly return on investment to the investor. MMIS 89 offered a target return of 12 per cent p.a. with monthly payout. MMIS 89 was to be redeemed on 31st March, 1993 has been extended up to 31st December, 1996 at a highly monthly payout of 15 per cent p.a. for those investors who have excercised the option of extension. MMIS 91 targets at a return of 13 per cent p.a. with monthly payout.

(C) 80 CC Schemes

These are tax saving schemes. MTSS 88-89 is called Magnum Tax Saving Scheme. It commenced from 1st April, 1989. Magnum Tax Saving Scheme—90 commenced from 1st April, 1990. The object of these two was to enable subscribers to benefit under Section 80 CC of the Income Tax Act, 1961.

(D) 80 CCB Schemes

These are like Magnum Equity Linked Schemes. The MELS-91 commenced from 1st April, 1991. Magnum Gifts commenced from 1st April, 1992. The investment objective is to enable subscribers to benefit under Section 80 CCB of the Income Tax Act, 1961. It aims at achieving substantial realised income and capital appreciation. To achieve the investment objective investments are made in equities and equity related instruments.

(E) Growth Schemes

The Growth Schemes are (i) Magnum Multiplier Schemes 90, Magnum Express 91, Magnum Multiplier Plus 93 and Magnum Taxgain 93. These growth schemes aim at providing long-term capital appreciation to the investor. The investment policy followed in this case is to invest funds primarily in equity and other related securities. In some cases and schemes, investments have also been made in OTCEI scrips.

(F) Cumulative Income Schemes

SBI Mutual Fund issued Magnum Triple as the cumulative income scheme. It commenced its operation on 20th November, 1991. The investment objective is to invest funds in such a way that the investor receives a sum equal to the amount invested or more at the end of 90 months from the date of allotment. In order to achieve this aim, the funds are mainly used in investing in equities and equity-related investments as well as in non-convertible debentures and in money market instruments.

Performance of Various Schemes

The basic objective of any Mutual Fund is to provide a vehicle for investors to avail of the opportunities offered by the capital and money market. State Bank of India Mutual Fund (SBI MF) was also formed with this fundamental objective. Its aim is to provide such opportunity even to the smallest investor in urban as well as rural areas and offer opening to employ his funds profitably. Returns, safety and liquidity packaged in different forms are the three main features which the SBI MF offers to investors.

SBIMF introduced as many as 20 schemes upto the end of 1995. Out of these, five schemes were redeemed and there are fifteen schemes working and Magnum Gifts 92 has two schemes, viz. Magnum Gifts 92-A and Magnum Gifts 92-B. In total, there were 16 schemes were in operation. Out of 20 different schemes, 5 schemes were in Regular Income category; 2 schemes each under monthly income, 80 CC, 80 CCB category; 4 schemes under Growth Schemes category; 3 schemes were in the category of Tax Savings and one each in the cumulative and open-end categories (Table 3.2).

Market Share of SBIMF

As on 31st December, 1995, 196 schemes launched by 20 Mutual Funds including UTI were in operation with a total corpus of Rs. 80,500 crores. With a market share of 4.3 per cent, SBI MF was next to UTI. Among the Mutual Funds launched by public sector banks, insurance companies and other private sector mutual funds, as on 31st March, 1995, SBI MF was on the top with a market share of 21.28 per cent. SBIMF's corpus is however declining due to redemption or repurchase of under certain schemes and not been matched by fresh schemes and has unable to mobilise funds from

Table 3.2
SBI Mutual Fund Schemes at a Glance

Year	Scheme	Nature	Face Value Rs.	Date of Commencement	Date of Maturity/ Duration	Minimum Lock-in-Period	No. of Investors	Investors Funds (Crores) Rs.	Dividend Payments	Redemption	NAV as on 31.03.1995
1	2	3	4	5	6	7	8	9	10	11	12
1987	—	—	—	—	—	—	—	—	—	—	—
1988	MRIS - 87	Regular Income	500	01.01.88						30.06.93 (Rs. 684)	
1989	MRIS- 89	Regular Income	100	01.01.89						31.03.94 (Rs. 153.85)	
	MMIS - 89	Monthly Income	100	01.09.89						31.03.94 (Rs.222)	
	MTSS - 88-89	Tax Saving 80 CC	100	01.04.89							
1990	MRIS - 70	Regular Income	100	01.08.90						31.07.95 (Rs.107.28)	
	MTSS - 90	Tax Saving 80 CC	100	01.04.90						01.04.95 (Rs.172)	

1991	MMIS - 91	Monthly Income	100	01.07.91	30.06.1997 6Yrs	2 Yrs 6 Mnts	54,000	150.52	13% p.a. Payable Monthly		81.00
	MTPL - 91	Cumu-lative	100	20.11.91	19.05.1999 7 ½ yrs	1 Yrs	1,80,000	190.98	—		173.59
	MELS - 91	Tax Sav-ing 80 CCB	100	01.04.91	31.03.2001 10 Years	3 Yrs	44,600	29.89	10 in 1995-96		169.33
	MMS - 90	Growth	10	01.01.91	31.12.1997- 31.12.1998 (7 Years)	NIL	4,00,000	210.00	15% in 1995-96		12.31
	MEX - 91	Growth	10	20.11.91	19.11.1996- 19.11.1997	(1 Year)	1,40,300	107.34	Cumulative Scheme		10.97
1992	Magnum 92 A Gifts	Tax Savi-ing 80 CCB	10	01.04.92	21.03.2002 10 years	3 Years	90,604	60.64	7% in	1995-96	96.03
	92 B	Tax Savi-ngs 80 CCB	10	01.04.92	31.03.2002 10 Years	3 Years	1,31,180	106.49	NIL		106.90
1993	MRIS - 93	Regular income	10	15.12.93	15.12.2000 7 Years	NIL	16,625	61.92 Crores	12.25%		8.61

(Contd.)

1	2	3	4	5	6	7	8	9	10	11	12
	MMPS - 93	Growth	10	01.03.93	28.02.1999	NIL	1,20,000	640.	Cumulative Scheme		12.81
	MTGS - 93	Tax Saving 88	10	01.04.93	31.03.2003 10 Years	3 Years	1,06,000	74.43 (as on 31.03.96)	10% in 2nd Year 8% in 3rd Year		9.42
1994	MGF - 94	Growth	10	01.10.94	30.09.1999 5 Years	NIL	93,432	102.13	NIL		7.09
	MTPS - 94	Tax Saving 88	10	01.04.94	31.03.2004 10 Years	3 Years	66,000	43.56	—		7.33
1995	MBF - 94	Regular Income	10	01.02.95	01.02.2000 5 Years	NIL	33,000	75.58	12.00%		9.26
	MELS - 95	Tax Saving	10	01.04.95	31.03.2005 10 Years	3 years	41,354	40.55	NIL		9.39
	MOF	Open-ended	10	12.10.95	Open-ended	—	9,307	55.73	NIL		11.34

Source : Various Issues of Annual Reports of SBI Mutual Fund.

new schemes due to slack market conditions and the general decline in the investor support.

There are 178 funds as at the end of 1994-95. The number of mutual schemes increased tremendously after 1989. Till 1989, there were only 47 schemes. Out of 178 schemes, as many as 36 were issued in 1991, the highest number in all the years till 1995. The same position was seen in the case of SBIMF which issued five schemes in 1991 as against 36 schemes issued at all India level by all the Mutual Funds.

SBIMF raised a corpus in different schemes, viz. growth schemes, income schemes, tax savings and cumulative schemes whose break up of corpus showed at 56.90 per cent, 16.37 per cent, 18.03 per cent and 8.70 per cent respectively. Highest position was occupied by growth schemes depicting at 56.90 per cent while the lowest position was captured by cumulative income schemes showing 8.70 per cent as at 31st March, 1996 (Table 3.6).

SBIMF had an investor base of 3,398 thousand in 1995-96 as at 31st March, 1996 rose from 90 thousand in 1988. It showed a tremendous increase in the investors base covering throughout the country. The highest investor base was found in 1993 showing 1,741 thousand investors. While the lowest was seen in 1996 at 18 thousand investors.

Total funds collected went up from 131 crores in 1988 to Rs. 3,128 crores in 1996 showing a good increase in collection of funds from the investors. The highest collection was seen in 1993 figuring at Rs. 1,103 crores. While the lowest went to Rs. 74 crores in 1996. It was found that ups and downs in collection of funds throughout the period under study.

Magnum Regular Income Scheme (MRIS 87) was the first scheme of the SBI MF. It commenced its operation in January, 1988. The target return specified was 12 per cent.

Year	*Return*
1988	13.5 per cent
1989	14.0 per cent
1990	16.0 per cent
1991	18.0 per cent
1992	20.0 per cent

It was redeemed at Rs. 136.80 giving capital appreciation of 36.80 per cent. Its CAGR (Compound Annual Growth Rate) was 17.98 per

Table 3.3
SBI Mutual Fund Schemes—Scheme-wise Break-up

Nature of Scheme	*Number of Funds*
Regular Income	5
Monthly Income	2
80 CC	2
80 CCB	2
Growth Schemes	4
Cumulative Schemes	1
Tax Saving Schemes	3
Open-Ended Schemes	1
Total	20

Source : Various Annual Reports.
Various Issues of the Magnum Investor.

Table 3.4
SBI Mutual Fund Schemes—Year-wise Distribution

Year	*Number of Mutual Funds*
1988	1
1989	3
1990	2
1991	5
1992	1 (A and B)
1993	3
1994	2
1995	3
Total	20

Source : Various Issues of Annual Reports.
Various Issues of the Magnum Investor.

Table 3.5
SBI Mutual Funds—Nature of Scheme-wise Break-Up

Scheme	*Number of Mutual Funds*	
Magnum Rising Income Scheme	(MRIS)	4
Magnum Monthly Income Scheme	(MMIS)	2
Magnum Bond Fund Scheme	(MBF)	1
Magnum Triple Plus Scheme	(MTPL)	1
Magnum Multiplier Scheme	(MMS)	1
Magnum Express Scheme	(MEX)	1
Magnum Multiplier "Plus" Scheme	(MMPS)	1
Magnum Tax Profit Scheme	(MTPS)	1
Magnum Global Fund Scheme	(MGF)	1
M T S S		2
Magnum Equity Linked Saving	(MELS)	2
Magnum Gifts A		
Magnum Gifts B		1
Magnum Tax gain	(MTGS)	1
Magnum Open Fund	(MOF)	1
Total		20

Source : SBI Mutual Fund—Annual Report (Various Issues).
The Magnum Investor—Various Issues.

Table 3.6
SBI Mutual Fund Redeemed Schemes as on 31.12.1995

Schemes	*Date of Commencement*	*Face Value Rs.*	*Date of Redemption*	*Redemption Price Rs.*	*Registrars*
MRIS - 87	01.01.88	500	30.06.93	684.00	Datamatics Limited
MRIS - 89	01.04.89	100	31.03.94	153.00	- Do -
MTSS - 88-89	01.04.89	100	31.03.94	222.00	M.N. Dastur & Co.
MTSS - 90	01.04.90	100	31.04.95	172.00	Mafatlal Computer Services
MRIS - 90	01.08.90	100	31.07.95	107.28	- Do -

Source : Annual Reports of SBI Mutual Fund.
The Magnum Investor—Various Issues.

Table 3.7
SBI Mutual Funds—Scheme-wise Corpus Break-up

Schemes	*As on 31.03.96*
Growth Schemes	56.90 Per cent
Income Schemes	16.37 Per cent
Tax Savings	18.03 Per cent
Cumulative Income Schemes	8.70 Per cent
Total	100.00 Percent

Source : SBI MF Annual Report 1995-96.

Table 3.8
SBI Mutual Fund Schemes—Number of Investors

Year	*Cumulative Thousand Investors (CF)*	*Frequency (F)*
1988	90	90
1989	265	175
1990	415	150
1991	1,015	600
1992	1,302	287
1993	3,043	1,741
1994	3,189	146
1995	3,380	191
1996	3,398	18
		3,398

Source : SBI Mutual Fund Annual Reports—Various Issues.

Table 3.9
SBI Mutual Fund Schemes—Total Funds Collected

(Rs. Crore)

Year	*Cumulative Total Funds (CF)*	*(F)*
1988	131	131
1989	422	291
1990	712	290
1991	1,383	671
1992	1,590	207
1993	2,693	1,103
1994	2,835	142
1995	3,054	219
1996	3,128	74
		3,128

Source : SBI Mutual Fund - Annual Reports - Various issues.

Table 3.10
Funds Mobilised by Can Bank MF

(Rs. Crore)

Year	*Rs.*	*Growth %*
1987-88	119.29	—
1988-89	183.74	154.03
1989-90	460.55	250.65
1990-91	997.87	216.67
1991-92	1,268.36	127.11
1992-93	15.82	1.24
1993-94	43.11	272.50
1994-95	180.00	417.54
Total	3,268.74	

Source : Annual Reports of Can bank MF. Results Computed.

cent. Its simple yield was 21.5 per cent. It was redeemed on 30.06.1993.

Magnum Regular Income Scheme (MRIS 89) 89 has been redeemed at a price of Rs. 153.85 ps on 31st March, 1994. Total dividend of 53.86 per cent was given. Capital appreciation of 53.85 per cent was made. Its CAGR was 19.61 per cent. Its simple yield was 21.52 per cent.

Magnum Regular Income Scheme 90 was redeemed on 31st July 1995 at a capital appreciation of 7.28 per cent and its simple yield was 14.44 per cent. The redemption price paid was Rs. 107.28 at the time of redemption. The Registrars of the scheme was Mafatlal Computer Services.

Magnum Monthly Income Schemes (MMIS) Mis-89 and MMIS-91 were the two monthly income schemes with target return of 12 per cent and 13 per cent respectively. MMIS-89 was to be redeemed in March, 1993 has been extended up to December 1996 at a higher monthly pay out of 15 per cent.

Magnum Tax Saving Scheme 88-89 (MTSS 88-89) was commenced from 1st April, 1989 having a face value of Rs. 100 and redeemed on 31st March, 1994 at a redemption price of Rs. 222 with a capital appreciation of 122.00 per cent and having a simple yield of 33.80 per cent per annum. MTSS-90 scheme was started from 1st April, 1990 with a face value of Rs. 100 and redeemed on 1st April, 1995 with a redemption price of Rs. 172. Is capital appreciation was figured at 72 per cent? Is simple yield stood at 20.90 per cent per annum? The registrars of the issue was Mafatlal Computer Services.

In regard to growth schemes the performance was nice and have outperformed the national indices consistently, when CAGR was calculated since inception of the scheme.

Organisational Network

SBIMF has a widely spread investor base of over 28 lakhs, prompt and quick response to investor queries has assumed prime importance. The fund has been established 13 focal points all over the nation: Bombay, Ahmedabad, Bangalore, Bhopal, Bhubaneswar, Calcutta, Chandigarh, Delhi, Hyderabad, Lucknow, Madras, Patna and Guwahati. While Bombay centre is located in the AMC office the other centres are located at the State Bank of India local head offices or at suitable prominent locations in the respective centres and funds as a investor support hand.

Canara Bank Mutual Fund

Canara Bank was founded on 1st July, 1906 as the Canara Hindi Permanent Fund Ltd. in Mangalore. It was changed to Canara Bank in 1910. The main activities of the Bank include commercial banking, credit card (in house), merchant banking, mutual fund (subsidiary), factoring (subsidiary), housing finance (subsidiary), leasing (subsidiary), venture capital fund (subsidiary) and Indo Hong-Kong International Finance Co. (Deposit taking company). Having a big background and nice track record, it acted as a sponsor bank for Canara Bank Mutual Fund. Can bank Mutual Fund was set up by it pursuant to the approval received by it from Government of India, Ministry of Finance, New Delhi vide their Letter No. D.O. No. F.1/65/SE/87 dated: 15th December, 1987 for making investment in equity and other securities. SEBI granted registration vide registration No. MF/004/93/4 dated 19.10.1993. The fund has also been recognised under section 10 (23 D) of Income Tax Act, 1961 vide Notification No. SO/1064/E dated 18.11.1988 issued by CBDT, Department of Revenue, Ministry of Finance, Government of India.

The basic objective of the Fund is to channelise the savings from a wide cross-section of the people and to provide them attractive returns by way of annual income distribution/capital appreciation by investment in capital market and to provide security and liquidity.

The Fund constituted a Board of Trustees to manage the fund. The board consisted of one Chairman and four Board of Trustees.

The Board of Trustees created Asset Management Company to entrust the day-to-day management of the fund. Can bank Investment Management Services Limited, a wholly owned subsidiary of Canara Bank (sponsor bank) has been set up as per the SEBI Regulations of 1993. An investment management agreement has been signed between the mutual fund and the investment manager whereby Can bank Investment Management Services Ltd. is empowered to manage the affairs of Can bank Investment Management Services Ltd. included the following:

One Chairman, one Vice Chairman and five Directors. Among Directors, one is the Managing Director.

Organisation Structure

The Chairman of the Asset Management Company is separate. The Chairman of Canara Bank is separate. Many of employees are direct recruits. There are two General Managers from the Bank. Of the Assistant General Managers, 2 are direct recruits and three are from the Bank. All other employees are direct recruits. The Canbank MF has 19 schemes. There are three open ended schemes and the rest of close ended schemes. The mobilisation of savings is made through the vast branch network of sponsor bank, viz., Canara Bank.

There is an in-house researach team. The investment decision is based on both fundamental and technical analysis by an in-house research team. The AMC has got an exclusive and full fledged research department headed by an Assistant General Manager and assisted by research professionals and an economist.

The fund has various schemes which are categorised into *(i)* Pure growth schemes, *(ii)* Income and growth schemes, *(iii)* High income and capital growth schemes, and *(iv)* Tax Planning and Growth schemes.

Schemes of Canbank MF

CANSHARE

It is the close ended scheme. It was launched in 1987. Face value of each unit is Rs. 10. The scheme is a "High growth scheme" with a thrust on maximum growth opportunities. The surplus distributable income of the scheme is distributed by way of dividend and bonus in the form of fully paid shares of both. It is highly a rewarding scheme to the investors which is evident from the distribution/payout policy in the last various years.

Year	*1998*	*1989*	*1990*	*1991-92*	*1992-93*
Income Distribution	20%	20%	15%	35%	15%
Bonus	2:5	—	2:5	—	—

CANSTOCK

It is a close ended scheme. It is "income and growth scheme". It was launched in 1987. The unit's face value is Rs. 100. This shall be redeemable on or after completion of five years. But before 7th year and the scheme has completed 5 years on 31.03.1993.

Income Distribution

Year	*1988*	*1989*	*1990*	*1991-92*	*1992-93*
Income	13.5%	14.5%	15.5%	21% (15 Months)	12.5%

CANGROWTH

This is a pure growth scheme launched in October, 1989. The face value of each unit is Rs. 10. The initial corpus was 60.17 crores. The redemption may be any time before 1996. This scheme was launched with an objective of long-term capital appreciation with an eye on the growth factor. The income distribution of the scheme would be by way of dividend or fully paid shares in the form of bonus or both.

CANCIGO

This is an income oriented scheme. This is an open ended scheme. The scheme is designed mainly to suit the requirements of individuals who wish to have assured returns at regular intervals.

CANGILT

It is an open ended scheme. It was launched in 1988. The scheme was targetted to the individual and corporate bodies who wish to invest large sums, has continued its good performance in the current year.

CAN 80 CC-90

It was launched in March 1990. Face value of each unit is Rs. 10. Initial corpus of the scheme was Rs. 158.78 crores. This is a growth cum tax planning scheme.

The objective of the scheme provides for investments of funds collected by the Mutual Fund only in shares/securities of such companies which were allowed certain benefits under the then Section 80 CC of the Income Tax Act. The tax benefits under the above provision were available for the investments made in capital issues of eligible new issues.

CANSTAR

It was launched in September, 1990. Its corpus size was Rs. 791 crore. This is a high income based capital growth fund. The main objective of the fund is to aim at generation of high income. The scheme provides for declaration of annual income distribution which will be reinvested. Face value of each unit is Rs. 10.

CANPEP - 91

It is a tax planning cum growth scheme. It is a growth oriented scheme. It was launched during March, 1991. Face value of each unit is Rs. 10. This offers twin benefits to the investors, saving in tax upto Rs. 10,000 under section 80 CCB at the time of investment and the capital appreciation on the same. Initial corpus was Rs. 206.57 crores. The scheme has long-term of 10 years and is to be redeemed in 2001.

CANPREMIUM

The scheme was in May 1991. The face value is Rs. 1 lakh per unit. The scheme is designed for a period of 60 months. Subsequently the units were split into Rs. 10,000 face value to make marketable lots.

CANBONUS

This was launched as a pure growth scheme as a preferential offer to reward the existing investors during May/June 1991. The income distribution in this scheme would be by way of fullypaid CANBONUS units. Initial corpus of the scheme was Rs. 106.34 crore. The investors in it are 3 lakhs. It shall be redeemed between 1998-2001.

CANTRIPLE

The scheme was launched with an objective of long-term growth designed in such a way that the income distribution in every will be reinvested.

CANPEP-92

It was launched in March 1992. Face value of each unit is Rs. 10. Initial corpus was Rs. 306.54 crores. Which is launched in terms of Equity Linked Savings Scheme as prescribed by the Central Government under the Income Tax Act, 1961. The scheme, interalia, provided for income tax benefit under section 80 CCB to the investors.

CANPEP-93

It was launched in February/March, 1993. It was the equity linked saving scheme. It has collected around Rs. 14.92 crores.

CANGANGA

It slated for launch in the second week of January, 1995.

Table 3.11
Various Schemes of Canbank MF at a Glance

Sl. No.	*Schemes*	*Nature*	*Month and Year of Launch*	*Number of Investors*	*Initial Corpus*	*Dividend Bonus*
1.	Canstock	Income-cum-Growth	Jan. 1988	11,869	102.87	Dividend
2.	Cancigo	Income-cum-Growth	Apr. 1988	3,063	33.77	Dividend
3.	Cangilt	Income-cum-Growth	Jun. 1988	4	4.53	Dividend
4.	Canshare	Growth	Jun. 1988	39,787	17.05	Dividend Bonus
5.	Cangrowth	Growth	Oct. 1989	1,40,221	48.13	Dividend Bonus
6.	Can double	Income-cum-Growth	Feb. 1990	1,39,506	254.19	Dividend
7.	Can 80CC (90)	Tax Planning	Mar. 1990	1,03,899	158.15	Dividend
8.	Can star	Income-cum-Growth	Sept. 1990	3,39,247	791.30	Dividend
9.	Can pep'91	Tax Planning	Mar. 1991	3,03,341	206.57	Dividend
10.	Can Premium	Income-cum-Growth	May. 1991	49	509.2	Dividend
11.	Can bonus	Growth	June. 1991	3,06,585	106.34	Dividend Bonus
12.	Can triple+	Income-cum-Growth	Dec. 1991	57,496	346.28	Dividend
13.	Can pep '92	Tax Planning	Mar. 1992	2,92,296	306.54	Dividend
14.	Can pep'93	Tax Planning	Mar. 1993	19,899	14.92	Dividend.

Note : Can Star (80 L) and Can star (CG)= 2 Schemes Combined.

Ind Bank Mutual Fund

Indian Bank Limited was incorporated on March 5, 1907. Its authorised capital was Rs. 20 lakhs and it commenced business on August 15, 1907. Later, it was nationalised and become Indian Bank on coversation into a public sector bank. From a modest beginning the bank has emerged as one of the major commercial banks in the country . It celebrated its platinum jubilee in 1982. The Bank of Tanjavur Ltd., with 157 branches and offices was amalgamated with the bank on February 20, 1990. The bank has crossed the Rs. 11,000 crores mark in terms of global deposits as at the end of March, 1993. Indian bank activities include commercial banking, mutual funds (subsidiary), merchant banking (subsidiary), housing finance (subsidiary), and cash card (in house).

Indian Bank has created a trust for the purpose of setting up a mutual fund. The trust pools the funds raised from the investors from the members of public for collective investment which would include subscription, acquisition, holding, management, trading or disposal of securities or any other assets whatsoever for the purpose of having the effect of providing facilities for participation by the persons as beneficiaries in profits or income arising therefrom. Indian Bank Mutual Fund has been set up, persuant to the approval received from the Reserve Bank of India vide their Letter No. DBOD No. ESC 139/C 469-89 dated 6th November 1989, as trust on 17.11.1989 with Indian Bank as settler and principal trustee. SEBI has also granted registration vide Regn. No. MF/011/94/7 dated 17.03.1994. Indian Bank Mutual Fund has also been recognised under Section 10 (23D) of Income Tax Act, 1961 vide Notification No. SO 268 (E) dated March 19, 1990 issued by CBDT, Department of Revenue, Ministry of Finance, Government of India. Indian Bank has made an initial contribution of Rs. 25 lakhs towards the trust. It has appointed a Board of Trustees to supervise the activities of the Indian Bank Mutual Fund. Indian Bank is the principal trustee of the MF.

Sri S. Rajagopal,
Chairman and Managing Director of Indian Bank
He acts as Chairman of the Board of Trustees.

Sri M.B. Nageswara Rao,
General Manager, Indian Bank, Madras
Trustee.

Sri K. R. Ramamani,
Advocate and Tax Consultant, Madras
Trustee.

Sri C. G. Rangabhasham,
Management Consultant,
Madras,
Trustee.

The Board of Trustee have entrusted the work of Management of the Fund to Indfund Management Limited, which is a wholly owned subsidiary of Indian Bank with a paid up capital of Rs. 5 crores, Investment Agreement has been signed between Indian Bank Mutual Fund and Indfund Management Ltd., the investment manager, whereby Indfund Management Limited is empowered to manage the affairs of Indian Bank Mutual Fund and operate its various schemes. It makes investment decisions and manages the Fund in accordance with the scheme's objectives, investment agreement and the trust deed. The Board of Directors include the following professionals:

Sri S. Arunachalam,
General Manager, Indian Bank

Dr. V. L. Mote,
Retd. Professor,
Indian Institute of Management, Ahmedabad
Director

Sri K. Venkatrama Iyer,
Management Consultant, Cochin, as Director

Sri K. M. Gopinath
Managing Director

Ind Ratna

Ind Ratna is a growth scheme. Units were allotted on 23rd February, 1990. The face value of unit is Rs. 10. The scheme shall be redeemed after the expiry of 5 years but not later than 6 years from the date of allotment. The investment objective of the scheme is to generate substantial capital appreciation. To achieve this objective, the policy of investment is to invest a relatively high proportion of funds in equities with good growth potential, for achieving capital appreciation and to invest a small portion of the fund in fixed income and other securities to generate current income. The trustees declared a dividend of 17 per cent p.a. for the first year (1990-91), 25 per cent p.a. for the second year (1991-92), 27 per cent p.a. for the third year (1992-93), 30 per cent p.a. for the fourth year (1993-94) and 35 per cent p.a. for the fifth year (1994-95).

As per the agreement, Ind Ratna scheme has been redeemed/ rolled over on the expiry of the scheme period. Under Ind Ratna scheme, 47.75 per cent (Rs. 14.54 crores in value) of the investors have opted for roll over the units. The trustees have declared a loyalty dividend @ 5 per cent per unit in respect of original allottees under the scheme, who have continued in the scheme till redemption/roll over date. The investor who has invested Rs. 10. in Ind Ratna scheme in 1990 has earned a total dividend of Rs. 14.07 till 22.02.1996, giving an annualised yield of 26.63 per cent. The unit holders who have opted for redemption, the units have been redeemed at the NAV of Rs. 14.14 per unit. The scheme has been rolled over for another five years. Under Ind Ratna (Roll Over) scheme, the Board of Trustees are pleased to declare a dividend of 15 per cent p.a. for the year 1995-96. The NAV as on March 31, 1996 stands at Rs. 11.94 ex-dividend.

Swarna Pushpa

Swarna Pushpa is an income scheme. Units were allotted on 23rd February, 1990. The face value of each unit is Rs. 100. The scheme shall be redeemed after the expiry of 5 years but not later than 6 years from the date of allotment. The investment objective of the scheme is to generate regular income for investors. To achieve this objective, the policy of investments is to invest a relatively high proportion of funds in fixed income and other securities, to generate high current income and to invest a small portion of funds in equities for achieving capital appreciation. The Board of Trustees have declared an income distribution of 14.25 per cent p.a. for the first year (1990-91), 18 per cent p.a. for the second year (1991-92), 19 per cent p.a. for the third year (1992-93), 20 per cent p.a for the fourth year (1993-94), and 21 per cent p.a. for the fifth year (1994-95). Swarna Pushpa has been redeemed/rolled over on the expiry of the respective scheme period. Under Swarna Pushpa scheme, 23 per cent (Rs. 12 crores in value) of the investors have opted for the roll over of the units. The investor who has invested Rs. 100. in 1990 has earned a total dividend of Rs. 104.14 till 31.01.1996. The unit holders have opted for redemption. The unit have been redeemed at the NAV of Rs. 101.72 per unit, giving an annualised yield of 17.84 per cent. This has been rolled over for another five years. Post dated warrants for the minimum assured dividend of 13 per cent have been provided for 12 months to the monthly unit holders.

Ind Jyothi

It is an income scheme. The face value of each unit is Rs. 10. The units were allotted on 1st December, 1990. The scheme shall be redeemed after the expiry of 7 years from the date of allotment but not later than 31st March, 1998. The investment objective is to generate regular income for investors. To achieve this objective, the policy of investment is to invest relatively high proportion of funds in mixed income and other securities to generate high current income and to invest a small portion of funds in equities for achieving capital appreciation. The Board of Trustees have declared an income distribution of 16.5 per cent p.a. for the first accounting year (01.12.90 to 31.03.92) and 18 per cent for the year (1992-93), 19 per cent for the third year (1993-94), 20 per cent for the fourth year (1994-95), and 14.75 per cent for the fifth year (1995-96).

This scheme has two plans, viz., under Plan A of the scheme, dividend declared is distributed and under Plan B of the scheme, dividend declared is reinvested in the scheme itself.

Ind Sagar

Ind Sagar is a Capital Gains Scheme. Its units were allotted on 1st September, 1991. The face value of each unit is Rs. 10. The scheme shall be redeemed on or after 31st March, 2001 but not later than 15th June 2001. The investment objective of the scheme is to generate substantial capital appreciation and therefore income generated every year will not be distributed until redemption but will be reinvested. To achieve this objective, the policy of investment is to invest a relatively high proportion of funds in equities with good growth potential for achieving capital appreciation and to invest a small portion of the funds in fixed income and other securities to generate current income. It is included in the Growth Scheme. As per the terms of the scheme, the net surplus generated by the scheme every year has been redeployed.

Ind Moti

Ind Moti is an equity growth scheme. Units were allotted on 1st September, 1991. It shall be redeemed on or after 31st March, 1997 but not later than 30th June, 1997.

The investment objective of the scheme is to generate substantial capital appreciation. To achieve this objective, the policy of investment is to invest a relatively high proportion of funds in equities with good growth potential, for achieving capital appreciation and to invest small portion of the funds in fixed income and other securities to generate current income.

The Board of Trustees have declared a dividend of 15 per cent p.a. for the current year, (01.09.91 to 31st March 1993), 18 per cent in second year (1993-94),21 per cent in third year (1994-95) and no dividend was declared in view of the provision made for depreciation in the value of investments.

Ind 88A

It is a tax saving scheme under Section 88A of the Income Tax Act, 1961. Units were allotted on 28th September, 1990. The face value of each unit is Rs.100. It shall be redeemed after the expiry of 5 years but not later than 31st March, 1996.

The investment objective of the scheme is to invest in "Eligible Securities" of capital under Section 88A of the Income Tax Act. It provides tax rebate to investors for the financial year ended 31st March, 1991. To achieve this objective, the policy of investments will be attuned to maximising capital appreciation of the fund by investing fully in securities that are eligible for tax rebate under Section 88A of the Income Tax Act and those securities that may be permitted by the appropriate authorities. The Board of Trustees have declared a dividend of 15 per cent p.a. for the first accounting year (1990-92), 18 per cent p.a. for the second year (1992-93), 21 per cent for the third year (1993-94), 24 per cent for the fourth year (1994-95).

Under Ind 88A scheme, the units allotted under the scheme, in terms of the offer document have become due for redemption on March 31, 1996. The investor who has invested Rs. 100 in Ind 88A scheme in 1990, has earned a total dividend of Rs. 78 till 31st March, 1996. The units under the scheme shall be redeemed at NAV of RFs. 128.07 per unit, giving an annualised yield of 19.14 per cent.

In view of the termination of the scheme, no dividend has been declared on Ind 88A.

Ind Shelter-Plan A

It is a tax saving scheme. The face value of each unit is Rs. 100. Units were allotted on 31st March, 1992. It shall be redeemed on 31st March, 2002.

The Investment Objective of the scheme is to enable investors to avail themselves of benefits under Section 80 CCB of the Income Tax Act, 1961 for the financial year ended 31st March, 1992 and to attempt at generation of capital growth. To achieve this objective, the policy of investment is to invest in equities, convertible debentures and other equity related securities and investments.

The Board of Trustees have declared a dividend of 24 per cent for the current year 1994-95.

Ind Shelter-Plan B

It is a tax saving scheme. Face value of each unit under the scheme is Rs. 100. Units were allotted on 31st March, 1992. It shall be redeemed on 31st March, 2002.

The investment objective of the scheme is to enable investors to avail themselves of benefits under Section 80CCB of the Income Tax Act, 1961 for the financial year ended 31st March, 1992 and to attempt at generation of capital growth. To achieve this objective, the policy of investment is to invest in equities convertible debentures and other equity related investments.

Ind Prakash

Ind Prakash is an income scheme. Face value of each unit under this scheme is Rs. 10. Units were allotted on 1st June, 1992. The units under this scheme shall be redeemed on 30th November, 1999.

The investment objective of the scheme is to generate regular income for investors. To achieve this objective, the policy of investment is to invest in fixed income and other securities to generate high current income and to invest a small portion of funds in equities for achieving capital appreciation.

The Board of Trustees have declared an income distribution of 12 per cent p.a. for the first year (1992-93), 18 per cent p.a. for the second year (1993-94), 19 per cent for the third year (1994-95), 15.75

per cent p.a. for the fourth year has been declared (1995-96).

As per the terms of "Plan A" of the scheme, dividend declared is distributed and under "Plan B" of the scheme, dividend declared is reinvested in the scheme itself.

Ind Tax Shield-Plan A

It is a tax savings scheme. The face value of each unit is Rs. 10. Units were allotted on 31st March, 1992. It shall be redeemed on 31st March, 2002. The investment objective of the scheme is to enable investors to avail themselves of benefits under Section 80 CCB of the Income Tax Act, 1961 for the financial year ended 31st March, 1992 and to attempt at generation of capital growth. To achieve this objective, the policy of investment is to invest in equities, convertible debentures and other equity related investments.

The Board of Trustees have declared a dividend of 24 per cent for the year 1994-95.

Ind Shelter-Plan B

It is a tax saving scheme. The face value of each unit is Rs. 10. Units were allotted on 31st March, 1992. The scheme shall be redeemed on 31st March, 2002. The investments objectives are same as 'Plan A'. As per the terms of the scheme, the net surplus generated by the scheme every year has been redeployed.

Ind Tax Shield-Plan 'A'

It is a tax saving scheme. Face value of each unit is Rs. 10. Units were allotted on 31st March, 1993. It shall be redeemed on 31st March, 2003.

The investment objective of the scheme is to enable investors to avail themselves of the benefits under Section 88 of the Income Tax Act, 1961 for the financial year ended 31.03.93 and to attempt to generate capital growth. To achieve this objective, the policy of investment is to invest in equities, convertible debentures and other equity related investments. The Board of Trustees have declared a dividend of 15 per cent p.a. for the first year (1993-94) and 18 per cent for the second year (1994-95).

Ind Tax Shield-Plan 'B'

It is a tax saving scheme. Face value of each unit is Rs. 10. Units were allotted on 31st March, 1993. The scheme shall be redeemed on

31st March, 2003. The investment objective is to enable investors to avail themselves of benefits under Income Tax Act under Section 89 for the financial year ended 31st March, 1993 and to attempt at generation of capital growth. To achieve this objective, the policy of investment is to invest in equities, convertible debentures and other equity related investments. As per the terms of the scheme, the entire surplus generated every year is redeployed in the scheme itself.

Ind Navratna

It is growth scheme. Face value of each unit is Rs. 10. Its units were allotted on 1st July, 1994. The scheme shall be redeemed after the expiry of 5 years on 1st July, 1999. The investment objective of the scheme is to generate substantial capital appreciation. To achieve this objective, the policy of investment is to invest a relatively high proportion of funds in equities with good growth potential, for achieving capital appreciation and to invest a small portion of the funds in fixed income and other securities to generate current income. The Board of Trustees have declared a dividend of 15 per cent p.a. for the first year (1994-95).

Bank of India Mutual Fund

Bank of India was founded on 7th September, 1906. It was under private ownership till it was nationalised in July, 1969. Besides commercial banking operations, it has merchant banking department. A fully owned subsidiary, the BOI Finance Ltd., has been taken over the work of merchant banking.

Bank of India established a BOI Mutual Fund, a trust and registered with SEBI. It also got approval from RBI to set up Mutual Fund Business. The trust is sponsored by Bank of India. BOI MF is registered under the Indian Trust Act, 1882. The trustee exclusive ownership of the trust fund and are vested with the general power of superintendence, direction and management of the affairs of the trust. The trustees appoint the asset management company and the custodian and have to ensure that they fulfill the functions assigned to them from time to time subject to the trust deed and mutual fund regulations and other laws in force. Bank of India Asset Management Company (BOIAMC0) was incorporated on December 24, 1993 by Bank of India to manage the operations and investment of BOIMF. The paid up capital of BOIAMC is Rs. 5 crores.

Table 3.12
Ind Bank Mutual Fund Schemes

Name of the Scheme	Face Value Rs.	Date of Allotment of Units
Growth Schemes		
Ind Ratna	10	23.02.90
Ind Sagar	100	01.09.91
Ind Moti	10	01.09.91
Ind Navratna	10	01.07.94
Income Schemes		
Swarna Puspa	100	23.02.90
Ind Jyothi - A	10	01.12.90
Ind Jyothi - B	10	01.12.90
Ind Prakash - A	10	01.06.92
Ind Prakash - B	10	01.06.92
Tax Saving Growth Schemes		
Ind 88 A	100	28.09.90
Ind Shelter - A	100	31.03.92
Ind Shelter - B	100	31.03.92
Ind Tax Shield - A	10	31.03.93
Ind Tax Shield - B	10	31.03.93

BOI Asset Management Company Limited is to operate and manage the scheme of BOI Mutual Fund. Of the 56 employees, 47 are recruited and 9 are on deputation from Bank of India. It has four analysts with about four years' experience. It collects the funds through the network of the sponsor bank through the designated branches of other nationalised banks like Punjab & Sind Bank and UCO Bank. Among foreign banks it has Bank of Tokyo and smaller banks like Bank of Sanghi. It caters services through the three registrar agents, viz., Karvy Consultants and IIT Corporate Services Ltd. With regard to investment management of the fund, Managing Director and Investment Chief manage solely. Investment can be made only in permitted securities viz., quoted shares and debentures, securitised debts, privately placed securities, unquoted securities, etc., subject to limits as prescribed by the SEBI (Mutual

Fund) Regulations 1993. There are separate committees for investment in *(i)* Primary Market; *(ii)* Secondary Market; *(iii)* Debt Market; and *(iv)* Money Market. All the committees are headed by Managing Director.

Scheme

The design of various schemes is done by a joint management team. All schemes have to be approved by BOI Mutual Fund and SEBI. Asset Management Company is to receive its management and advisory fees on the basis of performance measured by appreciation in NAV. BOI MF has 13,000 agent force. It has six different schemes. The schemes are:

(i) Double Square Plus (1990);

(ii) Rising Monthly Income-60 (RMI-60);

(iii) Festival Bonanza Growth Scheme, 1991;

(iv) BONANZA 80 CCB;

(v) Bonanza Equity Linked Saving on Tax Scheme, 1993 (BEST-1993); and

(vi) Bonanza Exclusive Growth Scheme.

BOI Double Square Plus (Double^{2+})

It is a close-end scheme. It is a growth scheme. Its face value is Rs.100. It opened for subscription from June 25 to August 31st, 1990. It collected Rs. 482 crores from over 45,000 investors. The scheme is to be redeemed on 31st August, 2000. It has two different schemes, viz. *(i)* Income Plan-A, and *(ii)* Growth Plan-B. Under Plan-A, it collected Rs. 247.77 crores and for Plan-A, an amount of Rs. 234.03 crores. The registrars for management of the scheme is Datamatics Limited, Mumbai.

Rising Monthly Income Scheme-60

It is a close-end balance fund. Its face value is Rs. 100. It was open for subscription from June 25 to August 31, 1990. The duration of the scheme was five years. The redemption shall be made on 31st August, 1995. It has two plans, viz. *(i)* Income Plan and *(ii)* Growth Plan. The corpus of Income Plan was Rs. 94.66 crores and growth plan amounted to Rs. 15.05 crores.

Table 3.13
BOI Mutual Fund Schemes at a Glance

Sl. No.	Name of Scheme	Nature	Date/Year of Commencement	Corpus	Redemption	Type of Scheme	Duration of Scheme	No. of Investors	Assured Return
1	2	3	4	5	6	7	8	9	10
1.	D2 Plus 1990 Growth B	Income Plan	September, 1990	247.73/ 234.03	31.08.2000	F.V. = Rs.100	10 Years	4,50,000	14.87
2.	RMI - 60 1990	Income Plan Growth Plan	September, 1990	94.66/ 15.05	31.08.1995	F.V. = Rs.100	5 Years	48,000	15.5
3.	F.B.G.S. 1991	Growth Plan A Income Plan B	December, 1991	33.63 7.44	December, 1996/97	F.V. = Rs. 10	5/6 Years	13,200	
4.	88 CCB	Growth Plan A Income Plan B	April, 1992	24.35 7.70	31.03.2002	F.V. = Rs. 10	10 Years	36,000	
5.	BEST 93	Growth Plan A Income Plan B	April, 1993	4.75	March, 2003		10 Years	9,150	
6.	RIPS 1990	Income	June, 1990	5,986.58 lakhs as on 31.03.94					

7.	ELSS, 1991	Tax Planning	February, 1991	7,743.18 lakhs as on 31.03.94
8.	Premium Plus	Income Growth	November, 1991	9,222.70 lakhs as on 31.03.94
9.	ELSS, 1992	Tax Planning	March, 1992	5,436.43 lakhs as on 31.03.94
10.	Equity Growth	Growth Tax Planning	March, 1993	2,516.28 lakhs as on 31.03.94

Table 3.14
PNB Mutual Fund Schemes at a Glance

Sl. No.	Name of Scheme	Nature	Date/Year of Commencement	Corpus	Redemption	Type of Scheme	Duration of Scheme	No. of Investors	Assured Return
1.	PNB Equity Linked Saving Scheme—1991 (80 CCB)	Tax Planning	February, 1991	17.44 crores	April, 2001	—	10 Years	—	—
2.	PNB Premium Plus—1991	Growth	October, 1991	—	—	—	6 to 8 Years	—	—
3.	PNB Equity Linked Saving Scheme—1992	—	April, 1992	—	April, 2002	—	10 Years	—	—
4.	PNB Equity Growth Fund	—	—	—	—	—	—	—	—
5.	PNB Rising Income Plus Scheme-1994	—	—	—	—	—	—	—	—
6.	PNB Regular Income Plus —1990	Income	June, 1990	63.3 crores	September, 1996	—	6 Years	—	12.5

Festival Bonanza Growth Scheme

It was floated in October, 1991. The face value of each unit is Rs. 10. The investors are 13,200. The registrars of the scheme is Karvy Con. Pvt. Ltd. Mumbai. It has two plans, i.e., *(i)* Growth Plan, and *(ii)* Income Plan. The corpus of Growth Plan-A is Rs. 33.63 crores. The corpus of Income Plan-B is Rs. 7.33 crores.

Bonanza 80 CCB

It is a tax planning scheme. It was launched in March 1992. Its face value is Rs. 10. It shall be redeemed on 2002. The duration of the scheme is 10 years. It is close-ended scheme. It has two plans, viz. Growth Plan-A and Income Plan-B. The initial corpus of growth plan is Rs. 24.35 crores and income plan-B is 7.7 crores.

Bonanza Equity Linked Savings on Tax Scheme

It is a tax planning scheme. It was launched in March, 1993. The investors were 9,150. The face value of each unit is Rs. 10. It has two plans, i.e., Growth Plan-A and Income Plan-B. Initial corpus of the scheme is Rs. 4.76 crores. The registrars are II Corp. Services Ltd.

Punjab National Bank Mutual Fund

Punjab National Bank has set up a PNB Mutual Fund in 1990.

Schemes

Regular Income Plus Scheme (RIPS) : It is a close-end scheme. It was launched in June, 1990. The objective of the scheme is to provide steady income to investors. The assured minimum annual rate of return is 12.5 per cent. The units of the scheme shall be redeemed in September, 1996. The duration of the scheme is 6 years. Initial corpus is Rs. 63.3 crores.

PNB Premium Plus : It is an income-cum-growth scheme. It was launched in November, 1991. The corpus of the scheme is Rs. 92.21 crores. The redemption date shall fall in January, 1997 and may be extended upto January, 1999. The duration of the scheme is 6 to 8 years.

PNB ELSS-91

It is an equity linked savings scheme. It was launched in 1991 February. The initial corpus of the scheme is Rs. 17.44 crore. The scheme is for 10 years duration having a lock-in-period of 3 years. The objective of the scheme is to offer tax benefits under Section 80 CCB. It shall be redeemed in April, 2001.

PNB-Equity Linked Savings Scheme : It is a tax planning scheme. It was launched in April, 1992. It is a ten year scheme. It shall be redeemed in 2002.

LIC Mutual Fund

Life Insurance Industry was nationalised and consequently Life Insurance Corporation of India (LIC) came into existence on 01.09.1956 by an Act of Parliament. Since then, it is doing Life Insurance business covering entire Indian Territory. LIC has to day the largest family of savers around 6 crore policy holders. It has nearly 2000 branches and 100 divisional offices. It has its Central Office in Mumbai and has 7 Zonal Offices at Mumbai, Delhi, Kanpur, Calcutta, Hyderabad and Chennai. It has 18,000 development offices and around 6 lakh agents. It renders multi-dimensional services such as, Life Insurance, Group-Insurance, Group Pension Plans, Individual Pension Plans, Social Security Schemes, annuity business etc.

Having such a track record in business activities, LIC established another new venture LIC Mutual Fund. It was established on 19.06.1989. The basic objectives are:

(i) to mobilise savings of people, especially, from rural and semi-urban areas;
(ii) to provide good returns on investment;
(iii) to assure safety, security and liquidity of capital.

LIC MF has, therefore, been established as a catalytic agent between investors and capital market. LIC MF has been recognised under Section 10 (23 D) of the Income Tax Act, 1961 vide Gazette S.O. 477 (E), Part II, Section 3, Sub-Section (II) dated 22.06.1989. LIC sponsored the LIC MF. The trust deed was executed by LIC as a settler. It contributed Rs. 2 crores in which it shall have no beneficial interest. It created a Board of Trustees. In terms of SEBI (Mutual Fund) Regulations, 1993, an Asset Management Company (AMC) called the Jeevan Bhima Sahayog Asset Management

Company Limited, with an authorised capital of Rs. 5 crores. It has separate Board of Directors.

The administration and the day-to-day operation of the MF is looked after by the AMC. AMC has the Chief Executive who looks after day-to-day affairs with the help of a dedicated team of employees drawn from LIC and some are directly recurited.

LIC MF has made an agreement with Central Bank of India for collection of subscriptions under its different schemes through designated branches. Funds collected are invested in the light of general guidelines of Government and SEBI and the predetermined objectives of the scheme.

Dhanvriddhi-1989

It was launched in June, 1989. It is an income cum growth scheme. It is an open-end scheme. The assured return is 12 per cent. The corpus of the scheme is Rs. 2.43 crore. The redemption duration is 7 to 8 years. It shall be redeemed in 1996-97.

Dhan 80 CC (I)

It was launched in March, 1990. It shall be redeemed in 1994-95. It is a growth-cum-tax savings scheme. The corpus was Rs. 23.16 crores.

Dhanvarsha (1) Option 1

It was launched in February, 1990. It shall be redeemed in 1995. It is a monthly income scheme. It is a close-ended scheme. The corpus of the scheme is Rs. 77.81 crores.

Dhanvarsha (2) Option 2

It was launched in October, 1990. It is a growth-cum-income scheme. The assured return was 12.5 per cent.

Dhansahayog

It was launched in January, 1991. It is an income-cum-growth scheme. It is an open-end scheme. It has collected a corpus of Rs. 61.43 crores.

Dhanashree-1989

It is an income and growth scheme. It was launched in June, 1989. The duration of the scheme is 6 to 7 years. It is a close ended scheme. The minimum assured return assured is 12 per cent The

Table 3.15
LIC Mutual Fund Schemes at a Glance

Sl. No	Scheme	Nature	Date and Year of Launch	Redemption
1	2	3	4	5
1.	Dhanashree 1989 Growth	Income and 1989	November,	1995-1996
2.	Dhanaraksha 1989 Growth	Income and	June, 1989	1999-2004
3.	Dhanavridhi 1989 Growth	Income and	June, 1989	1996-1999
4.	Dhan 80 CC (1) Tax Saving	Growth-cum-	March, 1990	1994-1995
5.	Dhanavarsha (1) Option 1	Income	May, 1990	Nov. 1995
6.	Dhanavarsha (1) Option 2	Income	May, 1990	Nov. 1995
7.	Dhanashree—1990 Growth	Income and 1990	September,	1996-1997
8.	Dhanavarsha (2) Option 1	Income and Growth	December, 1990	1996
9.	Dhanavarsha (2) Option 2	Income and Growth	December, 1990	1996
10.	Dhanavarsha (2) Option 3	Income and Growth	December, 1990	1996
11.	Dhanavarsha (2) Option 4	Income and Growth	December, 1990	1996
12.	Dhan 80 CCB (1) Plan A	Tax Planning	March, 1991	2001
13.	Dhan 80 CCB (1) Plan B	Tax Planning	March, 1991	2001
14.	Dhan 80 CCB (1) Plan C	Tax Planning	March, 1991	2001
15.	Dhanasahayog Plan A	Income and Growth	April, 1991	Open-end
16.	Dhanasahayog Plan B	Income and Growth	April, 1991	Open-end

(Contd.)

1	2	3	4	5
17.	Dhanasahayog Plan C	Income and Growth	April, 1991	Open-end
18.	Dhanavarsha (3) Option 1	Income and Growth	June, 1991	Sept. 1996
19.	Dhanavarsha (3) Option 2	Income and Growth	June, 1991	Sept. 1996
20.	Dhanavarsha (3) Option 3	Income and Growth	June, 1991	Sept. 1996
21.	Dhanavarsha (3) Option 4	Income and Growth	June, 1991	Sept. 1996
22.	Dhanashree—1991 Growth	Income and 1991	October,	1997-1998
23.	Dhanalakshmi (1) Option 1	Income and Growth	February, 1992	Feb. 1997
24.	Dhanalakṣhmi (1) Option 2	Income and Growth	February, 1992	Feb. 1997
25.	Dhanavidhya	—	1992	—
26.	Dhan 80 CCB (2) Plan A	Tax Planning	March, 1992	2002
27.	Dhan 80 CCB (2) Plan B	Tax Planning	March, 1992	2002
28.	Dhan 80 CCB (2) Plan C	Tax Planning	March, 1992	2002
29.	Dhan Vikas (1)	Growth 1993	February,	Apr. 1998
30.	Dhan 88 (1)	Tax Planning	March, 1993	2003
31.	Dhansamriddhi	Growth	August 1994	Aug. 1999
32.	Dhan Tax-Saver 1995	Tax Planning	March, 1995	2005

investor's funds Rs. 276.14 crores. The date and year of its redemption shall be 1995-96.

Dhanshree-1990

It was launched on July, 1990. It is a growth and income scheme. The duration of the scheme is 6 to 7 years. The assured rate of return is 12.5 per cent p.a. Total funds mobilised under the scheme was Rs. 118 crore. The redemption date and year shall be 1996-97. It is a close-end fund.

Dhanshree-1991

It was launched in September, 1991. It is an income scheme. It is a close-end scheme. The duration of the scheme is 6 to 7 years. The assured return is 13 per cent p.a. The corpus of the scheme was 13.09 crore.

Dhanraksha-1989

It was launched in June 1989. It is a growth cum income scheme. It is an open-ended scheme. This shall be redeemed in 1999-2000.

Dhanvidhya

It was launched in 1991. It is a tax-cum-growth scheme. It is an open-end scheme. It collected a corpus of Rs. 0.54 crore.

Dhanlakshmi

It was launched in November, 1991. It is an income scheme. It is targetted to ladies. The assured return is 15 per cent.

General Insurance Corporation Mutual Fund

The General Inssurance Industry was nationalised in 1973. It is undertaking all general insurance business activities. It has subsidiaries operating in various general insurance activities. GIC and its four subsidiaries launched the GICMF in 1990. The GIC Mutual Fund has been sponsored by General Insurance Corporation and its four subsidiaries. The sponsor has settled a sum of Rs. 2 crores as a corpus which will be converted as subscription into the Fund's scheme. A trust is created to manage the Fund. GICMF is registered as a Trust under the Indian Trust Act, 1882. The trusteeship functions of the GIC Mutual Fund are discharged by its Board of Trustees. The Trustees appointed GIC Asset Management Company and the custodian and have to ensure that they fulfill the functions assigned to them from time to time subject to the Trust Deed and Mutual Fund Regulations and other laws in force. The trustees have also to repeat at the end of every six months to SEBI and report annually to the investors on the functioning of the Fund. The Board is comprising of Board of Trustees. Four Board of Trustees and one Chairman. In order to look after the day-to-day affairs of the Fund, an Asset Management Company is formed by the Board of Trustees. GIC Asset Management Company Limited (GIC AMC) has been incorporated on 25th May, 1993. The paid-up capital of it is Rs. 5 crores of which 49 per cent is held by GIC and its subsidiaries, 33 per cent by Soros Fund Management, 17 per cent by GIC Housing Finance. In terms of a foreign collaboration agreement entered into between GIC and Soros Fund Management, USA (SMF), has contributed 33 per cent of share capital of AMC through SC Management Company Inc., which is a wholly owned subsidiary of SFM. SFM is the principal investment advisor to Quantum group of funds, which includes Quantum Fund, Quantum Emerging Growth Fund, Quasar International Fund and Quantum Reality Fund which together representing over 12 billion in fund assets. SFM has nominated two highly qualified and experienced specialist on emerging markets on the Board of GICMF's AMC.

The day-to-day function of the fund is looked after by the Chief Executive with the help of a team of select professionals and staff drawn both from the GIC subsidiaries and also directly recruited from the market. The collection of funds is being done through the designated branches of the nationalised banks like Punjab National Bank, SBI, Union Bank of India and foreign banks like Citibank and others.

GIC Safe-1991

It was launched in April, 1991. The date of maturity of the scheme shall be in 1996. The duration of the scheme is 5 years. It is an income scheme. It is a close-end scheme. Its corpus is Rs. 7.21 crore. Face value of each unit is Rs. 10.

GIC Rise 1991

It was launched on 30.04.1991. It is an income scheme. It is a close-end scheme. Its face value is Rs. 10. It shall be redeemed on 1st May, 1994. The corpus is Rs. 206.76 crores.

GIC Rise II

It is an income scheme and it is a close end scheme. Its face value is Rs. 10. The date of allotment of units was on 11th January, 1992. The date of redemption shall be on 1st April, 1995. The duration of the scheme is 8 years. The corpus of it is Rs. 197.49 crores.

GIC Big Value

It was launched in June, 1992. It is an income-cum-growth scheme. It is a close-end scheme. It is having a face value of each unit of Rs. 10/-. The date of allotment of the units is 30th June, 1992. The date of redemption shall be 30.06.1997. The corpus of the scheme is Rs. 130.61 crores. The duration of the scheme is 5 years.

GIC Balance Fund

It is an income-cum-growth scheme. It is a close-end scheme. Face value of each unit is Rs. 10. The date of allotment of units is 1st February, 1993. The date of redemption shall be 31st March 2000. The corpus of the scheme was Rs. 179.29 crores.

GIC Growth Plus

It is a growth scheme. It is close-end scheme. Face value of each unit is Rs.10. Date of allotment is 31st March, 1993. Date of redemption shall be 31st March, 2003. Corpus of the scheme is Rs. 60.87 crores.

GIC Growth Plus II

It is a growth scheme. It is a close-end scheme. Face value of each unit is Rs. 10. Units were allotted on 1st February, 1994. The redemption of the scheme shall be on 1stApril, 2004. Corpus of the scheme is Rs. 198.39 crores.

GIC Tax Savers Growth Plan

It is a growth scheme. It is close-end scheme. Face value of each unit is Rs. 10. Units were allotted on 31st March, 1994. The day and date of redemption of the scheme shall be on 1st April, 2004. The corpus of the scheme is Rs. 28.64 crores.

Unit Trust of India (Mutual Fund)

In order to recover from the adverse affects by war in 1962, resource crunch had to be garnished to a better economic condition, growth in industrial sector, new economic order for the country, a novel step forward would be establishment of an institution which would mobilise savings from the common man and then channelise them into the corporate sector, the then Prime Minister Pandit

Jawaharlal Nehru felt the need of such on the suggestion of Shri T.T. Krishnamachari, the then Finance Minister of India. The Reserve Bank of India was entrusted the task of setting up such an institution and Unit Trust of India bill was introduced in Parliament. It was introduced by the then Finance Minister. In the context of National Economic development, the concept of setting up UTI as a new institution combining the characteristics of Mutual Funds (MFs) of USA and Unit Trust of the UK to provide resource support for corporate growth through channelising household savings was the brain child of Shri T.T. Krishnamachari. A separate act was enacted in Parliament entitled Unit Trust of India Act, 1963.

Board of Trustees

Upon formation of Unit Trust of India, the general supervision and management of the UTI was entrusted to the Board of Trustees. The Board was expected to act on business principles, having regard to the interests of the unit holders. Chairman was appointed by the RBI. Four trustees to be nominated by RBI, one each to be nominated by LIC and SBI, two trustees to be elected by contributing institutions other than RBI, IDBI, LIC and SBI and one executive trustee appointed by RBI (IDBI now) since they are the contributors of the initial capital to the UTI.

Functions

UTI was empowered to sell and purchase units, introduce unit schemes, invest, acquire, hold and dispose of securities, keep money on deposit, formulate insurance linked savings, borrow money and issue bonds etc.

Management

UTI is managed by the Board of Trustees under a Chairmanship of Dr. S.A. Dave. There are nine Directors. It constituted an advisory Board of Mutual Fund and advisory Board of India Fund exclusively. Besides, a separate Board of Directors of India Growth Fund Inc.

UTI's corporate office is situated in Mumbai. It has four zonal offices and 49 branch offices and two collection centres. It has six subsidiaries.

Unit Trust of India (UTI) was founded in 1963 by the Parliament with the enactment of UTI Act, 1963. The objective of it was to provide an opportunity for the middle and lower income groups to acquire without much difficulty, property in the form of shares. This institution is intended to cater mainly to needs of individual investors whose means are small.

UTI came out with a maiden scheme captioned "Unit Scheme-1964" popularly known as US-64. It is an open-ended scheme. It was launched in 1964. In the very first year it raised Rs. 18.73 crores from 1.32 lakh investors and in the year ended 1964-65, it could raise Rs. 24.67 crores. Late Shri P.C. Bhattacharya the-then Governor of Reserve Bank of India, said "This response exceeded our most optimistic expectations." It was true. Slowly and steadily, the fund had grown in its size. Currently, US–64 is the largest fund with an investible corpus above Rs. 25,000 crores in its hand having a vast investor base. In 1971, the second fund was launched which is christened as "Unit Linked Insurance Plan-1971, popularly known as ULIP-1971 with both the schemes, UTI was much progressive in accumulating funds on massive way till 1980. In 1981, unit scheme for charitable and religious trusts was launched.

In 1983, Capital Gains Unit scheme was introduced. Upto 1986, there was no competition for it and acted a market monark in the mutual fund industry. From the modest figure of Rs. 24.67 crores investible funds in 1964-65, it rose upto an amount of Rs.11834.65 crores in 1988-89 disclosing a massive growth in investible funds, thus, the growth was significant during the period from 1964-65 to 1986-87.

In 1987, Government of India permitted two nationalised banks to commence mutual fund and later on another five public sector concerns were included in the list to become eight mutual fund organisations which are called "Big Eight". The Mutual Fund industry was thrown open to private sector in 1993. Thus, Indian Mutual Fund industry is comprised of special Parliament enatcment category, public sector bank sponsored mutual fund and insurance sector as sponsor and private sector mutual funds. Primarily, mutual fund industry is divided, broadly, into public sector and private sector.

Unit Trust of India progressed well in the mutual fund sector in India and became a market leader and continues to be a pioneer. The two key factors in the progress and success of UTI are: *(a)* competent, efficient and honest leadership; and *(b)* stability of leadership. For its success, the leadership is consistent. Only five chairmen in its history of thirty-four years.

Table 3.16
Mutual Fund Schemes of UTI at a Glance

Sl. No.	Scheme	Date of Introduction	Nature	Type	Date of Termination	Inoperation upto (period)
1	2	3	4	5	6	7
1.	Unit Scheme, 64	01.07.1964	Income	Open-ended	—	—
	(a) Reinvestment Plan—1966	01.07.1966	Post Retirement	Open-ended	—	—
	(b) Children's Gift Plan—1970	01.07.1970	Plan for Children	Open-ended	June, 1986	—
2.	Unit Scheme, 1971	01.10.1971	Income-Cumulation with Life and Insurance Cover	Open-ended	—	—
3.	Unit-Scheme for Charitable & Religious Trusts and Registered Societies, 1981	01.10.1981	Income	Open-ended	—	—
4.	Capital Gains Unit Scheme, 1983	01.12.1983	Capital Gains	Open-ended	September, 1992	—
5.	Children's Gift Growth Fund Unit Scheme, 1986	14.04.1986	Plan for Children	Open-ended	—	—

(Contd.)

1	2	3	4	5	6	7
6.	Mutual Fund (Subsidiary) Unit Scheme, 1986 (Master share)	19.09.1986	Growth Scheme	Close-ended	—	October, 2008
7.	India Fund Unit Scheme, 1986	July, 1986	Off-shore Fund	Close-ended	—	—
8.	Growing Income Unit Scheme, 1987 (III)	01.09.1987	Growing Income	Close-ended	—	May/June, 1993
9.	Monthly Income Unit Scheme with extra Bonus plus Growth (II), 1988	01.11.1988	Monthly Income	Close-ended	—	December, 1993
10.	India Growth Fund Unit Scheme, 1988	August, 1988	Off-Shore Fund	Close-ended	—	—
11.	Monthly Ircome Unit Scheme with extra Bonus Plus Growth (12), 1989	01.05.1989	Monthly Income	Close-ended	—	June, 1994
12.	Monthly Income Unit Scheme with extra Bonus Plus Growth (13), 1989	01.09.1989	Monthly Income	Close-ended	—	December, 1994
13.	Growth Income Unit Scheme, 1989	01.01.1989	Growing Income	Close-ended	—	June/July, 1994
14.	Growing Income Unit Scheme, 1989 (II)	01.11.1989	Growing Income	Close-ended	—	April/May, 1995
15.	Venture Capital Unit Scheme, 1989	28.02.1989	Venture Capital	Close-ended	—	—

16.	New-7-Year Monthly Income Unit Scheme with Yearly Bonus and Growth with 1990	01.04.1990	7-Year Monthly Income	Close-ended	—	April/May June, 1997
17.	7-Year Monthly Income Unit Scheme with Bonuses and Growth (II), 1990	01.11.1990	7-Year Monthly Income	Close-ended	—	November/ December, 1997/Jan., 1998
18.	Growing Income Scheme, 1990	01.01.1990	Growing Income	Close-ended	—	June,1995
19.	Unit Growth Scheme, 2000	01.09.1990	Growth Scheme	Close-ended	—	December, 2000
20.	Deferred Income Unit Scheme, 1990					
	(1) 5-Year Option	20.08.1990	Deferred Income	Close-ended	—	Aug./Sept., 1995
	(2) 7-Year Option	20.08.1990	Deferred Income	Close-ended	—	Aug./Sept., 1997
21.	Venture Capital Unit Scheme (II), 1990	29.03.1990	Venture Capital	Close-ended	—	—
22.	OMNI Plan, 1992	16.08.1991	Feeder Fund	Open-ended	—	—
23.	7-Year Monthly Income Unit Scheme with Yearly Bonuses	01.04.1991	7-Year Monthly Income	Close-ended	—	June, 1998

(Contd.)

1	2	3	4	5	6	7
24.	Deferred Income Unit Scheme, 1991	01.08.1991	Deferred Income	Close-ended	—	August,1996
25.	Growing Monthly Income Unit Scheme, 1991	01.10.1991	Growing Monthly Income	Close-ended	—	Nov. 1996
26.	Master Equity Plan, 1991	15.02.1991	Growth Scheme	Close-ended	—	March, 2001
27.	Capital Growth Unit Scheme, 1991 (Mastergain)	15.04.1991	Growth Scheme	Close-ended	—	June, 1998
28.	Unit Growth Scheme, 5000	01.09.1991	Growth Scheme	Close-ended	—	December, 2001
29.	Master share plys Unit Scheme, 1991 (Master Plus)	09.12.1991	Growth Scheme	Close-ended	—	December, 1998
30.	Venture Capital Unit Scheme (III), 1991	29.10.1991	Venture Capital	Close-ended	—	—
31.	Housing Unit Scheme, 1992	25.06.1992	Special Purpose	Open-ended	June, 1994	—
32.	Rajalakshmi Unit Scheme, 1992	02.10.1992	Plan for Children	Open-ended	—	—
33.	Deferred Income Unit Scheme, 1992	10.08.1992	Deferred Income	Close-ended	—	August,1992
34.	Growing Monthly Income Unit Scheme, 1992	03.02.1992	Growth Monthly Income	Close-ended	—	March, 1997

35.	Growing Monthly Income Unit Scheme, 1992 (II)	16.04.1992	Growing Monthly Income	Close-ended	—	June, 1997
36.	Growing Monthly Income Unit Scheme with Bonus, 1992	07.09.1992	Growing Monthly Income	Close-ended	—	October, 1997
37.	Growing Monthly Income Unit Scheme with Bonus, 1992 (II)	16.12.1992	Growing Monthly Income	Close-ended	—	January, 1998
38.	Master Equity Plan, 1992	01.01.1992	Growth Scheme	Close-ended	—	March, 2002
39.	Capital Growth Unit Scheme, 1992 (Mastergain)	20.04.1992	Growth Scheme	Close-ended	—	July, 1999
40.	Unit Scheme, 1992	02.09.1992	Growth Scheme	Close-ended	—	Not Specified
41.	Bhopal Gas Victims Monthly Income Plan, 1993	25.01.1993	Special Monthly Income	Open-ended	—	—
42.	Institutional Investors Special Fund Unit Scheme, 1993	01.03.1993	Special Purpose Fund	Open-ended	—	—
43.	Senior Citizens' Unit Plan, 1993	03.05.1993	Post-Retirement Medical Benefit Career	Open-ended	—	—

(Contd.)

1	2	3	4	5	6	7
44.	Children's College and Career Fund, 1993	12.07.1993	Plan for Children	Open-ended	—	—
45.	Monthly Income Unit Scheme with Bonus, 1993 (MISB-93)	05.04.1993	Monthly Income Scheme	Close-ended	—	July, 1998
46.	Monthly Income Unit Plan with Bonus, 1993	16.09.1993	Monthly Income	Close-ended	—	October, 1998
47.	Deferred Income Unit Plan, 1993	03.08.1993	Deferred Income	Close-ended	—	September, 1998
48.	Master Equity Plan, 1993	15.01.1993	Growth	Close-ended	—	March, 2003
49.	Master Growth, 1993	18.01.1993	Growth	Close-ended	—	April, 2003
50.	Grand Master, 1993	29.04.1993	Growth Scheme	Close-ended	—	July, 2000
51.	Master Equity Plan, 1994	27.12.1993	Growth Scheme	Close-ended	—	April, 2004
52.	Monthly Income Unit Plan, 1994	03.01.1994	Monthly Income	Close-ended	—	February, 1998
53.	Monthly Income Unit Plan, 1994 (II)	23.05.1994	Monthly Income	Close-ended	—	June, 1998
54.	Growing Corpus Growing Income Plan, 1994	02.04.1994	Income-cum-Growth	Close-ended	—	June, 2004

Source : Annual Reports of UTI. Various Issues.

Number of schemes introduced have been increased during the period from 1989-90 to 1994-95 which rose from 30 schemes in 1989-90 to 59 in 1994-95. Number of open ended schemes were 8 in 1989-90 increased to 21 in 1994-95. Number of close ended schemes increased from 22 schemes in 1989-90 to 38 in 1994-95. Number of schemes introduced in each year increased. Thirteen schemes each were introduced in 1989-90 and 1990-91. Eighteen schemes each were introduced in 1991-92 and 1993-94, 21 schemes were introduced in 1992-93 and 19 schemes were introduced in 1994-95.

Unit Trust of India has 20 offices in 1989-90 increased to 48 offices in 1994-95. Number of employees of 1506 in 1989-90 grown to 2,381 in 1994-95. Agent base also grown alarmingly from 55,000 in 1989-90 to 85,000 in 1994-95.

Outstanding unit capital grown from Rs. 13,392 crores in 1989-90 to Rs. 45,433 crores in 1994-95. It has grown three and half times the figure in 1989-90. Total investible funds grown from a figure of Rs. 17,651 crores in 1989-90 to Rs. 59,619 crores in 1994-95.

Management Style

The chairman is the fund manager. As per the UTI Act, only chairman has the authority to sanction investment decisions. He is effectively in charge of and responsible for, the management of the funds. He decides the type of scheme to be launched and generally plans the future strategy.

UTI funds manager handles in different way. Fund managers are divided into *(i)* fund manager of primary market, *(ii)* fund manager for secondary market, and *(iii)* fund manager for money market. Primary Market fund manager is incharge of investing in primary market instruments—primary market instruments include equity shares, preference shares, debentures and bonds. It includes the Government dis-investment of public sector units. This manager sanctions term loans and undertakes underwriting obligations. He also takes quarterly view on his cash requirements and accordingly requests the money market fund manager to create for him the required liquidity. The primary market fund managers are supported by 10 analysts. The secondary market fund manager is in charge of secondary market instruments, both equity and debt. He trades on the secondary market. He allocates to the various schemes the new issues subscribed to by the primary market fund managers. He executes inter-schemes sales at prevailing market prices. The money market fund manager is primarily responsible for the liquidity of UTI funds.

Progress

UTI commenced its operations in 1964 with a maiden scheme of US-64. It mobilised massive funds through the plan successfully. In 1971, another significant plan was started called Unit Linked Insurance Plan (ULIP) which provided not only growth in the value of investment for the contractual period of 10 years (15 years option was introduced later) but also insurance benefit. By June, 1980, with four offices UTI had been operating 6 schemes and plans with an outstanding investible funds of Rs. 467.04 crores having 10 lakh unit-holding accounts. The unit capital at the 1979-80, figured at Rs. 391 crores.

During eighties, UTI introduced more than 20 new open-ended and close-ended schemes and plans. The investible funds as at the year ended 1989-90 revealed Rs. 17,650.92 crores from an amount of Rs. 523.22 crores in 1980-81.

During the period 1990-94, UTI witnessed high rate of growth in its operation. Investible funds increased from Rs. 21,376.48 crores in 1990-91 to Rs. 51,708.88 crores in 1993-94 showing a significant growth. Outstanding unit capital increased from Rs. 13,392 crore in July, 1990 to Rs. 16,409 crore in 1991 and further to Rs. 39,303 crores in June, 1994.

As at the end of 1993-94 accounting year, UTI has 54 schemes and plans. Out of these, 12 were open-ended and 42 were close-ended schemes. Upto the year 1980, there were only five schemes. Gradually, the number of schemes/plans enhanced. In 1990, there were 32 schemes and increased to 56 schemes in 1994.

Sales under all schemes increased from Rs. 19.14 crores in 1964-65 to Rs. 10,711.55 crores in 1993-94. Outstanding unit capital grown from Rs. 18.73 crores in 1964-65 to Rs. 39,297.95 crore in 1993-94. Outstanding unit holding accounts rose from 1.32 lakhs in 1964-65 to 378.14 lakhs in 1993-94. Investible funds rose from Rs. 24.67 crores in 1964-65 to Rs. 51,708.88 crores in 1993-94. Reserves and Provisions grown from Rs. 0.07 crores in 1964-65 to Rs. 9,874.15 crores in 1993-94. Thus, it showed an overall growth over the period 30 years of its tenure.

Table 3.17
UTI MF Schemes—Type-wise and Nature-wise

Open End Schemes	12
Close End Schemes	42
Total	54 in operation

Break-up of Close-end Schemes

1.	Monthly Income Unit Schemes (MIS Pool & MISB)	=	4
2.	Monthly Income Unit Plan (MIUP)	=	3
3.	7 Year Monthly Income Schemes (MISG-90-Pool)	=	3
4.	Growing Income Unit Schemes (GIUS Pool)	=	4
5.	Deferred Income Unit Scheme	=	4
6.	Growing Monthly Income Unit Schemes (GMIS Pool & GMIS-B Pool)	=	5
7.	Growth Scheme	=	13
8.	Income-cum-Growth Scheme	=	1
9.	Off-Shore Fund	=	2
10.	Venture Capital	=	3
	Total	=	42

Table 3.18
UTI MF Scheme—Year-wise Break-up

Year	*Schemes (F)*	*(F)*
1964	1	1
1966	1	2
1970	1	3
1971	1	4
1981	1	5
1983	1	6
1986	3	9
1987	1	10
1988	1	11
1989	5	16
1990	7	23
1991	9	32
1992	10	42
1993	11	53
1994	3	56
	56	

Note : Unit, 64 Includes:

(*a*) Reinvestment Plan 66, and
(*b*) Children's Gift Plan —1970. Thus it is having three schemes in total.

Table 3.19
UTI's Investment Funds

(Rs. Crore)

Year	*Investible Funds (Rs.)*	*Growth*
1964-65	24.67	—
1965-66	25.94	5.15
1966-67	33.86	30.53
1967-68	48.7	43.83
1968-69	65.4	34.29
1969-70	88.15	34.83
1970-71	105.14	19.23
1971-72	119.26	13.43
1972-73	141.96	19.03
1973-74	172.09	21.22
1974-75	169.95	–1.24
1975-76	184.57	8.61
1976-77	214.41	6.17
1977-78	288.18	34.41
1978-79	402.43	39.65
1979-80	467.04	16.05
1980-81	523.22	12.03
1981-82	679.24	29.82
1982-83	870.24	28.12
1983-84	1,261.33	44.94
1984-85	2,209.61	75.18
1985-86	3,218.34	45.65
1986-87	4,563.68	41.80
1987-88	6,738.81	47.66
1988-89	11,834.65	75.62
1989-90	17,650.92	49.15
1990-91	21,376.48	21.11
1991-92	31,805.69	48.79
1992-93	38,976.81	22.55
1993-94	51,708.88	32.67

Source : Various Issues of Annual Reports of UTI.
Results Computed

Table 3.20
Investible Funds—Comparison

(Rs. Crore)

	1988-89	1989-90	1990-91	1991-92	1992-93	1993-94
UTI	11,835.00	15,892.00	21,377.00	31,806.00	38,977.00	51,709.00
	(87.95)	(91.48)	(94.73)	(84.86)	(82.95)	(84.72
)						
Other	1,621.00	1,480.00	1,188.89	5,672.08	8,011.21	9,323.92
MFs	(12.05)	(8.52)	(5.27)	(15.14)	(17.05)	(15.28)
Total	13,456.00	17,372.00	22,565.89	37,479.08	46,988.21	61,032.92
	(100.00)	(100.00)	(100.00)	(100.00)	(100.00)	(100.00)

Source : Various Annual Reports of Different MFs and UTI.
Results Computed.
Figures in Parenthesis indicate percentages.

Table 3.21
Investments

(Rs. Crore)

	1990-91	1991-92	1992-93	1993-94
Unit Trust of India	13,720.10	21,157.64	30,370.42	43,493.84
(% of Total Instruments)	90.24	78.74	78.07	80.93
Other Mutual Funds	1,483.56	5,713.19	8,530.88	10,246.67
(% of Total Investments)	9.76	21.26	21.93	19.07
Total	15,203.66	26,870.83	38,901.30	53,140.51
	100.00	100.00	100.00	100.00

Source : Annual Reports.
Results Computed.

CHAPTER FOUR

Investment Procedure of Mutual Funds

Introduction on Investment Procedure of MF

Chapter four deals with 'Investment Process' of mutual fund organisations in India. A study on 'big eight' mutual funds have been analysed and results computed and interpreted to arrive at concluding remarks on the investment pattern over a few years span. For business, trade, commerce and industry, capital is needed to establish and make run its operations after gathering and acquiring fixed assets. Besides fixed assets, working capital is essential to meet day-to-day operations of business activities. Fixed assets are acquired to use permanently to reap returns while current assets (or working capital) is required to meet immediate and daily expenses for the organisation. Thus, these fixed and current assets are a must for a success of business entity. Capital is one of the factors of production, a due and diligent care in getting and using is essential since it is a scarce item in the materialistic and economic world. Proper tapping sources should be planned and achieved. There are different variety of sources of capital needs of an entity. To suit the need, a choice of securities among many alternatives to be made (See Chart 4.A. Securities). Each security has its own features and merits. Picking up proper suitable security is essential task of a financial executive.

Chart 4.A
SECURITIES

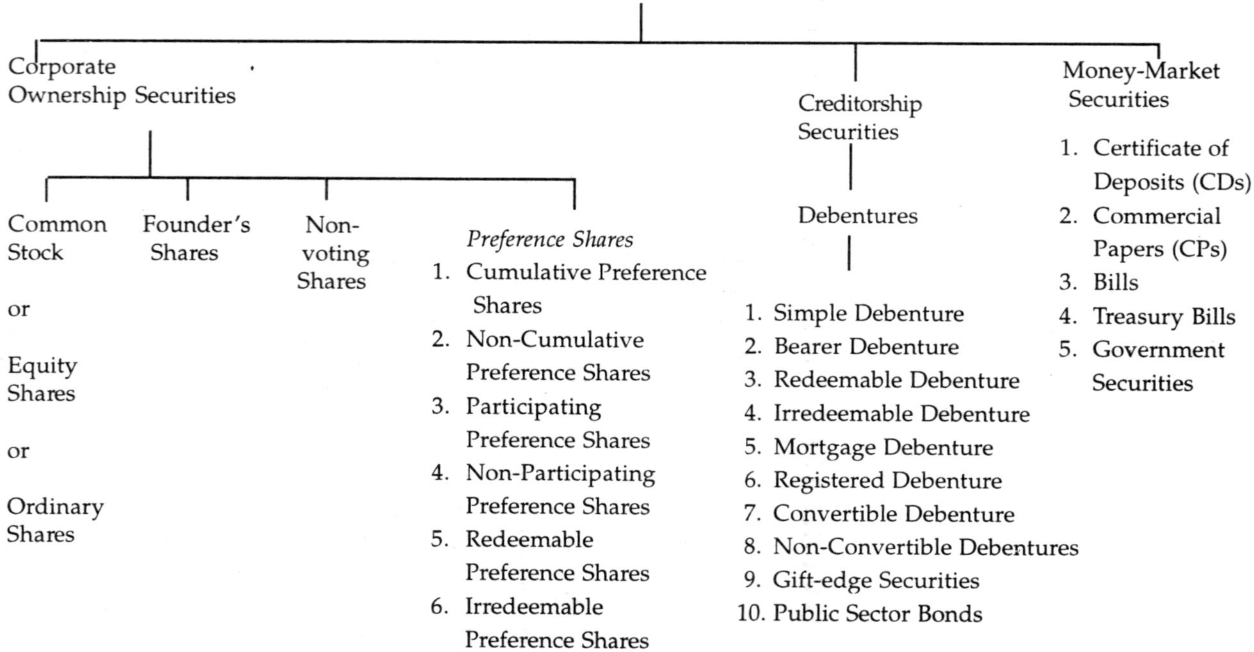

Household Sector

During the past one/two decades (after independence of India), household sector used to have funds out of its income and invest the modest amounts in acquiring shares and securities of corporations and other variety of savings schemes available to it from time to time. For instance, total savings of household sector grown up from 35,920 crores in 1985-86 to 1,57,349 crores in 1993-94 revealing four and half times increase over the tenure of five years. Household sector is naturally, playing a good role in pumping out its funds to industry through purchasing shares and securities. The acquisition of financial assets increased in shape of shares, securities and certificates, etc. Around 50 of the savings of household sector goes to purchase of financial assets which is an encouraging picture in the investment climate of the country.

Mobilisation of Savings by Mutual Funds

Upon starting of Unit Trust of India and public sector mutual funds and private sector mutual funds, investments attitude of Indian households sector was radically changed. Mutual Funds could mobilise savings of Indian household sector very fast. An amount of Rs. 2,017.9 crores was mobilised in 1987-88 by all the mutual fund organisations of India which rose up to a figure of Rs. 7,750.3 crores in 1994-95 disclosing three and half fold rise over the span of eight years. At the same time, investible funds grown from a figure of Rs. 13,456 crores in 1988-89 to Rs. 61,032.92 crores in 1993-94 exhibiting four and half times increase. Thus mutual funds are mobilising a huge amount of capital through various mutual fund schemes. These funds are pumped into industrial sector of the country in different forms and modes, which, indirectly catalyses the industry for a positive growth. A lot of funds are invested through purchasing equity shares, preference shares, debentures, convertible debentures, non-convertible debentures, bonds of various categories, certificate of deposits, commercial papers, money market instruments, treasury bills, bills of exchange, government securities, gilt-edged securities and others.

Investments

Before investment of scarce resource like funds or money or capital, an investor (or an economist) looks into various factors such as industry at metro level; factors of production, particularly availability of raw materials, machines, land and buildings, man power, managerial personnel etc, selection of past records, past performance, prospects for growth and political and economic stability; nature of investment, time span of investment, returns, risks etc. All these are looked into before investment.

A saver who is pumping out his savings for productive purposes is called investment. An investment does not necessarily originate from savings. There are so many, who inherit wealth, or receive unexpected bonus at work, or win lotteries and cross word puzzles. In these cases, the individuals would be investing for earning profit. Whatever may be the source, for investment, return is of primary concern in form of change in capital value or income or both:

$$\text{Return (P.C)} = \frac{V_1 - V_0 + D}{V_0} \times 100\%$$

Where V_0 = Value of Investment at the beginning
V_1 = Value of Investment at the end
D = Income received during the period.

Illustration

An equity share is purchased at a price of Rs. 80 (V_0). After a year t is sold at Rs. 120 (V_1). During the year, a dividend of Rs. 6 (D) has been received. The return in this case would be:

$$\text{Return (\%)} = \frac{120 - 80 + 6}{80} \times 100 = 57.5$$

According to Frank K. Reilly* an 'Investment' may be defined as the current commitment of funds for a period of time. The funds are committed for an expected rate of inflation, and also for the uncertainty involved in the future flow of funds. This encompasses all types of investments, whether these be corporate investments in machinery, plant and equipment, or government investments in flood control; or investment by individual in stocks, bonds, commodities or real estates.

---

* Reilly, Frank K., *Investment*, The Dry den Press, USA, 1982, p. 7.

Features are:

(i) Current Commitment of funds for a future period of time.
(ii) The funds are committed for an expected rate of inflation.
(iii) The funds are committed for an expected uncertainty involved in the future flow of funds.
(iv) This covers all types of investments such as corporate investments, government investments, investment by individual, etc.

Types of Investments

Direct Investments

A company borrows money for expansion of production capacity. The Government borrows money to invest in for providing to the citizens-hospitals, boards, wells and infrastructural facilities etc.

Indirect Investments

An indirect investment is made through financial intermediaries such as Banks, Unit Trusts, Mutual Funds, Investment Companies and Housing Banks etc.

Investment in Marketable Securities.

Investment in Non-Marketable Securities.

Investment in Financial Assets of:

(a) Fixed Income bearing,
(b) Non-fixed income bearing,
(c) Capital appreciable securities, and
(d) Regular income bearing securities.

Investment in real estate includes property, antique, gold, furniture etc.

Investment in financial assets like Cash Deposits, Gilts, Stocks, Securities etc.

Investment Choice

The underlying factor are influencing the choice for an investment:

(a) Investor's Personal Profit,
(b) Investor's Age,

(*c*) Investor's Marital Status,
(*d*) Investor's Children,
(*e*) Investor's Family Responsibility,
(*f*) Investor's Financial Status,
(*g*) Investor's Income,
(*h*) Investor's Savings,
(*i*) Investor's Financial Commitments,
(*j*) Investor's Tax Position, and
(*k*) Investor's Attitude towards risk.

An Investor's plan for investment is developed on the underlying basis:

(*i*) Need for liquidity,
(*ii*) Time duration,
(*iii*) Allocation of requirements between regular income and capital appreciation diversification, and
(*iv*) Minimum tax liability.

Risk

Risk in finance and financial management is an uncertainty of return and variability in probable outcomes. In finance, some control is exercised for variable risk like diversification in investment or opportunity to find exit route on even minor downtrend by disinvestment. But non-diversible risk is the key to which any fund manager is always concerned about. In a formal sense, there is difference between 'risk' and 'uncertainty'. But, the tendency is to use these two concepts as same. High degree of uncertainty gives rise to increased risk. Higher the rate assets risk, lower is its market value. In order to compensate high risk on low market value of a share or investment is the higher return. The larger the range of uncertainty in regard to the return, greater is the risk involved in investment.

Following items of uncertainty make the investment risky. The sources of uncertainty such as:

(*a*) Interest rate risk;
(*b*) Purchasing power risk;
(*c*) Management risk;
(*e*) Default risk;
(*f*) Liquidity risk;

(g) Convertible risk;
(h) Political risk;
(i) Industrial risk; and
(j) Other risks.

Combination of all these above taken together is 'Total Risk'. All these elements of uncertainties give rise to total variation in the rate of return.

A fund manager constructs the prudent investment pattern through port folio by thorough analysis, field surveys, equity research, elements of uncertainties, issue terms and conditions of mutual fund schemes. More diversification of portfolio is the factor that minimises the riskiness of investments in mutual fund. Portfolio coverage should comprise of a wide variety of financial instruments such as equity shares, preference shares, debentures, bonds, government securities, money market instruments etc.

The objectives of Portfolio management is to invest in securities in such a way that one maximises one's returns and minimises risks in order to achieve one's investment objectives. These are:

(a) Safety of Investment;
(b) Stable Current Returns;
(c) Appreciation in the Value of Capital;
(d) Marketability;
(e) Liquidity; and
(f) Tax Planning.

In Mutual Fund Organisations, Mutual Fund Trust appoints Asset Management Company (AMC) to look after the funds of Trustees of MF. The asset management company is incharage of funds management and allocation of assets of unit holders. Such allocation of assets involves a judicious investment pattern of mutual fund. The investment pattern of a mutual fund scheme is to a large extent determined by the broad guidelines issued by SEBI which are general in nature which are applicable to all mutual funds. Of course, these are strictly adhered to while chalking out investment pattern or portfolio section. Besides, primarily, each individual scheme/plan has its own objectives different from one another. Accordingly fund manager frames and builds a suitable portfolio to deploy funds to reap optimum return and capital appreciation.

SEBI Guidelines on Investment Pattern of Mutual Fund

Securities and Exchange Board of India (SEBI) has issued guidelines through an enactment captioned "Securities and Exchange Board of India (Mutual Funds) Regulations, 1993. It was notified on 20th January, 1993 which are applicable to all Mutual Funds except:

(*i*) Money Market Mutual Funds established for investments exclusively in Money Market Instruments; and

(*ii*) Mutual Funds established outside India.

Regulation 40 (1) of Chapter V and Schedule VI of the SEBI (Mutual Funds) Regulations, 1993 deal exclusively on investment pattern. Regulation 40 (1) says that the money collected under any scheme of a Mutual Fund shall be invested only in transferable securities whether in the money market or in the capital market or in privately placed debentures or securitised debts. Regulation 41 indicates that any investments to be made in pursuance to Regulation 40 shall be invested subject to the investment restriction mentioned in Schedule VI. Schedule VI of SEBI (Mutual Funds) Regulations, 1993 deals with 'Restrictions on Investments' vide Regulation 41 of the SEBI.

Restrictions are

Debt instruments should be rated as investment grade by a credit rating agency. Credit rating agencies are CRISIL, ICRA etc. If the debt instrument is not rated, the specific approval of the Board of Asset Management Company should be taken for investment.

No term loans for any purpose may be advanced by Mutual Funds.

Investments by way of privately placed debentures, securitised debts and other unquoted debt instruments shall not respectively exceed 10 per cent of the total assets of the scheme in case of growth schemes and 40 per cent of the total assets of the relevant scheme in case of income scheme.

No individual scheme of the Mutual Fund should invest more than 5 per cent of its corpus in any one company's shares.

No Mutual Fund under all its should own more than 5 per cent of any company's paid up capital carrying voting rights.

No Mutual Fund under all its schemes taken together should invest more than 10 per cent of the funds in the shares, debentures or other securities of a single company.

No Mutual Fund under all its schemes taken together should invest more than 15 per cent of its funds in the shares and debentures of any one industry.

Provided that provision shall not apply to a scheme which has been floated for investments in one or more specified industries and a declaration to the effect has been made in the offer letter.

Transfers of investments from one scheme to another scheme in the same Mutual Fund shall be allowed only if :

(a) Such transfers are done at the prevailing market price for quoted instruments on spot basis.

(b) The securities so transferred shall be in with the investment objective of the scheme to which such transfer has been made.

No scheme shall invest in or lend to another scheme under the same Asset Management Company.

Mutual Funds shall not be allowed to borrow funds to finance its investments.

The initial issue expenses in respect of any scheme may not exceed 6 per cent of the funds raised under that scheme.

Notwithstanding anything contained in paragraphs 1 to 12 the total expenses charged to the fund, except the initial issue expenses, shall not exceed three per cent of the weekly average net assets outstanding during the accounting year.

SEBI's guidelines for investment in money market instruments have been relaxed on the occasion of Union Budget for 1994-95. The more was designed to give greater flexibility to mutual funds for deployment of resources.

The Revised Norms are

1. During the first six months from the date of allotment of units, mutual funds can invest upto 100 per cent in these instruments, upto 30 per cent during the next six months, and upto 25 per cent thereafter to meet their short-term liquidity requirements.
2. Mutual Fund can also invest upto 100 per cent of their resources in various money market instruments during the terminal six months to facilitate redemption.
3. However, money market mutual funds can be started only

after prior permission of the R B I. The more was welcomed by MFs although the yield from the money market instruments is much lower which may affect the returns to the investors' funds.

Instruments of Investment

1. Equity
2. Convertible Debentures
3. Fixed Income Securities
   - *(a)* Debt Instruments, i.e., non-convertible debentures;
   - *(b)* Bonds of public sector; and
   - *(c)* Government Securities of "gilts".
4. Money Market Instruments
   - *(a)* Certificate of Deposits (CDs);
   - *(b)* Treasury Bills;
   - *(c)* Bill discounting;
   - *(d)* Commercial paper; and
   - *(e)* Call money
5. Unit-64 (US-64)

Investment Mix

Obviously, the investment pattern of mutual fund scheme is governed by the type of scheme. A growth scheme would have a predominant accent on equities. For an income scheme, high degree of investment in debt instruments is required to generate a steady flow of returns to investors. In case any predetermined rate is indicated in the offer document of a scheme, it stands to reason that the equity element would be still lower. Such situation takes place in the case of monthly income schemes. The same situation is to the miscellaneous types of schemes.

Investment Pattern

Investment policy of a mutual fund changes from time to time. Investments of Unit Trust of India (UTI) and other mutual funds over the period four years from 1990-91 to 1993-94 discloses in Table-4.1. Investments in real terms of rupees grown up significantly showing an increasing trend during the period under review.

Investments in 1990-91 amounting to Rs. 13,720.10 crores in UTI rose to Rs. 43,493.84 crores in 1993-94 which increased to 3 1/2 times. In 1990-91, UTI invested to Rs. 13,720.10 crores revealing that 90.24 per cent of total investments of Rs. 15,203.66. crores. In 1991-92 it declined to 78.74 per cent although investments in real terms increased. In 1992-93, investments of UTI disclosed at 78.07 per cent despite of increase in funds in absolute terms. In 1993-94, it revealed 80.93 per cent although investments in real terms increased. On percentage wise, UTI disclosed ups and downs. Other mutual funds displayed a different picture. In terms of rupees, investments showed an increasing tendency over the period. Investments in 1990-91 revealed Rs. 1,483.56 increased to Rs. 10,246.67 in 1993-94. Percentage wise, other mutual funds displayed an increasing trend. It increased from 9.76 per cent in 1990-91 to 21.93 per cent in 1992-93 and slightly depressed to 19.07 per cent in 1993-94. However, it revealed an increasing trend. It can be inferred that other mutual funds fared well than UTI.

Broadly, investments are classified under equity shares (equity and preference), debentures and bonds, government securities (including treasury bills), public sector bonds, commercial papers (CPs), Certificate of Deposits (CDs) and others. UTI used to invest its funds in four different categories. Its investment in equity over the period of four years revealed an increasing growth trend which increased from Rs. 3,862.45 crores in 1990-91 to Rs. 20,379.60 crores in 1993-94. In absolute figures it increased significantly. It took risk in its investment policy. In terms of percentage, it disclosed 28.15 per cent in 1990-91 to 47.26 per cent in 1992-93 and subsequently declined to 46.86 per cent in 1993-94. At about 28 per cent to 47 per cent of investible funds were invested in equity shares by UTI with regard to investment in Debentures and Bonds, Rs. 4,371.55 crores in 1990-91 increased to Rs. 11,101.84 crores in 1993-94 showed an increasing trend. Around 28 per cent of investments were deployed in this category of fixed income bearing securities. In the third category, UTI invested Rs. 3,561.66 crores in 1990-91 to Rs. 7,877.49 crores in 1993-94 revealing our increased trend. Around 11 per cent of fund were deployed in government securities. In the fourth category, it invested Rs. 1,728.44 crores in 1990-91 to Rs. 4,081.74 crores in 1993-94 disclosing a growth during the period. Thus, UTI adopted risk investment for growth in its fund's capital appreciation. Simultaneously, it invested in fixed income group of securities to invest regular income (Table 4.10).

Table 4.1. shows Aggregate Investment of all mutual funds including UTI. The total investment in 1993-94 is to the tune of Rs. 53,740.51 crore compared to Rs. 15,203.66 crore in 1990-91. MFs investment in 1993-94 is to the tune of Rs. 10,246.67 crore compared to Rs. 1,483.56 crore in 1990-91. The mean aggregate investment for all four years come together revealed a figure at Rs. 6,493.58 crore recording 18.01 per cent of total investment. In terms of percentage it accounted 9.76 per cent in 1990-91 rose to 21.26 per cent in 1991-92 and further enhanced to 21.96 per cent in 1992-93 but a sudden fall to 19.07 per cent in 1993-94 is noticed. On an average, UTI's investment recorded at 81.95 per cent for the 4 years period. It showed 90.24 per cent in 1990-91 came down to 78.74 per cent in 1991-92 and further declined to 78.07 per cent in 1992-93 and sudden increase was found in 1993-94 recording at 80.93 per cent.

Table 4.1
Aggregate Investments of All MFs

(Rs.Crore)

	1990-91	*1991-92*	*1992-93*	*1993-94*	*Mean*
Mutual Funds	1,483.56	5,713.19	8,530.88	10,246.67	6,493.58
	(9.76)	(21.26)	(21.93)	(19.07)	(18.01)
Unit Trust of	13,720.10	21,157.64	30,370.42	43,493.84	27,185.5
India	(90.24)	(78.74)	(78.07)	(80.93)	(81.99)
Total	15,203.66	26,870.83	38,901.30	53,740.51	33,679.08
	(100.00)	(100.00)	(100.00)	(100.00)	(100.00)

Note : Figures in Brackets indicate percentages to total.
Results Computed.

Source : Annual Reports of Mutual Funds—Various Years.

A detailed break-up of security-wise investment pattern of all mutual funds is exhibited in Table 4.2. The mean investment in equity figured at Rs. 15,139.80 crore over the period of 4 years span showing 41.82 per cent, a highest per cent in the equity. The next position has gone a debentures, bonds etc. showing investment of Rs. 9,668.92 crore recording 2.65 per cent. Third position has been occupied by Government securities to the tune of Rs. 5,208.58 crore recording at 17.08 per cent. Fourth position has been occupied by "Others" category showing Rs. 3,557.36 crore recording 10.92

per cent. It can be concluded that Mutual Funds are inclined to invest their investment in equity shares on a first property.

Table 4.2
Investment Pattern of Mutual Funds—Security-wise Aggregates

(Rs. Crore)

	1990-91	*1991-92*	*1992-93*	*1993-94*	*Mean*
Equity Shares	4,436.11	11,020.28	18,535.86	26,566.95	15,139.80
	(29.18)	(41.01)	(47.65)	(49.44)	(41.82)
Debentures/ Bonds including privately placed	4,877.48	8,476.42	11,075.12	14,246.67	9,668.92
	(32.08)	(31.55)	(28.47)	(26.51)	(29.65)
Government Securities (including Treasury bills)	3,627.95	5,147.38	4,007.09	8,051.91	5,208.58
	(23.86)	(19.16)	(10.30)	(14.98)	(17.08)
Public Sector Bonds	71.34	66.26	142.38	131.12	102.78
	(0.47)	(0.25)	(0.37)	(0.24)	(0.33)
CDs/CPs	0.00	0.00	225.24	107.42	83.17
	(0.00)	(0.00)	(0.58)	(0.20)	(0.20)
Others	2,004.78	3,177.15	4,464.23	4,583.26	3,557.36
	(13.19)	(11.82)	(11.48)	(8.53)	(10.92)
Total Investments	15,203.66	26,870.83	38,901.29	53,740.51	33,679.07
	(100.00)	(100.00)	(100.00)	(100.00)	(100.00)

Note : Figures in Brackets indicate percentages.
Source : Annual Reports of Mutual Funds, Various Years. Results Computed.

Investment Pattern of SBI MF

Mutual Funds mobilise funds from various mutual fund schemes. Those funds are invested in different categories such as equity shares, debentures, bonds, money market instruments, etc. Table 4.3 shows investment pattern of funds of SBI MF for the consecutive years from 1991-92 to 1993-94. Investments over the three years increased from Rs. 875.80 crores in 1991-92 to Rs. 2,389.16 crores in 1993-94 which displayed increasing trend. Turning to year wise break-up, an amount of Rs. 321.34 was deployed in equity out of total investment of Rs. 875.80 crores in 1991-92 recording 36.69 per cent. As much as Rs. 518.64 crores was

Table 4.3
Investment Pattern of SBI MF

(Rs. Crore)

	1991-92	*1992-93*	*1993-94*
Equity Shares	321.34	850.07	1,704.07
	(36.69)	(59.71)	(71.32)
Debentures/Bonds including	518.64	366.72	442.33
Privately placed	(59.22)	(25.76)	(18.51)
Government Securities	0.00	154.07	136.84
(Including Treasury Bills)		(10.82)	(5.73)
CDs/CPs	0.00	47.67	105.92
		(3.35)	(4.44)
Others	35.82	5.02	0.00
	(4.09)	(0.36)	(0.00)
Total Investments	875.80	1,423.55	2,389.16
	(100.00)	(100.00)	(100.00)

Note : Figures in paranthesis indicate percentages.
Source : Mutual Funds in India Fact Book, UTI-CM, Mumbai, 1995 p. 46. Results Computed.

invested in debentures/bonds etc., out of Rs. 875.80 crores recording 59.22 per cent. But amount of Rs. 35.82 crores was invested in other item showing 4.09 per cent. Thus, portfolio of SBI MF covered equity, debentures, bonds and others. Risk free investments was preferred. In 1992-93, the portfolio pattern was changed. Out of total investment of Rs. 1,423.55 crores, Rs. 850.07 crores was deployed in equity shares; Rs. 366.72 was invested in debentures bonus etc. Rs. 154.07 was invested in Government securities; Rs. 47.67 crores was invested in CDs/CPs and Rs. 5.02 crores was invested in other miscellaneous items. Thus, 59.71 per cent in equity, 25.76 per cent in debentures, bonds etc. 10.82 per cent in CDs/CPs and 0.36 per cent in others was portfolio. In 1993-94, the investment amounted to Rs. 2,389.16 crores. Out of total amount of Rs. 1,704.07 crores was invested in equity shares Rs. 442.33 in debentures/bonds etc. Rs. 136.84 crores in Government securities and Rs. 105.92 crores in CDs/CPs. Thus, 71.32 per cent was invested in equity while 18.51 per cent in debentures and bonds. During the 3 years of duration, SBI MF changed its portfolio emphasizing on equity than debentures and bonds. It stressed on growth and risk.

A comprehensive break-up of Canbank Mutual Fund investment pattern is exhibited in Table 4.4. The major asset in Canbank MF is equity shares. The table discloses that the proportion of investment in equity shares has gone up from 41.37 per cent in 1990-91 to 62.95 per cent in 1993-94. In absolute terms, equity share increased from Rs. 123.70 crore in 1990-91 to Rs. 1,476.70 in 1991-92 and further rose to Rs. 1,859.16 crores in 1992-93 and sudden increase has been noticed in 1993-94 showing Rs. 2,384.28 crore. A significant change in the Canbank Mutual Fund's investment policy is that during the last four years period, investment in bonds and debentures and Government securities have gone down to 33.40 per cent and 0.86 per cent respectively from a significantly higher proportion of 51.22 per cent and 7.35 per cent in 1990-91. Mainly the shift has taken place from the Government securities and bonds and debentures to equity shares. This change might have necessitated owing to launch of a more and more growth funds.

Table 4.4
Investment Pattern of Canbank MF

(Rs. Crore)

	1990-91	*1991-92*	*1992-93*	*1993-94*	*Mean*
Equity Shares		123.70 (41.37)	1,476.70 (57.41)	1,859.16 (52.86)	2,384.28 (62.95)
Debentures/Bonds including private placed		153.13 (51.22)	1,070.02 (41.60)	1,361.62 (38.71)	1,264.95 (33.40)
Government Securities (Treasury Bills)		21.98 (7.35)	12.93 (0.50)	123.59 (3.51)	32.77 (0.86)
Others		0.18 (0.06)	12.14 (0.49)	167.00 (4.92)	105.31 (2.79)
Total Investments		298.98 (100)	2,572.34 (100)	3,517.37 (100)	3,787.31 (100)

Note : Figures in brackets indicate percentages.
Source : Fact Book of Mutual Funds, UTI CM, Mumbai, 1995, Edn., p.43. Results Computed.

A detailed break-up of Indian Bank Mutual Fund investment pattern is given in Table 4.5. The major asset in Indbank Mutual Fund's portfolio is equity shares. The table shows that the proportion of investments in equity shares has gone up from 44.86 per cent in 1991-92 to 58.31 per cent in 1993-94. A significant change in the Indbank Mutual Fund investment policy is that during the last four years period, investment in debentures and bonds have gone down to 36.03 per cent in 1993-94 from 52.25 per cent in 1991-92. Primarily the shift has taken place from the debentures and bonds to equity shares. This change might have necessitated owing to launch of more growth funds.

Table 4.5
Investment Pattern of Indian Bank Mutual Fund

(Rs. Crore)

	1990-91	*1991-92*	*1992-93*	*1993-94*
Equity Shares	46.67	137.25	301.36	375.35
	(52.17)	(44.80)	(52.02)	(58.31)
Debentures/Bonds (including	42.74	160.08	229.45	231.94
privately placed)	(47.78)	(52.25)	(39.61)	(36.03)
Government Securities	0.00	0.00	0.00	0.00
(including Treasury Bills)	(0.00)	(0.00)	(0.00)	(0.00)
CDs/CPs	0.00	0.00	17.62	0.00
	(0.00)	(0.00)	(3.04)	(0.00)
Others	0.04	9.03	30.93	36.43
	(0.05)	(2.95)	(5.33)	(5.66)
Total Investments	89.45	306.35	579.32	643.73
	(100.00)	(100.00)	(100.00)	(100.00)

Note : Figures in Brackets indicate percentages.
Source : Mutual Funds in India—Fact Book, UTI-CM, Mumbai, 1995, p. .44. Results Computed.

A detailed break-up of BOI Mutual Fund investment pattern is exhibited in Table 4.6. The major asset in BOI Mutual Fund's port folio is equity shares. The table shows that the proportion of investments in equity shares has gone up from 62.09 per cent in 1990-91 to 78.00 per cent in 1993-94 showing an increasing trend. A significant change in the BOI MF's investment policy is that during the last four years period, investment in debentures and bonds and Government securities have gone down to around 20.16 per cent and 0.52 respectively in 1993-94. Primarily the shift has taken place from the debentures and Government bonds to equity shares. This change and shift might have necessitated owing to launch of more growth fund.

Table 4.6
Investment Pattern of BOI Mutual Fund

(Rs. Crore)

	1990-91	*1991-92*	*1992-93*	*1993-94*
Equity Shares	354.36	517.55	603.48	709.58
	(62.09)	(69.77)	(74.85)	(78.00)
Debentures/Bonds (including	209.49	198.68	178.71	183.42
private placed)	(36.71)	(26.78)	(22.16)	(20.16)
Government Securities	5.00	4.80	4.80	4.80
(Including Treasury Bills)	(0.88)	(0.65)	(0.60)	(0.52)
Others	1.83	20.77	19.29	12.02
	(0.32)	(2.80)	(2.39)	(1.32)
Total Investments	570.67	741.81	806.28	909.82
	(100.00)	(100.00)	(100.00)	(100.00)

Note : Figures in paranthesis indicate percentages.
Source : Mutual Funds in India, Fact Book, UTI-CM, Mumbai, 1995, p.43. Results Computed.

A detailed break-up of a PNB Mutual Fund is given in Table 4.7 in regard to Investment Pattern. PNB MF's port folio discloses that the major asset is equity shares. The table shows that the proportion of investments in equity shares increased to 72.12 per cent from 19.61 per cent in 1990-91. A significant change in PNB MF's investment policy is that during the last four years period, investment in debentures and Government securities have gone down to 26.40 per cent and 0.00 per cent respectively in 1993-94 from 71.87 per cent and 8.34 per cent respectively in 1990-91. Primarily the shift has been taken place from the government securities and debentures to equity shares. The change might have necessitated owing to launch of more growth funds.

A detailed study on LIC MF investment policy is given in Table 4.8. The assets in LIC MF's portfolio are equity shares, debentures and bonds, government securities, public sector bonds and others totally spread. Investment in equity shares has gone up from 9.33 per cent in 1990-91 to 33.71 per cent in 1993-94 showing increasing trend. Investment in debentures and bonds has gone up from 19.17 per cent in 1990-91 to 37.09 per cent in 1993-94 revealing an increasing trend. Investment in government securities has gone down from 7.49 per cent in 1990-91 to zero in 1992-93 and 1993-94. Investment in public sector bonds has gone down to 6.98 per cent in 1993-94 from 13.60 per cent in 1990-91. Similarly, investment in

Table 4.7
Investment Pattern of PNB MF

(Rs. Crore)

	1991-92	*1992-93*	*1993-94*
Equity Shares	25.86	136.28	170.27
	(19.61)	(62.01)	(72.12)
Debentures/Bonds (including privately placed)	94.75	60.32	62.33
	(71.87)	(27.45)	(26.40)
Government Securities (including Treasury Bills)	11.00	0.00	0.00
	(8.34)	(0.00)	(0.00)
CDs/CPs	0.00	12.00	0.00
	(0.00)	(5.46)	(0.00)
Others	0.23	11.16	3.50
	(0.18)	(5.08)	(1.48)
Total Investments	131.84	219.76	236.10
	(100.00)	(100.00)	(100.00)

Note : Figures in brackets indicate percentages.
Source : Annual Reports of PNB—Various Issues.
Results Computed.

"others" category has gone down to 22.22 per cent in 1993-94 from 50.44 per cent in 1990-91. There is a shift in investment pattern due to slow down of investment in Government securities and public sector bonds to enhancing investment in equity and debentures. This shift might have necessitated owing to launch of, both, growth schemes and income schemes.

Table 4.8
Investment Pattern of LIC MF

(Rs. Crore)

	1990-91	*1991-92*	*1992-93*	*1993-94*
Equity Shares	48.94	113.68	280.34	487.92
	(9.33)	(16.10)	(21.98)	(33.71)
Debenture/Bonds (including private placed)	100.56	199.25	332.49	536.99
	(19.17)	(28.23)	(26.07)	(37.09)
Government Securities (including Treasury Bills)	39.31	34.78	0.00	0.00
	(7.49)	(4.93)	(0.00)	(0.00)
Public Sector Bonds	71.34	66.26	101.03	101.03
	(13.60)	(9.38)	(7.92)	(6.98)
Others	274.30	307.54	561.43	321.61
	(50.44)	(41.36)	(44.03)	(22.22)
Total	524.45	705.89	1,275.29	1,447.56
	(100.00)	(100.00)	(100.00)	(100.00)

Note : Figures in brackets indicate percentages.
Source : Mutual Funds in India-Fact Book, UTI-CM, Mumbai,1995, p.45.
Results Computed.

A detailed break-up of GIC MF investment pattern is given in Table 4.9. The assets in GIC MF's portfolio is consisting of equity, debentures, public sector bonds and others. Investment in equity has gone up from 18.80 per cent in 1990-91 to 42.72 per cent in 1993-94. Investment in debentures has gone up from 138.69 per cent to 50.76 over the term of three years. Investment in public sector bonds has declined to 3.61 per cent from 5.81 per cent during last two years. Investment CDs/CPs has gone down to 0.18 per cent in 1993-94 from 20.81 per cent in 1992-93. Investment in "Others" category has declined from 38.55 per cent in 1991-92 to 2.73 in 1993-94. Mainly the shift has taken place from the public sector bonds, CDs/CPs and others to equity shares and debentures. This change might have been necessitated owing to launch of more and more growth schemes and income schemes.

Table 4.9
Investment Pattern of GICMF

(Rs. Crore)

	1991-92	1992-93	1993-94
Equity Shares	70.58 (18.80)	152.15 (21.39)	355.88 (42.72)
Debentures/Bonds (including private placed)	158.99 (42.35)	275.10 (38.69)	422.87 (50.76)
Government Securities (including Treasury bills)	0.00 (0.00)	0.00 (0.00)	0.00 (0.00)
Public Sector Bonds	0.00 (0.00)	41.35 (5.81)	30.09 (3.61)
CDs/CPs	0.00 (0.00)	147.96 (20.81)	1.50 (0.18)
Others	145.85 (38.85)	94.52 (13.30)	22.65 (2.73)
Total Investments	375.43 (100.00)	711.07 (100.00)	833.00 (100.00)

Note : Figures in paranthesis indicate percentages.
Source : Annual Reports of GIC MF-Various Issues.
Results Computed.

A detailed break-up of UTI investment pattern is given in Table 4.10. The major asset in UTI's portfolio is equity shares. The table shows that the proportion of investments in equity shares has gone

Table 4.10
Investment Pattern of UTI Mutual Fund

(Rs. Crore)

	1990-1991	*1991-92*	*1992-93*	*1993-94*
Equity Shares	3,862.45	8,357.32	14,353.02	20,379.60
	(28.15)	(39.50)	(47.26)	(46.86)
Debentures/Bonds (including	4,371.55	6,076.00	8,270.72	11,101.84
privately placed)	(31.86)	(28.72)	(27.23)	(25.53)
Government Securities	3,561.66	5,083.87	3,724.63	7,877.49
(including Treasury bills)	(25.96)	(24.03)	(12.26)	(18.11)
Others	1,728.44	2,645.77	3,574.90	4,081.74
	(12.60)	(12.51)	(11.77)	(9.38)
Total	13,720.10	21,157.64	30,370.42	43,493.84
	(100.00)	(100.00)	(100.00)	(100.00)

Note : Values in paranthesis indicate the percentage of total investments.

Source : Annual Reports of various MFs and UTI.

up from 28 per cent in 1990-91 to around 47 per cent in 1992-93 and 39 per cent in 1993-94. A significant hang in the UTI's investment policy is that during the last four years period, investment in bonds and government securities have gone down to around 25.53 per cent and 18.11 per cent respectively from a significantly higher proportion of 31.86 per cent and 25.96 per cent in 1990-91. Primarily the shift has taken place from the government securities and bonds to equity shares. This change and shift might have necessitated owing to launch of more and more growth funds.

CHAPTER FIVE

Accounting and Reporting Practices in Mutual Funds

This Chapter deals with 'Accounting and Reporting Practices in Mutual Funds' in India. For the purpose the various annual reports, half-yearly reports and relevant accounting records are considered for analysis. Wherever necessary, personal contacts and interviews with the executives and accountants of respective mutual funds have been made for better picture. Principally, this chapter covers:

(i) Legal Aspect,
(ii) Accounting Aspect,
(iii) Analysis of Incomes and Expenses, and
(iv) Reporting Practices and Disclosure Practices.

Legal Aspect of Accounting in Mutual Funds

Guidelines for Mutual Funds issued by the Ministry of Finance, Department of Economic Affairs (Investment Division) are: According to guideline 13, Mutual Funds should be required to segregate their earnings as current income, short-term capital gains and long-term capital gains. Thus, incomes earned by Mutual Funds are comprising of:

(a) current incomes,
(b) short-term capital gains as per the provisions of the Income Tax Act, 1961, and

(c) long-term capitals gains as per the provisions of Income Tax Act, 1961.

Accounting for all the mutual fund schemes should be required to be done for the same year ending.

For all quoted instruments, mutual fund must compute weekly NAV at the last available closing market prices.

For unquoted investments, the valuation may be done once weekly either at cost or by any other method authorised by SEBI.

For investments considered doubtful, the directors' best estimate may be accepted, subject to the auditor's certificate of reasonability.

Guideline 14 of the said Guidelines of Government are provisions regarding to 'Disclosures and Reporting'. They are:

(i) Every mutual fund should prepare and submit copies of duly audited annual statements of accounts including balance sheet and the profit and loss account for the fund for each scheme. It must be submitted once a year.

(ii) Six monthly unaudited accounts as above are to be furnished.

(iii) A statement of movements in net assets for each of the schemes of the fund, every quarter.

(iv) A portfolio statement, including changes from the previous periods, for each scheme, every quarter.

All mutual funds should submit the following:

(a) accounting policies adopted by MFs,

(b) texts of the marketing literature and advertisements issued to the investors,

(c) offer documents,

(d) advertisement literature, and

(e) marketing and publicity brochures of each scheme.

In this connection, SEBI has framed a separate 'regulations' under SEBI (Mutual Fund) Regulations, 1993 for more emphasis on maintenance of accounts and reporting practices for mutual funds operating in India. According to Regulation 47, every mutual fund should maintain proper books of accounts records and documents for each individual scheme. Books of accounting and records should be such as to explain its transactions and to disclose at any point of time the financial position of the Mutual Fund in general and in particular give a true and fair view of the state of affairs of the Mutual Fund. A mutual fund should intimate the SEBI the place where the books of accounts, records and documents are maintained. A Mutual Fund should follow consistent accounting policies and accounting standards and uniform accounting practices so as to provide appropriate details of the scheme-wise disposition of the assets of the fund at the relevant accounting data and the performance during that period together with information regarding distribution or accumulation of income accruing to the unit holder in a fair and true manner. Regulation 48 indicates the 'Accounting year'. The accounting year for all the schemes shall end on the same date which shall be March 31. If a new scheme is commenced during the accounting year, the disclosure and reporting requirements would apply for the period beginning from the date of its commencement and ending on the last date of the relevant accounting year of the mutual fund. For instance, if fund commenced its scheme in September, 1996, it should provide and close accounts on 31st March, 1997. Regulation 49 indicates on classification of earnings. Earnings should be, for each scheme, segregated into *(i)* short-term capital gains, *(ii)* long-term capital gains, and *(iii)* other incomes.

Auditor's Report

According to Regulation 53, Accounts of the scheme shall have to be audited by the auditor who shall be different from the auditor of the Asset Management Company. For the purpose, auditor means a person who is qualified to audit the accounts of a company under Section 224 of the Companies Act, 1956. An auditor shall be appointed by the Trustees. The auditor shall forward his report to the trustees. Such report shall form part of the Annual Report of the Mutual Fund.

Publication for Annual Report and Summary thereof is dealt under Regulation 54. The schemewise annual report of a Mutual Fund or an abridged summary thereof shall be published through an advertisement as soon as possible but not later than six months from the date of closure of relevant financial year. For the purpose, Schedule VII and VIII shall be followed.

Disclosure

A Mutual Fund shall furnish the following periodic reports to the Board, namely:

- *(i)* copies of duly audited annual statements and accounts including Balance Sheet and the profit and loss account. For each scheme once a year;
- *(ii)* a copy of six monthly unaudited accounts;
- *(iii)* a quarterly statement of movements in net assets for each of the schemes of the fund; and
- *(iv)* a quarterly portfolio statement, including changes from the previous period, for each scheme.

A Mutual Fund shall before the expiry of two months from the close of each half year that is on 31st September publish through an advertisement, its unaudited financial results in one English daily newspaper circulating in the language of the region where the Head office of the Mutual Fund is situated. The unaudited report shall contain details as specified in Schedule VIII and shall provide a true and fair view of the operations of the Mutual Fund.

Schedule VII of SEBI (Mutual Fund) Regulations, 1993 details the provisions and rules regarding to 'Annual Report' as per Regulation 54.

Schedule VIII of the SEBI (Mutual fund) Regulations,1993 indicates the'Half Yearly Financial Results ' as per Regulation 58.

Accounting Aspect

A Accounting Cycle of Mutual Fund for each individual mutual fund scheme shall be adopted since account and records for each scheme must be exclusively and separately maintained at the Head Office or Corporate Office as per the regulations of SEBI, Guidelines of Government of India and Companies Act, etc. The accounting cycle consisting of transactions, journal, subsidiary books, ledger (i.e., personal ledger, impersonal ledger and allied ledgers which the Mutual Fund deem fit), Registers such as Assets Register, Non-Performing assets register, Investment register, Equity portfolio register, Debenture portfolio register etc., trial balance, Revenue Account, Balance Sheet and Auditor's report.

Concepts and Accounting policies usually adopted by mutual fund organisations are comprising of going concern concept, Entity concept, Accounting year concept, Dual Aspect concept, Revenue Recognition, Accrual accounting, Depreciation accounting standard, cash basis of accounting, merchantile system, valuation of assets, valuation of investments, valuation of inventories, valuation of intangible assets, treatment of deferred revenue expenses, treatment of initial expenses, treatment of brand development expenses, computation of net assets value profit and loss account and balance sheet.

Annual Report

According to Regulation 54 of the SEBI (Mutual Fund) Regulations, 1993, annual report shall contain:

(i) Report of the Board of Trustees on the operations of the various schemes of the Fund as a whole during the year and the future outlook of the fund;

(ii) Balance sheet and Revenue Account in accordance with paras 2 and 3 of the schedule;

(iii) Auditor's Report in accordance with the paragraph 4 of this schedule;

(iv) Brief Statement of the Board of Trustees on aspects, namely:

(a) liabilities and responsibilities of the Trustees and Settler;

(b) Investment objective of each scheme;

(c) Basis of investment underlying the scheme;

(d) If the scheme permits investment partly or wholly in shares, bonds, debentures and other sectors or securities whose value can fluctuate, a statement on the following line; "The price and redempion value of the units and income from them, can go up as well as down with the fluctuations in the market value of its underlying investments;

(v) Statement giving relevant perspective historical 'per unit' statistics in accordance with paragraph 5 of this schedule; and

(vi) Statement on the following: "On written request, present and prospective unit holder/investors can obtain copy of the trust deed, the annual report and the text of the relevant scheme".

Analysis of Incomes and Expenses

In this section, we attempted to analyse various components of income generated by mutual fund industry. The mutual fund industry has various sources of income. The main sources of income include:

(a) Profit on sale of investments,
(b) Dividend,
(c) Interest,
(d) Other incomes.

Other incomes include profit from redemption of investments, profit on transfer of investments and other income.

For the industry as a whole, the dominant source of income is interest. More than 60 per cent of the income comes as interest income. Surprisingly, income from trading is not much. Dividend income is 3.86 per cent of the total income as an aggregate basis. Dividend yield as percentage of total investments is only 0.7 per cent. Dividend yield as a percentage of total investment in equity works out to be 1.44 for the year 1993-94. Therefore, dividend is not the main source of income for the purpose of distribution of income. For distribution of income, the mutual funds have to depend either on interest income or on profits from market operations.

Unit Trust of India generates 83.79 per cent of the total income of the industry as an average over the period of four years under review. It was 89.10 per cent in 1990-91 which declined to 83.35 per cent in 1991-92 and further came down to 82.21 per cent in 1992-93 and still decreased to 80.51 per cent in 1993-94. Thus, it revealed declining trend. Still it is dominating the whole industry. this is keeping the market leadership.

Balance Sheet of ....
As at ....

Liabilities	*P.Y. Rs.*	*C.Y. Rs.*	*Assets*	*P.Y. Rs.*	*C.Y. Rs.*
Unit Capital			Investments		
Reserve and Surplus			Deposits		
Loans			Other Current Assets		
Current Liabilities and Provisions			Fixed Assets		
			Deferred Revenue Expenditure		
Total			Total		

Revenue Account of ....

For the Year ended ....

Expenditure and Losses	*P.Y. Rs.*	*C.Y. Rs.*	*Income*	*P.Y. Rs.*	*C.Y. Rs.*
1. Provision for Depreciation in Value of Investments			1. Dividend		
2. Provision for outstanding Accrued income considered doubtful.			2. Interest		
3. Provision for Doubtful Deposits and Current Assets			3. Profit on Sale/ Redemption of Investments (Other than inter scheme Transfer/Sale)		
4. Loss on Sale/Redemption of Investments (Other than inter-scheme transfer/sale)			4. Profit on Inter-Scheme Transfer/Sale of Investments		
5. Loss on Inter-Scheme Transfer/ Sale of Investments			5. Other Income		
6. Management Fees					
7. Trusteeship Fees					
8. Staff Cost including Salary, Allowances, Contribution to Provident Fund, Gratuity etc.					
9. Office and Administrative Expenditure					
10. Registration and Legal Expenses					
11. Commission to Agents					
12. Audit Fees					
13. Other Operating Expenses					
14. Deferred Revenue Expenses W/O					
15. Depreciation on Fixed Assets					
16. Income Distribution/Dividend					
17. Transfer to General Reserve					
Total			Total		

PY = Previous year
CY = Current year

Liabilities-Schedules

Schedule—1 Unit Capital

	P.Y.	C.Y.
(a) Initial Capital		
(b) Unit Capital		

Schedule—2 Reserves and Surplus

	P.Y.	C.Y.
(a) Unit Premium Reserve		
(b) General Reserve Relating to initial capital		
(c) General Reserve relating to Unit Capital		
(d) Dividend Equalisation Reserve		
(e) Any other reserve		
(f) Appropriation account		

Schedule—3 Loans

	P.Y.	C.Y.
Loans from :		
(a) Settlor		
(b) Other commercial banks		
(c) Others		

Schedule—4 Current Liabilities and Provisions

	P.Y.	C.Y.
A. *CURRENT LIABILITIES*		
(a) Sundry Creditors		
(b) Interest payable on loans		
(c) Contract for purchase of investments		
(d) Bank account over drawn as per books		
(e) Unclaimed distributed income		
(f) Others		

B. *PROVISIONS*

(*a*) Provision for loss/depreciation in value of investments
(*b*) Provision for doubtful deposits
(*c*) Provision for outstanding and accrued income considered doubtful
(*d*) Provision for gratuity
(*e*) Provision for staff welfare fund
(*f*) Proposed income distribution on initial capital and unit capital
(*g*) Other provisions

Assets—Schedules

I. Invstments

(*a*) Equity shares
(*b*) Preference shares
(*c*) Privately placed debentures/bonds
(*d*) Debentures and bonds listed/awaiting listing on the recognised stock exchange
(*e*) Cash paid in advance
(*f*) Term loans
(*g*) Central and State Government Securities (including treasury bills)
(*h*) Commercial paper
(*i*) Others

II. Deposits

(*a*) Deposits with scheduled banks
(*b*) Deposits with companies/institutions
(*c*) Others

III. Other Current Assets

(*a*) Balance with banks in current account
(*b*) Cash on hand
(*c*) Sundry debtors
(*d*) Contracts for sale of investments
(*e*) Outstanding and accrued income
(*f*) Advance, Deposits etc.
(*g*) Basic Finance
(*h*) Shares/debentures application money, pending adjust
(*i*) Others

IV. Fixed Assets

(*a*) Leasehold land

(*b*) Freehold land
(*c*) Office Building and Premises
(*d*) Furnitures and Fixtures and Office equipment
(*e*) Other Assets

V. Deferred Revenue Expenditure

(*a*) Opening Balance
(*b*) Addition during the year
(*c*) Amount Written off during the year
(*d*) Amount deferred to subsequent years

Historical Per Unit Statistics

(*a*) Net Asset Value (NAV) (after dividend)

(*b*) (*i*) Income Other than Profit on Sale of Investment
(*ii*) Income from Profit on inter-scheme sales/transfer of investment
(*iii*) Income from profit on sale of investment to third party
(*iv*) Transfer to Revenue Account from Past year's reserve
(*v*) Gross Income [Total of (i) to (iv)]

(*c*) (*i*) Aggregate of expenses, write off, depreciation, amortisation and charges
(*ii*) Provision for depreciation in value of investments
(*iii*) Gross expenditure [Total of (i) and (ii)]

(*d*) Net Income before dividend (b - c)

(*e*) Unrealised appropriation/unprovided depreciation in value of investments

(*f*) (*i*) Repurchase Price
(*ii*) Reissue Price
(*iii*) Trading Price
1. Highest during the year
2. Lowest during the year
(*iv*) Price-Earning Ratio

Statement of Accounting Policies and Notes Attached to and Forming Part of the Accounts

A. Accounting Policies

1. Valuation of investments
2. Recognition of Revenue/Expenses
3. Non-performing assets
4. Provision for depreciation in the value of investments.

B. Investments

Name of Investment	Cost	Market Value	Appreciation/ Depreciation	Provision for loss/ depreciation in the value of investments	Unrealised appropriation (+)/ Unprovided depreciation (–)
1. Equity					
2. Preference Schemes					
3. Privately placed debentures/Bonds					
4. Debentures and Bonds listed/awaiting for listing quoted					
5. Call others paid in advance					
6. Term loans					
7. Central and State Government Securities					
8. Commercial Paper					
9. Others					

Non-Performing Investments

An investment is regarded as non-performing, if it has provided no returns in the form of dividend or interest for more than two years as at the end of the current accounting year.

Name of Investment	Cost	Market Value	Appreciation/ Depreciation	Provision for loss/ depreciation in the value of Investments	Unrealised appropriation (+)/ Unprovided depreciation (–)
1. Equity Shares					
2. Long-term Capital Gains					
3. Debentures and Bonds listed/awaiting for listing					
4. Others					

Income generated by all mutual funds is analysed in Table 5.1. Unit Trust of India is remaining as a pioneer by generating income of 8.379 per cent over the tenure of 4 years from 1990-91 to 1993-94. It generated income of 89.10 per cent in 1990-91, 83.35 per cent in 1991-92, 82.21 per cent in 1992-93 and 80.51 per cent in 1993-94. This income generation is, indeed, depends on investment. When investment is more, income generation is more and *vice versa* keeping risk factor as same. Income generation declined consistently over the years from 89.10 per cent to 80.51 per cent during the period under review still it is dominating in the mutual fund industry although income in real terms enhanced. Other mutual funds income increased from 10.90 per cent in 1990-91 to 19.49 per cent in 1993-94 revealing an increasing trend. Over the period of 4 years term, 16.1 per cent of income is reported on an average.

Table 5.1
Income Generated by All Mutual Funds

(Rs. Crore)

	1990-91	*1991-92*	*1992-93*	*1993-94*	
Mutual Funds	336.40	972.38	1,176.94	1,850.63	
	(10.90)	(16.65)	(17.79)	(19.49)	(16.21)
Unit Trust of India	2,749.24	4,868.48	5,437.17	7,644.59	
	(89.10)	(83.85)	(82.21)	(80.51)	(83.79)
Total	3,085.63	5,840.86	6,614.11	9,495.22	
	(100.00)	(100.00)	(100.00)	(100.00)	(100.00)

Note : Figures in brackets indicate percentages.
Source : Annual Reports of UTI and MFs—Various Issues. Results Computed.

Table 5.2 exhibits Income Generated by all Mutual Funds—Headwise Break-up. From it, income generated is comprising of dividend, interest, profit on sale/redemption of investments, profit on inter-scheme transfers/sale of investments and other income. Out of all the various incomes 61.12 per cent generated from interest income, 28.29 per cent from profit on sale/redemption of investments, 5.45 per cent from others, 3.86 per cent from dividends and 1.28 per cent from profit on inter-scheme transfers/sale of investments. Thus, interest income is the major source of income generation, and second position is occupied by profit on sale/redemption of investments.

Table 5.2
Income Generated by All Mutual Funds–Head-wise Break-up

(Rs. Crore)

Head-wise Break-up of Income	*1990-91*	*1991-92*	*1992-93*	*1993-94*	
Dividend	125.32	177.32	288.18	383.10	
	(4.06)	(3.04)	(4.36)	(3.99)	(3.86)
Interest	2,319.47	3,132.02	4,254.13	4,878.78	
	(75.17)	(53.62)	(64.32)	(51.38)	(61.12)
Profit on Sale/Redemption of Investments	535.72	2,274.47	1,676.33	2,993.43	
	(17.36)	(38.94)	(25.34)	(31.52)	(28.29)
Profit on Inter-Scheme Transfers/Sale of Investments	12.91	31.32	136.20	281.62	
	(0.42)	(0.53)	(2.06)	(2.09)	(1.28)
Other Income	100.30	196.11	196.20	1,046.83	
	(2.99)	(3.87)	(3.92)	(11.02)	(5.45)
Total	3,085.63	5,840.85	6,614.11	9,495.22	
	(100.00)	(100.00)	(100.00)	(100.00)	(100.00)

Note : Figures in brackets indicate percentages.
Source : Annual Reports of all Mutual Funds—Various Issues. Results Computed.

Turning to individual performances of mutual funds, SBI mutual fund position is depicted in Table 5.3. Interest income is the main source of income. Second position is occupied by profit on sale/redemption of investments. Table 5.4. reveals income generated by Canbank Mutual Fund. Interest income is the main primary source. Second position is occupied by profit on sale/redemption of investments and profit on inter-scheme transfers/sale of investments. Position of Indbank Mutual Fund is exhibited in Table 5.5. Top position is taken by profit on sale/redemption of investments and second position is occupied by interest income. Table 5.6. exhibits income generated by BOI Mutual Fund. Top position is occupied by profit on sale/redemption of investments and second position went to interest income. Table 5.7. depicts income generated by PNB Mutual Fund. Interest is the prime source of income generation second source of income is profit on sale/redemption of investments. Table 5.8. exhibited income generated by LIC Mutual Fund. Interest income is the main source of income and second position is taken by profit on sale/ redemption of investments. Table 5.9. discloses income generated by GIC Mutual Fund. Income from interest is the top source of income. Profit on sale/redemption of investments occupies the second position. Table 5.10. reveals the position of income generated by UTI Mutual Fund. Interest income is the main source of income at the top. Second position is taken by profit on sale/ redemption of investments. Thus, interest income is the prime source in almost all mutual funds for income distribution. Dividend income is a negligible source in all the mutual funds. profit on sale/redemption of investments the second source of income is 6 mutual funds out of organisations.

Disclosure Practices in Mutual Funds

Like any business organisation, mutual funds are required to state in the 'Notes to the Accounts in their Annual Reports', significant accounting policies that have been adopted by them, in arriving at the accounting information that is reported. Materials alterations to reported income should be sufficiently disclosed. Changes in accounting policies should be disclosed.*

An analysis and indepth study of accounting policies and practices disclosed in the Annual Reports of "Big Eight" mutual funds and clarification obtained by accounts and auditors was made to ascertain if accounting policies adopted by mutual funds are similar. The impact of differential treatment was explained.

The following are the major areas where differential treatments were odserved.

Incomes

The usual contents of Revenue Account discloses:

---

* Accounting Standard No. 1 (As-1), "Discloure of Accounting Policies," The Institute of Chartered Accountants of India, New Delhi.

(i) Dividend;

(ii) Interest;

(iii) Profit on sale/redemption of investments (other than inter scheme transfers/sale);

(iv) Profit on inter-scheme transfer/sale of investments;

(v) Other income (indicating nature).

All these are reflected in the Revenue Account of each scheme individually by the Mutual Fund. Revenue Account is a nominal Account in nature and the rules of nominal account are strictly adopted. They are: 'All income and gains are credited and all expenses and losses are debited'. Thus, on credit side, all incomes are recorded while on debit side, all expenses, losses are reflected.

Table 5.3
Income Generated—SBI Mutual Fund

(Rs. Crore)

Headwise Break-up of Income	*1991-92*	*1992-93*	*1993-94*
Dividend	4.17 (3.73)	10.35 (4.44)	22.80 (5.12)
Interest	56.22 (50.28)	114.84 (49.14)	173.75 (39.03)
Profit on Sale/Redemption of Investments	32.08 (28.69)	90.66 (38.79)	186.33 (41.85)
Profit on Inter-Scheme Transfer/ Sale of Investments	0.52 (0.47)	13.00 (5.57)	42.94 (9.65)
Other Income	18.83 (16.83)	4.84 (2.06)	19.28 (4.35)
Total	111.82 (100.00)	233.70 (100.00)	445.19 (100.00)

Note : Figures in brackets indicate percentages.
Source : Annual Reports of Mutual Funds—Various Issues.
Results Computed.

Table 5.4
Income Generated—Canbank Mutual Fund

(Rs. Crore)

Head-wise Break-up of Income	*1990-91*	*1991-92*	*1992-93*	*1993-94*
Dividend	1.25	14.18	22.50	27.71
	(1.29)	(2.98)	(5.51)	(4.25)
Interest	68.38	267.91	243.00	206.54
	(70.73)	(56.30)	(59.55)	(31.67)
Profit on Sale/Redemption of Investments	12.41	146.92	18.53	87.52
	(12.83)	(30.87)	(4.54)	(13.42)
Profit on Inter-Scheme Transfer/Sale of Investments	12.30	27.43	108.02	175.90
	(12.72)	(5.77)	(26.47)	(26.97)
Other Income	2.33	19.43	14.65	145.46
	(2.43)	(4.08)	(3.93)	(23.69)
Total	96.68	475.88	408.04	652.08
	(100.00)	(100.00)	(100.00)	(100.00)

Note : Figures in brackets indicate percentages.
Source : Annual Reports of Mutual Fund—Various Issues. Results Computed.

Table 5.5
Income Generated—Indbank Mutual Fund

(Rs. Crore)

Head-wise Break-up of Income	*1990-91*	*1991-92*	*1992-93*	*1993-94*
1	2	3	4	5
Dividends	1.46	2.01	5.17	4.25
	(5.92)	(2.45)	(4.40)	(2.95)
Interest	7.38	26.75	39.07	45.70
	(29.96)	(32.63)	(33.28)	(31.73)
Profit on Sale/Redemption of Investments	15.39	50.17	69.39	80.10
	(62.48)	(61.20)	(59.11)	(55.61)

(Contd.)

1	2	3	4	5
Profit on Inter-Scheme Transfers/Sale of Investments	0.00 (0.00)	0.00 (0.00)	2.31 (1.96)	11.50 (7.98)
Other Income	0.41 (1.64)	3.05 (3.72)	1.46 (1.25)	1.26 (1.76)
Total Income	24.63 (100.00)	81.98 (100.00)	117.40 (100.00)	144.04 (100.00)

Note : Figures in brackets indicate percentages.
Source : Annual Reports of Mutual Funds—Various Issues.
Results Computed.

Table 5.6
Income Generated—BOI Mutual Fund

(Rs. Crore)

Head-wise Break-up of Income	*1990-91*	*1991-92*	*1992-93*	*1993-94*
Dividend	2.52 (2.35)	6.67 (5.47)	11.75 (8.35)	7.13 (7.77)
Interest	87.46 (81.38)	35.47 (29.10)	33.11 (23.54)	16.75 (18.26)
Profit on Sale/Redemption of Investments	15.72 (14.63)	77.88 (63.89)	92.33 (65.65)	65.01 (70.88)
Profit on Inter-Scheme Transfer/Sale of Investment	0.61 (0.56)	0.00 (0.00)	1.73 (1.23)	0.71 (0.77)
Other Income	1.16 (1.08)	1.87 (1.54)	1.72 (1.23)	2.11 (2.32)
Total	107.47 (100.00)	121.89 (100.00)	140.64 (100.00)	91.72 (100.00)

Note : Figures in brackets indicate percentages.
Source : Annual Reports of BOI MF—Various Years.
Results Computed.

Table 5.7
Income Generated—PNB Mutual Fund

(Rs. Crore)

Head-wise Break-up of Income	*1991-92*	*1992-93*	*1993-94*
Dividend	0.15	1.12	2.25
	(0.61)	(3.63)	(3.62)
Interest	18.18	21.20	14.12
	(73.54)	(68.67)	(22.72)
Profit on Sale/Redemption	4.81	3.23	25.48
of Investments	(19.46)	(10.46)	(41.00)
Profit on Inter-Scheme Transfers/	0.68	3.34	17.41
Sale of Investments	(2.75)	(10.82)	(28.01)
Other Income	0.91	1.98	2.87
	(3.64)	(6.42)	(1.78)
Total	24.72	30.87	62.14
	(100.00)	(100.00)	(100.00)

Note : Figures in brackets indicate percentages.
Source : Annual Reports of PNB MF—Various Years.
Results Computed.

Table 5.8
Income Generated—LIC Mutual Fund

(Rs. Crore)

Head-wise Break-up of Income	*1990-91*	*1991-92*	*1992-93*	*1993-94*
Dividend	0.67	3.28	4.92	12.29
	(1.47)	(3.30)	(3.49)	(4.17)
Interest	27.23	76.75	104.80	186.87
	(59.70)	(77.12)	(74.34)	(63.39)
Profit on Sale/Redemption	17.71	16.80	26.89	88.08
of Investments	(38.83)	(16.87)	(19.07)	(29.88)
Profit on Inter-Scheme	0.00	2.69	3.91	6.73
Transfers/ Sale of Investments	(0.00)	(2.71)	(2.77)	(2.28)
Other Income	0.00	0.00	0.51	0.87
	(0.00)	(0.00)	(0.33)	(0.28)
Total	45.61	99.53	140.98	294.78
	(100.00)	(100.00)	(100.00)	(100.00)

Note : Figures in brackets indicate percentages.
Source : Annual Reports of LIC MF—Various Years.
Results Computed.

Table 5.9
Income Generated—GIC Mutual Fund

(Rs. Crore)

Head-wise Break-up of Income	*1991-92*	*1992-93*	*1993-94*
Dividend	0.4,569	1.4,469	2.9,104
	(0.81)	(1.3,731)	(1.8,129)
Interest	44.9,521	78.3,083	103.7,908
	(79.46)	(74.3,604)	(64.5,943)
Profit on Sale/Redemption of Investments	8.1,920	17.0,706	22.2,658
	(14.18)	(16.2,099)	(13.8,571)
Profit on Inter-Scheme Transfer/ Sale of Investments	0.0,000	3.8,782	26.4,289
	(0.000)	(3.6,826)	(16.4,854)
Other Income	2.9,657	4.6,052	5.2,850
	(5.25)	(4.3,740)	(3.2,503)
Total	56.5,665	105.3,091	160.6,811
	(100.00)	(100.00)	(100.00)

Note : Figures in brackets indicate percentages.
Source : Annual Reports of GIC Mutual Fund - Various Years. Results Computed.

Table 5.10
Income Generated—UTI Mutual Fund

(Rs. Crore)

Head-wise Break-up of Income	*1990-91*	*1991-92*	*1992-93*	*1993-94*
Dividend	119.43	146.41	230.93	303.76
	(4.34)	(3.00)	(4.25)	(3.97)
Interest	2,129.02	2,605.78	3,619.80	4,131.26
	(77.44)	(53.52)	(66.57)	(54.04)
Profit on Sale/Redemption of Investments	474.50	1,937.62	1,358.24	2,438.64
	(17.25)	(39.79)	(24.98)	(31.90)
Other Income	96.40	149.05	166.44	869.69
	(3.50)	(3.69)	(3.20)	(10.09)
Total	2,749.24	4,868.48	5,437.17	7,644.59
	(100.00)	(100.00)	(100.00)	(100.00)

Note : Figures in brackets indicate percentages.
Source : Annual Reports of UTI—Various Years. Results Computed.

Table 5.11
Break-up of Expenses—Mutual Fund Industry Total

(Rs. Crore)

Break-up of Expenses	*1990-91*	*1991-92*	*1992-93*	*1993-94*	*Mean*
Provision for Depreciation in value of Investments	1.61 (2.29)	133.71 (45.62)	210.07 (47.39)	71.06 (17.59)	104.11 (28.22)
Management Fees	9.22 (13.16)	41.91 (14.30)	32.27 (7.28)	99.41 (24.61)	45.70 (14.84)
Trusteeship Fees	0.09 (0.12)	9.75 (3.33)	17.33 (3.91)	10.54 (2.61)	9.43 (2.49)
Staff Cost	10.78 (15.38)	10.71 (3.65)	14.05 (3.17)	18.97 (4.70)	13.63 (6.73)
Office and Administ-ration Expenses	24.08 (34.37)	47.97 (16.37)	55.28 (12.47)	81.01 (20.06)	52.08 (20.82)
Registration and Legal Expenses	0.06 (0.09)	0.45 (0.15)	1.69 (0.38)	8.68 (2.15)	2.72 (0.69)
Publicity/Agents Com-mission	12.02 (17.15)	19.59 (6.68)	50.96 (11.50)	51.73 (12.81)	33.57 (12.03)
Audit Fees	0.18 (0.26)	0.09 (0.03)	0.46 (0.10)	0.34 (0.08)	0.27 (0.12)
Other Operating Expenses	12.05 (17.19)	28.93 (9.87)	61.16 (13.80)	62.14 (15.39)	42.95 (14.06)
Total	70.08 (100.00)	293.12 (100.00)	443.27 (100.00)	403.87 (100.00)	302.59 (100.00)

Note : Figures in brackets indicate percentages.
Source : Annual Reports of Mutual Funds.
Results Computed.

Table 5.12
Income and Expenses—Industry Total

(Rs. Crore)

	1990-91	*1991-92*	*1992-93*	*1993-94*	*Mean*
Income	3,085.63	5,840.86	6,614.11	9495.22	6,258.955
Expenses	70.08	293.12	443.27	403.87	302.585
Expenses % of Income	2.27	5.02	6.70	4.25	4.56

Source : Annual Reports of Mutual Funds.
Results Computed.

Funds derive profits from sale of investments to third parties. Funds derive profits from sale of investments to another scheme in their own fund. Profits from both these sources are needed to be separately disclosed in the Revenue Account. Inter-scheme transfer is widely practiced by Indian Mutual Funds. There are certain stigma in the secondary market operation of Indian Stock Exchanges. They are:

(i) lack of adequate floating stock;
(ii) delays in settlement and registration;
(iii) liquidity constraints imposed due to trading a thin market.

Inter-Scheme Transfer

(i) Inter-Scheme transfer for quoted securities can be made basing on market prices. These market prices can be taken from the quotes of various stock exchanges, especially Bombay Stock Exchange. The market quotes of National Stock Exchange can also be marked.
(ii) Inter-scheme transfer for unquoted instruments need more care and caution. Such transfers are made by the best judgment of Investment managers with consultation of the Board. These are to be certified by the auditor of the scheme and such is mentioned in the auditor's certificate.

Dividend

Income from dividend is nothing but dividend received from the equity shares and preference shares from various companies. Dividend is of two types such as *(i)* interim dividend, and *(ii)* final dividend. The companies distribute dividends and pay after deducting income tax from the sources itself. Net amount is given to the investors. The investor is the Mutual Fund who receives the dividend in net. Such is 'grossed up' for the purposes of Income Tax computation.

Interest

Income from interest is the major and vital source of income to the Mutual Funds. It arises from debentures, bonds, convertibles, non-convertibles, public sector bonds, commercial papers, certificate of deposits etc. It is also subject to deduction of income tax. Net amount is derived from the source. It is to be 'grossed up' for the income tax purposes.

Profit on Sale of Investments

Profits are arising on sale of investments. Proper allocation of such profits is essential. The revenue profit is separated from the capital profit and proper record is made in the revenue account and accounting records.

Underwriting Commission

This is treated as income, provided there are no transfers on the mutual fund. If there is a transfer, the commission earned on the transferred investments, is reduced from the cost of the investments.

For instance, the scheme earned an income under this head amounted to Rs. 1 lakh as underwriting commission. With an agreement, it devolved 25 per cent of the issue to another company. An equal proportion of commission, i.e., Rs. 25,000 to be shunned and given to the other. Such an amount be reduced from the total income and properly recorded in the books of accounts. Finally, the fund shall show Rs. 75,000 as underwriting commission in the final accounts.

It is apparent that a mutual fund may have underwriting commitments on the balance sheet date, a liability arising if the issue devolves. It may have to be seen if such commitments should be disclosed as contingent liabilities on the balance sheet date, on the presumption that the entire issue may devolve. If information on the extent of develvement is known, that can be disclosed in the annual report. Liabilities arising out of partly paid share may also have to be separately disclosed.

Front End Fee

Some mutual funds treat front end fees received on equity investments as income. It can be adjusted in the acquisition cost. Some funds uniformly capitalise front end fees. Some funds treat as revenue item and charge to revenue account.

Other Income

Mutual Funds are income from the following activities. They are :

(*i*) Front end fees,

(ii) Service charges,
(iii) Commitment charges on firm allotments and private placements, and
(iv) Interest on advance subscriptions.

Expenses

Principally, expenses are categorised into 'revenue' and 'capital' expenses in the accounting jargon and language and the same concept is adopted here, too for accurate treatment. The treatment of expenses in the mutual funds accounts has a hearing on the determination of distributable surplus, on the one hand, and the evaluation of the capital gains/losses on the investment, on the other. Mutual Funds differentiate and distinguish between three types of expenses, viz:

(a) Expenses that are initially capitalised, and amortised and charged to the individual schemes over years. These include initial issue expenses, agents' commissions and incentives to investors;
(b) Direct Expenses; and
(c) Indirect Expenses.

Initial Expenses

Mutual Funds issue units to the public for their investment through offer document setting terms and conditions, objects, etc. Mutual Funds incur certain expenses towards public issue of units of the schemes. These expenses include brokerage, commission and incentives. Brokerage and commission can be recurring in case of open-ended schemes. These expenses are capitalised. These are written off over the tenure of the scheme. These expenses are capitalised by Mutual Funds as 'Deferred Revenue Expenditure' by all the existing mutual funds in India. But the manner in which the expenditure is amortised is not uniform. The treatment is different from one organisation to another. Some funds write off the incentives over the first three years and mortise rest of expenses like commission and brokerage over the tenure of the scheme. Some funds amortise all the expenses over the lock in period of the scheme. Some other funds, amortise these expenses over the tenure of the scheme. Of course, trust may decide to amortise such expenses in a particular year depending upon the earnings of that scheme.

SEBI stipulated a ceiling of 6 per cent of the funds raised for the initial expenses of the scheme. When it is not mentioned whether it is for open-ended or close-ended scheme, it is presumed that it is universally applicable to the schemes. The stipulation is applicable to initial expenses only. For close-ended scheme, the stipulation is alright since the issue of the scheme closes after an agreed period of the scheme as per offer document. In case open-ended fund schemes, the stipulation need clarification since the scheme is open continuously. The application of the 6 per cent limit would be unrealistic on amounts raised, since it may be too small. Since unit capital in an open-ended scheme would vary almost continuously, the basis on which the 6 per cent ceiling would apply, has also be clarified.

Commissions payable for initial issue of units, such an item is directly amortised in the same accounting year in which it is incurred in regard to open-ended funds. In regard to close-ended funds, commission on issue of units is treated as Deferred Revenue expenditure and be amortised over the lock-in-period. If commissions incurred on an on going basis can be charged to the revenue account as direct expense, as is done in established open ended schemes. If the commission of initial issue is included in Deferred Revenue Expenditure, it would cause to understatement of expenses. Another suggestive alternative could be to charge half of agent commission to revenue account of the initial year and the balance be amortised over the next three years period or over the tenure of the scheme. Yet another alternative could be charged one-half of initial expenses in the current year Revenue Account and rest of half would be amortised over the entire tenure of the scheme in case of close ended fund scheme.

Direct Expenses

These are direct and easily identifiable with the scheme. They are directly charged to revenue account on a regular basis. However, there are certain items of direct expenses whose treatment is varying from one fund to another. *(i)* The stamp duty payable on acquisition of securities is usually charged to the revenue account. There are some direct expenses including brokerage are treated as deductions from the capital. Some funds treat stamp duties as adjustable against the acquisition cost;

(iii) Depreciation is another major item for discussion. As per the 52 of SEBI Regulations, before declaring dividend in respect of any scheme, every Mutual Fund shall provide for depreciation on investments and also make a provision for bad and doubtful debts, to the satisfaction of its auditors and shall disclose the method of depreciation in the notes to the accounts; *(ii)* Every Mutual Fund shall create, in respect of every open-ended scheme, a dividend equalisation reserve by suitable appropriation from the income of that scheme; and *(iii)* The dividend warrants shall be dispatched within forty-two days of the declaration of the dividend. Thus, a mutual fund should create and charge depreciation to the revenue account suitable depreciation to make and arrive at surplus correct. Depreciation on investments should be created. The extent of depreciation would however be decided by the funds themselves; *(iii)* Provisions: When there is doubt about the realisability of incomes, provisions are created for the same. Provisions may be created for the investments' lose market values significantly which may require such provisions to qualify the investments and securities; *(iv)* Dividend Equalisation Reserve: Every Mutual Fund organisation shall create, in respect of every open-ended fund scheme, a dividend equalisation reserve in each current year's revenue account. Such is created by suitable appropriation from the income of that scheme. Such provision is created to meet the future shortages in dividend whenever there is shortage of dividend but the schemes wishes to declare dividends uniformly to maintain a sound track in dividend declaration to its unit holders; *(v)* Mutual Funds usually provide for depreciations on investments, if the market value of the investments falls below the cost of acquisition. The comparisons are made on global basis by most funds, without category-wise comparisons. But there are a few funds, compare category-wise with the cost and market values to provide depreciation. For instance, cost of acquisition of investments is Rs. 100 Lakhs and of such is Rs. 90 lakhs, the difference being depreciation in value of investments which is treated as 'depreciation'. Such is charged to revenue account after proper adjustments of provision for depreciation.

Indirect Expenses

Items of indirect expenses are allocated to various schemes. The basis of appropriation varying across funds. The most popular basis is the corpus of the fund. This is easy to use.

Items of indirect expenses, including fees to Asset Management Company, Board of Trustees, Custodians and Registrars etc., are negotiated in advance and they are subject to SEBI's regulations.

Conclusions

Accounting policies of a concern, including a mutual fund, involves the selection of certain specific methods of measuring, reporting and disclosing of financial information, from amongst alternatives that may be available. Selecting a common and suitable method of accounting and continuously maintaining the same one, at least for so many years, consistently is prime need which results positively to all the parties concerned to it. The implications are positively beneficial. The benefits are:

1. accounting information can be compared from year to year;
2. Inter-firm comparisons are easily made; and
3. Universalisation of accounting procedures help many a party for better reliability, acceptability, etc.
4. It helps in full disclosure of accounting information;
5. The reliability of accounting records are well accepted by Government and Tax collecting authorities;
6. The disposition of the assets and their performance have to be known to the unit holders whose money the mutual funds hold in trust;
7. The financial statements, i.e.

Balance Sheet and Revenue Account should enable evaluation of income earned on the amounts that have been placed with the mutual fund, for management. Such evaluations are expected to assist choice amongst completing financial products to the investor and facilitate efficient allocation of resources.

There are well accepted accounting principles and policies, both at international and national level. At international level, the generally accepted accounting principles (GAAP) and at national level, especially in India, accounting standards. As of ICAI. All these are adopted by mutual funds in India while preparing and presenting financial statements. Besides mutual funds strictly follow the regulations of SEBI. Of course, there are no specific standards for accounting of mutual funds are laid down by SEBI, almost uniform accounting standards and systems are adopted by all mutual funds.

Since SEBI has not spelt specific accounting standards exclusively for mutual funds, amount of variation is found to happen in treating certain transactions which are subject to some alterations. They are relating to revenue recognition, distinction between capital and revenue, allocation and apportionment of common expenses, provision for depreciation, treatment of initial issue expenses, treatment of underwriting commission, determination of profit/loss on sale of investments, etc.

The Accounts of Mutual Funds are maintained on historical cost method. Net Asset Values (NAV) are required to be calculated on market value basis or realisable value basis.

CHAPTER SIX

Investors' Perceptions on Mutual Funds

Introduction on Investors' Perceptions on Mutual Funds

Capital market and financial market in India have been comprehensively reformed consequent upon government's liberalised economic policies. As a result, a good number of mutual fund organisations came into existence adding a very large number of organisations to the existing Unit Trust of India (UTI) which was only the MF in India till 1986. From 1987 to 1996, over a period of 10 years span, as many as 22 MFs were added to make a big list. Indian Mutual Fund industry is comprising of Government enacted mutual fund (UTI), public sector mutual funds (seven in number), and private sector mutual funds. Mutual Funds are ideally suited to Indian economy due to presence of a large chunk of small and marginal investors who have ability to save and willingness to enter the capital market through mutual funds; the mutual funds provide professional management to their funds; they provide good returns; they assure safety in the capital; and capital appreciation. Thus, in view of the increasing significance of Mutual Funds in the context of Indian economy, it becomes much necessary to examine and infer the perception of household savers of India.

Objectives

This present study has been undertaken with the object of examining, analysing and inferring the perceptions of the investors on mutual funds which addresses the following issues:

(*a*) Which Mutual Fund is popular amongst the investors?
(*b*) Which factors govern the choice of a mutual fund organisation?
(*c*) What type of scheme/schemes are preferred by households?
(*d*) Which type of financial asset is opted by investors?
(*e*) How private sector is boosting competition?
(*f*) How UTI is pioneer in the Mutual Fund Industry?
(*g*) How MFs are helping to enhance capital market activities in India?

Methodology

A questionnaire was prepared by consulting various experts like, financial executives of various mutual fund organisations, academics and researchers and finalised. Copies were served to households of various places of the country by mailing. Follow-up letters were sent to remind them to speed up their valuable response. In all 400 copies of questionnaires were distributed to various investors. After repeated visits and requests, only 120 completed questionnaires were received (giving response rate of 30 per cent).

Investment in Different Mutual Funds

The respondents were requested to check from the list of different mutual funds (Amongst 'big eight'), in which they had invested (or proposing to invest) during the last three years. Table 6.1 shows three different choices opted. As it is clear from their table that a vast majority of respondents (96%) invested in Unit Trust of India followed by SBI MF (53%) and Canbank MF (41%). The least preferred is BOI MF (16.5%). The study shows that a vast majority of respondents preferred in investing in UTI, the reason which sounds more logical is , comparatively the better service and return given by this organisation. Therefore Rank 1 is assigned to UTI.

Table 6.1
Households Preference in Selection of MF Organisation

(In Per cent)

Sl. No.	*Name of Organisation*	*Households Choice*				*Ranks*
		Ist Choice	*IInd Choice*	*IIIrd Choice*	*Total (3+4+5)*	
1	*2*	*3*	*4*	*5*	*6*	*7*
1.	SBI MF	5.00	28.00	20.00	53.00	2
2.	Canbank MF	2.00	24.50	15.00	41.50	3
3.	Indbank MF	4.00	10.50	10.00	24.50	5
4.	BOI MF	5.00	6.50	5.00	16.50	8
5.	PNB MF	6.00	7.50	10.00	23.50	6
6.	LIC MF	1.5	10.5	15.00	27.00	4
7.	GIC MF	0.5	2.5	15.00	18.00	7
8.	UTI	76.0	10.00	10.00	96.00	1
	Total	100.00	100.00	100.00		

Number of Households analysed: 120.

Note : "Preference Score" indicates the total top three choices. For instance, in case of UTI, 76 per cent assign Ist preference, 10 per cent assign 2nd preference and 10 per cent prescribe third preference, adding up to a total of 96 per cent of investors. But the average choice comes to 32 per cent (96 3).

Ranks are assigned on the total percentages in column 6.

The respondents were requested to check from the list of various financial assets in which they had invested during the last three years. Table 6.2 shows that the households or investors had three different choices. As it is clear from this table the vast majority of respondents (66%) invested in UTI units and products be followed by Debentures (57%) and products of Mutual Funds (49%). The least preferred was Government bonds (13%). This study shows that a vast majority of investors preferred in putting their savings in UTI products due to its many advantages like prompt service, protection, quick redemption etc.

Table 6.2
Households' Investment Preferences of Financial Assets

Sl. No.	*Name of Financial Asset*	*Percentage of Households opting for*				*Ranks*
		Ist Choice	*IInd Choice*	*IIIrd Choice*	*Total (3+4+5)*	
1	2	3	4	5	6	7
1.	UTI Units					
2.	UTI Products	30	26	10	66	1
3.	Products of Mutual Fund Organisations	22	20	7	49	3
4.	Shares	5	10	12	27	5
5.	Debentures	22	15	20	57	2
6.	Government Bonds	3	6	4	13	8
7.	Bank Fixed Deposits	3	7	26	36	4
8.	LIC Policies	4	4	10	18	6
9.	Recurring Deposits	4	8	6	18	6
10.	National Savings Certificates	7	4	3	15	7
11.	Public Provident Fund	—	—	—	—	—
12.	Company Deposits	—	—	—	—	—
	Total	100	100	100	—	—

Note : Number of households analysed : 120.
Ranks are assigned on Aggregate percentages.

Table 6.3 reveals 'Geographic spread of individual households' which is broadly bifurcated into shareholders and unit-holders.Highest concentration was seen in metros amounting to 75 per cent followed by mega cities at 50.5 per cent The least position was found in rural at 6 per cent.

Table 6.3
Geographic Spread of Individual Households

(Per cent)

Sl. No.		*Share holders*	*Unit holders*
1.	Metros	50.5	24.5
2.	Mega Cities	25.00	25.5
3.	Big Cities	10.50	10.0
4.	Medium Size Cities	5.00	10.00
5.	Small Town	5.00	20.00
6.	Semi-Urban	3.00	5.00
7.	Rural	1.00	5.00
	Total	100.00	100.00

Number of Households analysed : 120.

Table 6.4 discloses the 'Household Classification on Income Basis'. The respondents numbering 30 were in the income group upto Rs. 2,000 p.m. showing 25 per cent. Similarly, respondents numbering 30 were found in the income group of Rs. 4,001 to 6,000 p.m. As much as 66.67 per cent was concentrated in the income upto Rs. 6,000 p.m.

Table 6.4

Households Classification on Income Basis

Income Rupees per month		%
Upto 2,000	30	25.00
2,001 — 4,000	20	16.67
4,001 — 6,000	30	25.00
6,001 — 8,000	15	12.50
8,001 — 10,000	20	16.67
10,001 and above	5	4.16
	120	100.00

Number of Households analysed : 120.

The respondents were asked to give their opinion about different factors which influence their choice of mutual fund organisations. They were asked to specify whether a particular factor is "very important", "important", "not much important", or "not important at all" in selecting mutual fund. Accordingly weights 3, 2, 1 and 0 were assigned to "very important", "important", "not much important", "not Important at all" respectively. For the purpose of analysis, Average Weighted Scores (AWS) calculated.

Table 6.5 shows the responses of respondents factors which affect their advice of a Mutual Fund. Table clearly shows that the two factors viz., "Investor's Services" (Average weightage score 2.625) and "Income-cum-Growth" (Average weightage score 2,500) are very important to the respondents while choosing a mutual fund. "Capital appreciation", "Tax Benefits" and "1-year lock-in-period" are important to them as average weightage score in all these three stood same at 2.333.

Table 6.5
Factors Affecting Investors Choice of MF Organisation

Sl. No.	*Factors*	*Very Important*	*Important*	*Not Much Important*	*Not at all Important*	*Total (1+2+3+4)*	*AWS*	*Ranks*
1	*2*	*3*	*4*	*5*	*6*	*7*	*8*	*9*
1.	Capital appreciation	60 (50.00)	42 (35.00)	16 (13.33)	2 (1.67)	120 (100)	2.333	3
2.	Better annual dividend	50 (41.67)	52 (43.33)	18 (15.00)	— —	120 (100)	2.267	4
3.	General Reputation and Goodwill	39 (32.5)	51 (42.5)	20 (16.67)	10 (8.33)	120 (100)	1.992	8
4.	Suiting the needs	40 (33.34)	60 (50.00)	10 (8.33)	10 (10.83)	120 (100.00)	2.083	7
5.	Advertisements	34 (28.33)	66 (55.00)	20 (16.67)	— —	120 (100.00)	2.117	6
6.	Previous experience with the Organisation	39 (32.5)	41 (34.17)	25 (20.83)	15 (12.5)	120 (100.00)	1.867	9
7.	Early third incentive	20 (16.67)	50 (41.67)	25 (20.83)	25 (25.83)	120 (100.00)	1.541	12

(Contd.)

1	2	3	4	5	6	7	8	9
8.	Agent's Recommendation	20 (16.67)	60 (50.00)	20 (16.67)	20 (16.66)	— (100.00)	1.667	11
9.	Friends's Suggestion	38 (31.67)	42 (35.00)	26 (21.67)	14 (11.66)	120 (100..)	1.783	10
10.	Tax benefits	40 (33.33)	80 (66.67)	— —	— —	120 (100.00)	2.333	3
11.	Income-cum-Growth	60 (50.00)	60 (50.00)	— —	— —	120 (100.00)	2.500	2
12.	Investors' Service	75 (62.5)	45 (37.5)	— —	— —	120 (100.00)	2.625	1
13.	1-Year Lock-in-period	60.00 (50.00)	40.00 (33.33)	20 (16.67)	— —	120.00 (100.00)	2.333	3
14.	3-Year Lock-in-period	50.00 (41.66)	50.00 (41.66)	20 (16.68)	— —	120.00 (100.00)	2.250	5

Number respondent analysed : 120.

Note : Figures in brackets indicate percentages.
AWS indicates average weighted score.

There are a number of mutual funds introduced by different mutual fund organisation in Indian Mutual Fund industry. It is very essential to know the preferences of the respondents for different schemes of mutual funds. The respondents were asked to assign ranks to a given list of various schemes in which they would like to invest during next coming years, weights are assigned to "Choice I", "Choice II", and "Choice III" as 3, 2 and 1 respectively and average weighted score were computed for each individual scheme.

Table 6.6 clearly reveals that close-ended schemes are more popular among investors (Average weighted score (2.825) followed by quarterly income scheme (Average weighted score 2.667) and yearly Regular Income scheme (Average weighted score 2.583). The least preferred by respondents is Regular Monthly Income scheme (Average weighted Score 2.166).

Table 6.6
Choice of MF Schemes by Investors

(Per cent)

Sl. No.	Mutual Fund Schemes	Ist Choice	IInd Choice	IIIrd Choice	Total (3+4+5)	AWS	Ranks
1	2	3	4	5	6	7	8
1.	Tax Planning	52 (43.333)	38 (31.667)	30 (25.60)	120 (100.00)	2.183	8
2.	Growth	60 (50.00)	36 (30.00)	24 (20.00)	120 (100.00)	2.300	6
3.	Income	50 (41.667)	50 (41.667)	20 (16.666)	120 (100.00)	2.250	7
4.	Income and Growth	80 (66.667)	30 (25.00)	10 (8.333)	120 (100.00)	2.583	3
5.	Regular Income (a+b+c+d)	50 (43.333)	50 (43.333)	20 (16.666)	120 (100.00)	2.250	7
	(a) Monthly	50 (41.667)	40 (33.333)	30 (25.00)	120 (100.00)	2.166	9
	(b) Quarterly	80 (66.667)	40 (33.333)	— —	120 (100.00)	2.667	2
	(c) Half-yearly	60 (50.00)	— —	60 (50.00)	120 (100.00)	2.500	4
	(d) Yearly	80 (66.667)	30 (25.00)	10 (8.333)	120 (100.00)	2.583	3
6.	Close-ended	90 (82.500)	21 (17.500)	— —	120 (100.00)	2.825	1
7.	Open-ended	55 (45.833)	60 (50.000)	5 (4.167)	120 (100.00)	2.416	5

Note : Number of respondent analysed are : 120.
Figures in brackets indicate percentages.
Ranks are assigned as per average weighted score.

Table 6.7. deals with a statement that "Private Sector MFs will give better facilities like rate of returns than public sector MFs, around 75 per cent of respondents agree to this. Table 6.8. indicates that 85 per cent on an average agreed that frauds, mis-management and corruption would decrease with entry of private sector MF into MF industry. Table 6.9. disclosed that with the entry of Private sector MFs investing mass would be benefited by confidence in the whole mutual fund industry. Around 78 per cent agreed positively. Table 6.10. revealed that at about 60 per cent respondents agreed that large number of investors stock to the public sector Mutual Funds. Some statements indicating the potentialities in the Mutual Funds were chalked out in a questionnaire form. The respondents were requested to give their valuable opinions to indicate their agreement level to each and every statement in the Table on a five point scale. The five point scale is comprising of strongly agree, agree, uncertain, disagree and strongly disagree (Table 6.11).

Table 6.7

Statement No.1:

Private Sector MFs will give Better Facilities Like 'Rate of Return' than Public-Sector MFs

(Per cent)

Monthly Income Category Rs.	*Agree*	*Disagree*	*No Opinion*	*Total (2+3+4)*
1	2	3	4	5
Upto 2,000	80.00	20.00	00.00	100.00
2,001 to 4,000	70.00	22.00	8.00	100.00
4,001 to 6,000	60.00	30.00	10.00	100.00
6,001 to 8,000	75.00	25.00	00.00	100.00
8,001 to 10,000	82.00	18.00	00.00	100.00
10,001 and above	76.00	14.00	10.00	100.00

These five points scales were corrupted by applying weighed Average entitled "Average Weighted Scale" (AWS) assigning +2, +1, 0, –1, –2 respectively to SA, A, U, D and SD respectively.

$$\overline{X}_w = \frac{\Sigma xw}{N}$$

Where $\overline{X}_w$ represents the weighted arithmetic mean

X represents the values of variables, i.e., $x_1, x_2, x_3 ..., x_4$
W represents weights attached to variables, i.e., $w_1, w_2, w_3 ...... w_4$
N represents number of observations.

Table 6.8
Statement No. 2:
Frauds, Mismanagement and Corruption would Decrease with the Entry of Private Sector into MF Industry

(Per cent)

Monthly Income Category Rs.	*Agree*	*Disagree*	*No Opinion*	*Total (2+3+4)*
1	2	3	4	5
Upto 2,000	90	5	5	100.00
2,001 to 4,000	75	15	10	100.00
4,001 to 6,000	80	10	10	100.00
6,001 to 8,000	72	18	—	100.00
8,001 to 10,000	90	10	—	100.00
10,001 and above	89	6	5	100.00

Table 6.9
Statement No.3
Private Sector Mutual Funds would Enjoy as Widespread Investor Confidence as Public Sector MFs

(Per cent)

Monthly Income Category Rs.	*Agree*	*Disagree*	*No Opinion*	*Total (2+3+4)*
1	2	3	4	5
Upto 2,000	74.00	26.00	00.00	100.00
2,001 to 4,000	73.00	17.00	10.00	100.00
4,001 to 6,000	77.00	10.00	13.00	100.00
6,001 to 8,000	67.00	23.00	10.00	100.00
8,001 to 10,000	68.00	21.00	11.00	100.00
10,001 and above	71.00	19.00	10.00	100.00

Table 6.10
Statement No. 4 :
A Large Number of Small Investors Stick to Public Sector Mutual Funds

(Per cent)

Monthly Income Category Rs.	Agree	Disagree	No Opinion	Total (2+3+4)
1	2	3	4	5
Upto 2,000	60.00	30.00	10.00	100.00
2,001 to 4,000	75.00	19.00	6.00	100.00
4,001 to 6,000	69.00	20.00	11.00	100.00
6,001 to 8,000	71.00	19.00	10.00	100.00
8,001 to 10,000	19.00	61.00	20.00	100.00
10,001 and above	29.00	61.00	10.00	100.00

Analysis

1. It can be observed from Table 6.11 that a vast majority of respondents (93.33%) fully agree with the statement that 'For the growth of Indian Capital Market, Mutual Funds are desirable and necessary' (Average weighted score of 1.383).
2. A majority of respondents (79.17%) agree with the statement that "For the Growth of Indian Money Market, Mutual Funds are desirable and necessary". (Average weight score 1.266).
3. Most of the respondents (76.67%) agree that "Mutual Funds should make full disclosure of entire portfolio to investors periodically" (Average Weighted Score 1.350).
4. A majority of respondents (88.33%) agree with statement that "Investment in MFs is less risky in comparing to shares" (Average weighted score 1.650).
5. Most of the respondents (80%) agree with the statement that "MFs are more suitable to small investors who are otherwise shy of entry in capital market" (Average weighed score 1.200).
6. Respondents (58.32%) agree that "Mutual Funds are better than RDs and TDs of Banks" (Average weighed score 0.833).

Table 6.11
Opinion of Investors Towards Mutual Funds

Sl. No.	*Statement of Opinion*	*Strongly Agree*	*Agree*	*Uncertain*	*Disagree Disagree*	*Strongly Wrighted Score*	*Average*	*Ranks assigned to each statement*
1	2	3	4	5	6	7	8	9
1.	For the growth of Indian Capital Market, Mutual Funds are desirable and necessary	70 (58.33)	30 (25.00)	16 (13.33)	4 (3.34)	— —	1.383	4
2.	For the growth of Indian Money Market, Mutual Funds are desirable and necessary	60 (50.00)	35 (29.17)	22 (18.33)	3 (2.5)	— —	1.266	6
3.	Mutual Funds should make full disclosure of entire portfolio to investors periodically	80 (66.67)	12 (10.00)	18 (15.00)	10 (8.33)	— —	1.350	5
4.	Investment in MFs is less risky in comparing to shares	96 (80.00)	10 (8.33)	10 (8.33)	4 (3.34)	— —	1.650	2
5.	MFs are more suitable to small investors who are otherwise shy of entry in capital market	60 (50.00)	36 (30.00)	12 (10.00)	12 (10.00)	— —	1.200	8
6.	Mutual Funds are better than RDs and TDs of Banks	50 (41.66)	20 (16.66)	30 (25.00)	20 (16.68)	— —	0.833	12

(Contd.)

1	2	3	4	5	6	7	8	9
7.	MFs are better than MMFs	60 (50.00)	30 (25.00)	15 (12.5)	15 (12.5)	— —	1.125	10
8.	Investing in MF should get more relief from Income Tax	70 (58.33)	20 (16.66)	20 (16.67)	10 (8.34)	— —	1.250	7
9.	Entry of Private Sector Mutual Funds is desirable as there will be more competition hence more profits and returns for investors	50 (41.66)	30 (25.00)	20 (16.66)	20 (16.68)	— —	0.916	11
10.	MFs will help in mobilising the savings of the rural investors towards corporate investment	70 (58.34)	15 (12.50)	25 (20.83)	9 (7.50)	1 (0.83)	1.200	8
11.	Income and returns from MFs should be fully exempted from taxation for individual investors	60 (50.00)	30 (25.00)	20 (16.66)	10 (8.34)	— —	1.167	9
12.	MFs should publish and advertise Half-yearly unaudited final statements in detail	80 (66.67)	15 (12.5)	25 (20.83)	— —	5	1.458	3
13.	Calculation of NAV on weekly basis and advertise throw national dailies	90 (75.00)	20 (16.67)	10 (8.33)	— —	— —	1.667	1

Note : Number of Investors investigated and analysed : 120.
Figures in bracket indicate percentages.
Average weighter score is computed on the bass of weighted arithmetic average.
Formula.

7. Majority of respondents (75%) agree that "MFs are better than MMFs (Average weighted score 1.125).
8. A vast majority of respondents (73.99%) fully agree with the statement that "Investing MF should get more relief from Income Tax" (Average weighted score 1.250).
9. Respondents (66.66%) agree that "Entry of Private Sector Mutual Funds is desirable as there will be more competition hence more profits and returns for investors" (Average weighted score 0.916).
10. Respondents (70.84) agree that "MFs will help in mobilising the savings of the rural investors towards corporate investment" (Average weighted score 1.200).
11. Most of the respondents (75%) agree that "Income and Returns from MFs should be fully exempted from taxation for individual investors" (Average weighted score 1.167).
12. A vast majority of respondents (79.170%) agree the statement that "MFs should publish and advertise half-yearly unaudited final statements in detail" (Average weighted score 1.458).
13. A vast majority of respondents (91.67%) agree fully that the statement "Calculation of NAV on weekly basis and advertise in leading daily newspapers" (Average weighted score 1.667).

Concluding Remarks

On an indepth analysis of the perceptions of respondents, the following conclusions can be drawn:

(i) The top most popular mutual funds amongst investors is Unit Trust of India, followed by State Bank of India Mutual Fund and Canbank Mutual Fund. The least preferred by investors is BOI MF.

(ii) The most popular financial asset preferred by the respondents is UTI products, followed by debentures and products of mutual funds. The least preferred financial asset is government bonds.

(iii) In regard to geographical spread of investors, highest concentration was seen in Metropolis viz. Calcutta, Madras, Delhi and Mumbai, followed by mega cities. Least concentration is found in rural areas.

(iv) Households classification on income basis revealed that 66.67 per cent concentration of respondents were found in the income class up to Rs. 6,000 per month.

(v) The most important factors for choice a mutual fund organisation amongst the correspondents is 'investors service', followed by 'income-cum-growth' and 'Tax benefits' and capital appreciation.

(vi) A vast majority of respondents choices close-ended funds as rank No.1, followed by Quarterly Regular income schemes and yearly regular income schemes.

(vii) A vast majority of respondents agreed that mutual funds are desirable and necessary for growth of Indian Capital and Money Markets.

(viii) Majority of the respondents showed their good willingness to invest their savings in private sector mutual funds.

(ix) Majority of respondents strongly agree that mutual funds should disclose full informations in their annual reports.

CHAPTER SEVEN

Financial System and Institutional Services

The financial system of any nation comprises of specialised and non-specialised financial institutions, of organised and unorganised financial markets, of financial instruments and financial services which aid in transfer of funds. Various procedures and practices adopted in the markets are integral part of the total system. The concept "financial system" is primarily bifurcated into two words, viz.," finance" and "system" implies a set of complex and closely connected or intermixed institutions, agents, practices, markets, transactions, claims, and liabilities in the nation's economy (Bhole, L.M., 1994)[1]. The financial system of a nation highly influences its economy. The close relationship between financial structure and economic development is reflected in the prevailing institutional arrangement, delivery system and intermediation process (Sadhak, H., 1997).[2] Financial institutions are business organisations that act as mobilisers and depositories of savings, and as purveyors of credit or finance. Besides, financial institutions provide various financial services. The financial institutions differ from non-financial (industrial and commercial) business organisations in respect of their wares, nature, and objectives. The activities of different financial institutions may be either specialised or they may overlap, quite often they overlap. Although, they overlap, we need to categorise financial institutions either on the basis of main activity, the degree of their specialisation or manner of their creation.

Besides, other factors such as the functional, geographic, sectoral scope of activity, type of ownership are often taken into consideration while classification. According to one classification, financial institutions are divided into the banking and non-banking ones. Though banking institutions have a few points of similarities with non-banking financial institution, the distinguishing character was in the payments mechanism. Financial institutions provide transaction services, their deposit liabilities constitute a major part of the national money supply, and they can, as a whole, create deposits or credit. On the other hand, Banks, subject to legal requirements, can advance credit by creating claims against themselves. Banking system in India is consisting of commercial banks, and co-operative banks. The non-banking financial institutions are Life Insurance Corporation of India (LIC), Unit Trust of India (UTI), and Industrial Development Bank of India (IDBI), Financial Institutions are also categorised as intermediaries and non-intermediaries. As the intermediaries, financial institutions intermediate between savers and investors. They lend money. They also mobilise savings. Their assets are from the investors or borrowers. Their liabilities are towards the ultimate savers. Non-intermediary institutions do the loan business but their resources are directly obtained from the savers. On the other side, non-intermediary institutions are comprising of IDBI, IFCI, and NABARD. They have come into existence because of Governmental efforts to provide assistance for specific purposes, sectors, regions etc. They are created as a result of policy decision of the Government. They are created to cater the needs of borrowers who are adequately getting financial assistance from the usual financial institutions. Since they have been setup by the Government, we would call them Non-Banking Statutory Financial Institutions (NBSFIs). Guerley and Show (1955)[3] view the role of financial institutions as one helping to realise the opportunities for savings and real investment in an economy. Mobilisation of funds and its creation took a different path, i.e., a shift from self-financing to direct financing and then to indirect financing. The suppliers of indirect financing are:

(i) Commercial banks,
(ii) Insurance and other, and
(iii) financial companies.

All these mediate between savers and borrowers of funds. Financial intermediaries play a pivotal role in eliminating market imperfections which arise out of non-dissemination of information about borrowing customers. Distortions in the market can be eliminated or mitigated by several institutional devices. It is in their respect that financial arrangements such as issuing market for securities and financial intermediaries plan their roles (Kaizuka, 1987).[4] According to Kaufman (1986)[5] financial institutions are expected to embody the essence of integrity and their entrepreneurial drive is well balanced by a strong sense of fiduciary responsibility and that as why financial regulations have always been a part of economic development.

Another category of financial institutions are mutual funds which play a dynamic role in an economy by mobilising savings and investing them in the capital markets. They establish a link between savings and the capital market. Therefore, the activities of mutual funds (a category of financial institutions, or FIs) have both short and long-term impact on the savings and capital markets, and national economy. Mutual funds mobilise funds in the savings market and act as a complimentary to banking and simultaneously they also compete with banks and other financial institutions. In the process the stock market activities also influenced by mutual funds since they invest funds in acquiring, trading in the shares and stocks of in Stock-Exchanges as a part of their portfolio investment management. Their scope, efficiency and working are totally influenced by over economic fundamental principles and factors of the nation. In other words, therefore, the interrelationship between the financial and real sector, the nature, process and development of savings and capital market, market structure, institutional arrangements, overall policy of the Government are very much influencing.

In India, the financial system has two broad segments, viz. organised and unorganised, organised sector is comprising of commercial banks, development financial institutions, insurance corporations, and other non-bank financial institutions, including mutual funds, unit trusts, etc. The presence of dominating role of public sector financial institutions since 1951. Commerical banks are categorised into public and private sector banks. Their nature of job is to mobilise the savings in terms of deposits and giving advances to needy public. Term lending development institutions are consisting of *(i)* the Industrial Development Bank of India (IDBI), Industrial Finance Corporation of India (IFCI) and Industrial Credit and Investment Corporation of India (ICICI). All these cater to the heads of long-term finance for the Indian corporate sector. Insurance Institutions, in India, are the government-owned Life Insurance Corporation of India (LIC), and General Insurance Corporation (GIC) and its subsidiaries. They mobilize funds and invest in capital markets. UTI and Mutual Funds are comprising of:

(i) Public Sector Mutual Funds,
(ii) domestic private sector mutual funds, and
(iii) foreign mutual funds.

All these have emerged as dynamic financial intermediaries. They are important institutional investors of the country. Pension and Provident Fund Trusts are important savings institutions. They are under the strict regulatory provisions. There other sectoral financial institutions, namely, Export Import Bank (Exim Bank), National Bank for Agricultures and Rural Development (NABARD), Industrial Reconstruction Bank of India (IRBI), State Financial Corporations (SFCs), State Industrial Development Corporations (SIDCs) and Technology Finance Corporation of India (TFCI). Reserve Bank of India (RBI) is the central bank of the country. It is the nerve centre of the monetary system of the nation. As the apex bank in the monetary and banking operations of the country, the Reserve Bank of India has been guiding, monitoring, regulating, controlling, and promoting the destiny of Indian financial system since its inception. RBI is performing various functions, viz., *(i)* note issuing authority, *(ii)* Government Banker, *(iii)* Bankers' Bank, *(iv)* Supervising Authority, (v) Promoter of the Financial system, and *(vi)* Regulator of money and credit. Broadly, RBI has two sections such as *(a)* Commercial Banks, and *(b)* Non-banking financial companies. The Securities and Exchange Board of India (SEBI) was set up in India in April, 1988 which has been entrusted with both the regulating and developmental functions. The objective of SEBI are :

(a) Investor protection,
(b) ensuring the fair practices by the issues of securities, namely, companies so that they can raise resources at least cost, and

(c) Promotion of efficient services by brokers, merchant bankers and other intermediaries so that they become competitive and professional.

SEBI Act was passed on 4th April, 1992 in the form of Securities of Exchange Board of India Act. The SEBI Act has seven chapters. Chapter one deals with preliminaries and definitions, Chapter two deals with establishment, incorporation, administration and management of Board of Directors etc. Chapter three deals with transfer of assets and liabilities of the existing Boards to the new Board, under the Act. Chapter four deals with the powers and functions of the SEBI, Chapter five deals with registration of stock brokers, sub-brokers, transfer agents etc., on which action was already taken by SEBI since May 1992. Chapter seven deals with powers to of Central Government to issue directions to SEBI Board etc. SEBI is controlling and managing *(a)* Mutual Funds , *(b)* Venture Funds, and *(c)* Capital Markets.

Capital Market

Capital is one of the factors of production, highly, essential to produce goods, to acquire machinery, to meet expenses etc. Capital market is a vehicle through which long-term finance is channelised for various requirements of industry, commerce, Government and local authorities. According to Husband and Dockerbay (1962).[6] "The capital market used to designate activities in long-term credit which is characterised mainly by securities of investment type." But the notion 'capital market' embraces a wider meaning in view of varied function. Livingston (1929)[7] remarked that in a developing economy, it is the business of capital market to facilitate the movement of the stream of command over capital to the point of highest yield. By doing so it enables control over resources to pass into the hands of those who can employ them most effectively, thereby increasing operative capacity and swelling the national divided . Arun K. Datta, Gupta (1963)[8] writes that "the capital market is a complex of institutions, investment and practices which established link between the demand for and supply of different types of capital funds." Therefore, its can be understood that in the capital market private savings both individual and corporate are mobilised and made available to the industry for meeting its long-term financial needs. The constituents of the capital market range from common man to specialised financial institutions. Generally, they include individual investors, investment and trust companies, banks, stock exchanges and specialist financial institutions. Indian capital market is bifurcated into organised and unorganised. The suppliers of funds to capital market are, namely, individual investors, corporate savings, government savings, foreign investments, banks, financial institutions, investment trusts, life insurance corporation, and international financial agencies. Potential users are consisting of Industry, Government and Semi-Government institutions in the organised sector of capital market. On the other hand, unorganised sector is comprising of indigenous bankers in towns and money-lenders in rural areas who supply funds. There is, absolutely, no link between unorganised and organised capital market. The users of finance are traders, industrial units etc. Two important constituents of the capital market are:

(i) Primary market (or new issue market), and
(ii) Secondary market.

The primary market helps both corporaters and the Government raise funds by issuing securities. The secondary market, through continuous trading activities provides liquidity in the system. It reflects the changing mood and perception of investors. Stability and growth in the capital market depend in the efficient functioning of both the markets since they are closely interdependent. At the same time Mutual Funds pay an all-important role in both the markets and strengthen the transfer mechanism. SEBI Act promulgated in January 1992 encompasses the entire gamet of securities industries in India. It has brought out several regulations to improve the efficiency and quality of the capital market. The other regulations are : SEBI (Stock Brokers and Sub-Brokers) Rules and Regulations, 1992, SEBI (Merchant Bankers) Rules and Regulations, 1993, SEBI (Registrars to an issue and share Transfer Agents) Rules and Regulations, 1993, SEBI (Insider Trading) Regulations, 1993, SEBI (Mutual Funds) Regulations, 1993, SEBI (Prohibition of Fraudulent and Unfair Trade Practices Relating to Securities Market) Regulations, 1995. Malegam Committee Report on disclosure norms aim at improving transparency, quality and completion in the capital market. Many steps have been initiated to improve the activities in the secondary markets. The removal of badla and introduction of revised carry forward, monitoring of price movement, introduction of capital adequacy norms for brokers, changes in listing rules, introduction of electronic trading, establishment of National Stock Exchange (NSE) and over the counter Exchange of India (OTCEI) are all good and encouraging steps have already altered the capital market scenario in India.

Capital market aids in the growth of savings and their mobilisation for investment. Borrowers with deficits can have funds from lenders with surplus in capital market . Capital market helps the corporate sector expand and grow and diversity leading to growth of output and income in the economy. Corporate bodies are now at liberty to enter into the capital market to raise any quantity of funds they can and price their securities at any price which are rational. In capital market financial institutions and banks lend long-term loans and act as intermediaries. Besides, the joint stock companies can raise funds through issue of equity and preference shares directly to the public at large through prospectus.

National Stock Exchange

Capital market is a broader concept used to consist of all operations in the new issues and stock market. New issues made by the joint stock companies constitute the primary market, while trading in the existing securities relates to the secondary market. Thus, capital market is, on an aggregate, bifurcated into primary market and secondary market while one can only buy in the primary market, one can buy and sell securities in the secondary market. The secondary market is for trading and imparting liquidity to existing securities. Secondary market structure is comprising of:

(a) Twenty-one Regular stock Exchanges,
(b) one over the counter Exchange of India, and
(c) one National Stock Exchange.

Following the Pherwani Committee recommendations, the Government have initiated steps for National Market System (NMS) and recognised the National Stock Exchange (NSE) in 1993 for setting of National Market System, in which electronic trading, and settlement is possible throughout the country on the basis of standard prices and fixed margin of service charges or commission for the broker. National Stock Exchange was the 22nd Stock Exchange to be recognised under Securities Contracts Regulations

Figure 7.1
INDIAN FINANCIAL SYSTEM

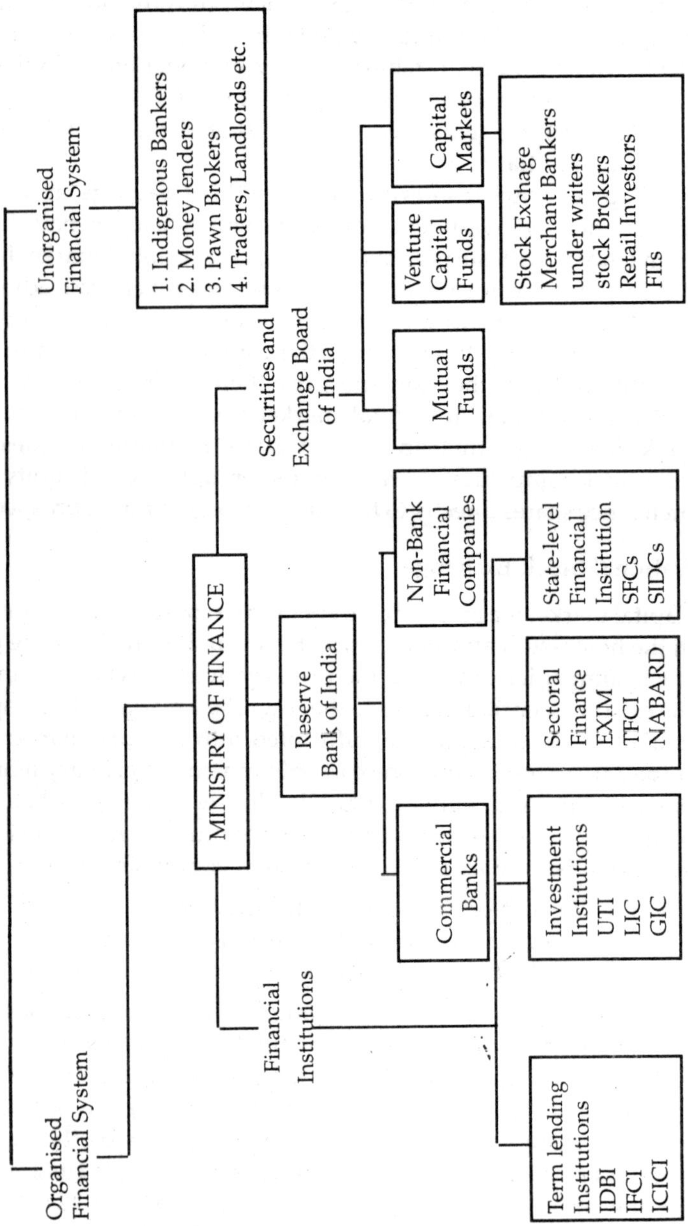

Figure 7.2
SECURITIES MARKET OF INDIA

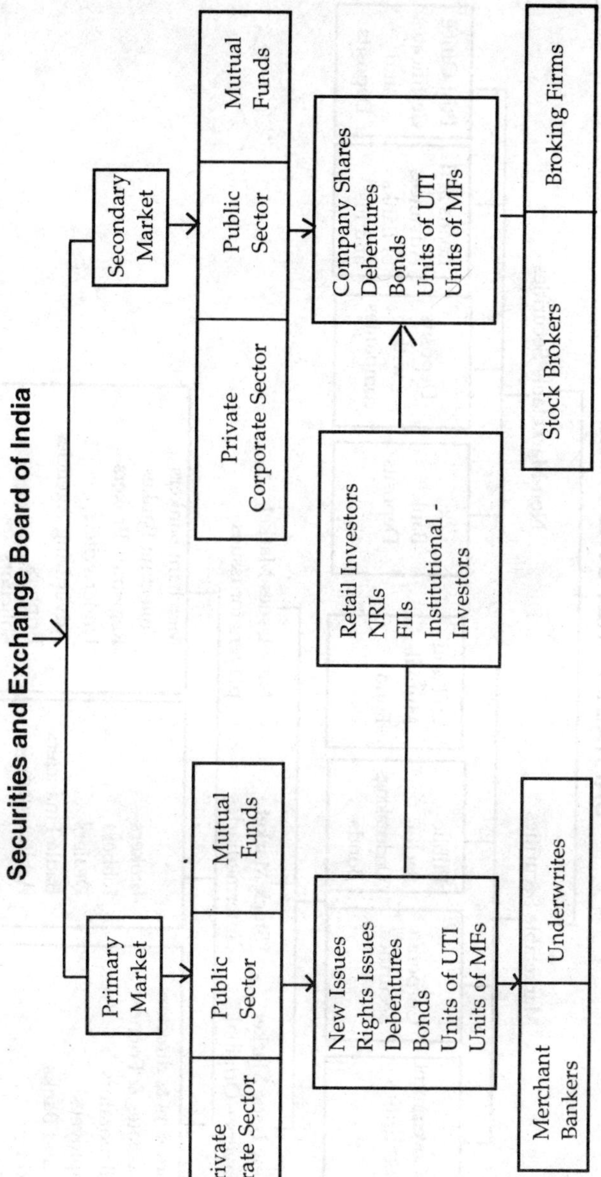

Source : H. Sadhark, p. 32.

Figure 7.3
CAPITAL MARKET STRUCTURE

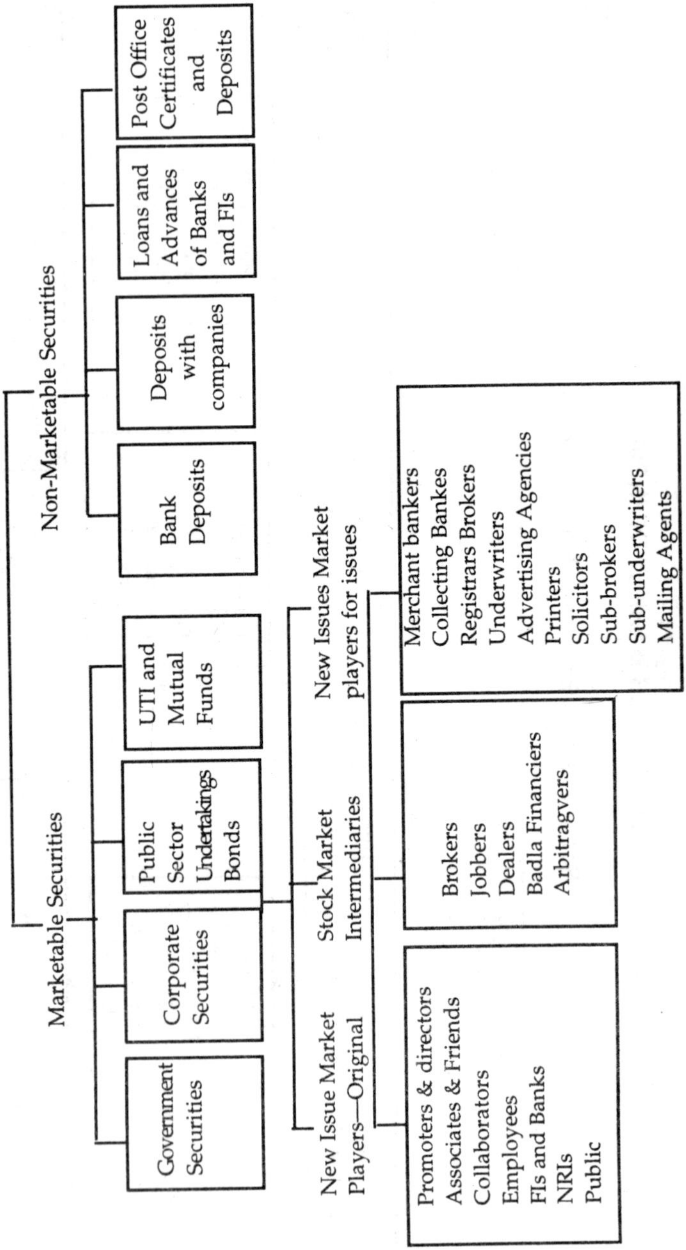

Act (see Appendix 1 for list of stock exchanges). The Pherwani Committee recommended the setting up of the national market system based on the Stock Exchange which was already set up in Mumbai. To make the national market system effective, the committee recommended several support agencies to provide high quality trading, settlement and depository services. In this connection, Pherwani Committee recommended that there should be three tiers, namely, stock exchange at Mumbai, Delhi, Calcutta, Chennai and Ahmedabad; regional stock exchanges like those in major stock capitals and additional trading floors sponsored or managed by Principal or Regional Stock Exchanges . The structure would be as:

(i) Regular stock markets which are 21 in number at present,
(ii) National Market System (NMS) with separate set of licensed brokers all over the country mostly banks and corporate units,
(iii) Retail broking through a series of registered sub-brokers attached to the regular stock markets or to NMS,
(iv) Additional Trading Floor licensed for trading in securities on the basis of a Regional / Stock Exchange quotations,
(v) OTCEI for risky and venture some companies and companies which cannot satisfy the listing requirements of regular Stock Exchanges, such as small companies.

Pherwani* recommended the setting up of a model National Stock Exchange at New Bombay (NSE) which will develop the National market system in the country. Any infrastructure in terms of space, Tele-commutation, computerisation, on live processing system, Library, Research facilities, Publicity Department, etc., are all recommended for the "National Market" to be set up by NSE. The market will have two types of members, namely, participating trading members who can only trade on their behalf and intermediary trading members (dealers) who can deal on behalf of their clients. Trading members will have computer terminals connecting to the other trading members (PTM) and to the central computer system at the NSE. Trading covers to buy and sell securities or to borrow and lend are entered into the computer

* Sri M.J. Pherwani, Chairman of a high powered study group on Establishment of New Stock Exchanges has submitted its report in June 1991.

system and stocked in its memory in an order book. Trading being order driven, it will be matched with a matching counter order . If matched, both the buyer and seller are informed by the NSE computer system. By the end of the trading day, the Exchange System will give out rates and a list of completed transactions for each trading member.

The characteristics of National Market System are :

1. Completely automated system in terms of trading and settlement procedures to be provided through the securities Facilities Supporting Corporation.
2. Compulsory market makers/jobbers to provide liquidity and ready market.,
3. The members would be as large as 1,000 and Corporate and Institutional members would also be there drawn from various parts of the country and to represent the professionals on an All India basis.
4. Only medium sized companies and Public Sector Undertakings are expected to be listed on their Exchange and it will complement the existing Exchange.
5. The NSE would have a separate trading time allotted for debt instruments in order to have the beneficial effect of creating an active secondary market in debt instruments.

The aims and objectives of NMS are :

(a) To help the privatisation of Public Sector Units through listing of their shares on this exchange,

(b) To spread the investment habit and cult to savers in the rural and semi-urban areas as well,

(c) To professionalise the members with a view to improve the investor services and make it comparable to international markets abroad,

(d) To create more employment opportunities in the service sector within the orbit of the capital market, and

(e) To promote the market for debt instruments.

Three Tier Structure of National Market System is comprising of:

(i) Principal stock Exchange comprising the five major Exchanges at Mumbai, Delhi, Calcutta, Chennai and Ahmedabad,

(ii) Regional Stock Exchanges in the country (i.e., sixteen),
(iii) Additional Trading Floors, sponsored and managed by the principal or a Regional Stock Exchange, as the case may be.

Nation Stock Exchange (NSE) was incorporated in November, 1992 and was recognised as stock Exchange in April, 1993 in the name of National Stock Exchange of India Limited (NSEIL). The promoters of NSEIL are IDBI, LIC, GIC, IFCI, ICICI, SBI, Bank of Baroda, Canara Bank, Punjab National Bank, Corporation Bank, Indian Bank, Oriental Bank of Commerce, Union Bank of India, SBI Capital Markets Ltd., Stock Holding Corporation of India Ltd., and Infrastructure Leasing and Financial Services Ltd.

Objectives of NSE are:

(i) To establish a nation wide trading facility for equities, debt instruments and hybrids,
(ii) To ensure equal access to investors all over the country through an appropriate communication network,
(iii) To provide a fair, efficient and transparent securities market to investors using electronic systems,
(iv) To enable shorten settlement cycles and book entry settlement system, and
(v) To meet the current international standards of securities markets.

The Board of NSEIL consisted of 12 directors, one Chairman, one Managing Director and one Deputy Managing Director. Its head office and registered office are located at Mumbai. It has set up facilities which serve as a model for the securities industry in terms of trading systems, practices and procedures. Though the impetus for its establishment came from policy makers in the country, it has been set up as a public limited company, owned by the leading institutional investors who promoted it is mentioned elsewhere in this chapter. NSC is different from most stock exchanges in India where ownership on an exchange also meant ownership of the exchange. The ownership and management of the Exchange in completely separated from the right on a trading members, to trade on the NSE. The Exchange is managed by a Board. Decisions relating to market operations are delegated by the Board to an Executive Committee which includes representation

Figure 7.4
NSE Membership

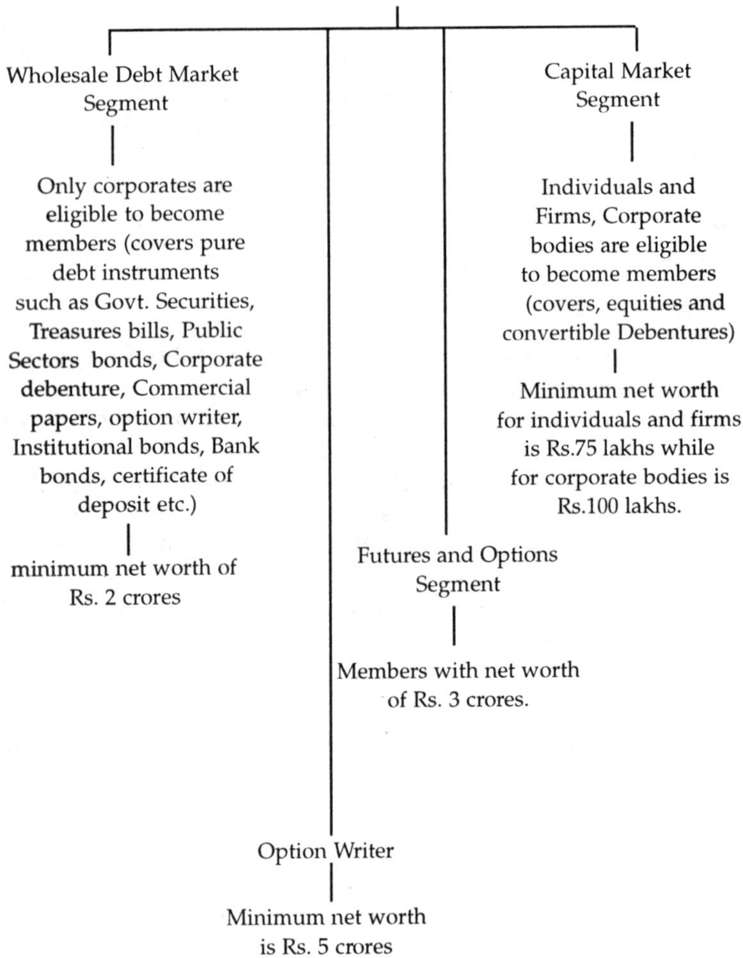

Source : Personal Survey.

Chart 7.1
Eligibility Criteria for Trading Membership in NSE

Trading Membership	*Eligibility Criteria*
1. Wholesale Debt Market (WDM)	*(a)* Body corporates, sub-sidiaries of Bank and Institutions. *(b)* The whole, time directors or the dealers should possess atleast two year's experience in any activity related to banking or financial services. *(c)* The applicant must possess minimum net worth of Rs. 2 crores. *(d)* The applicant must be engaged solely in the business of securities and must not be engaged in any fund based activities. *(e)* The minimum paid-up capital of a corporate body should be Rs. 30 lakh.
2. Capital Market (CM)	*(a)* Individuals, registered firms, bodies corporate and institutions. *(b)* The minimum net worth requirements for individuals and registered firms is Rs. 75

(Contd.)

Trading Membership	*Eligibility Criteria*
	lakhs while for corporate bodies, it is Rs. 100 lakhs.
	(c) The minimum prescribed qualification is graduation and two years experience of dealing in capital market must be fulfilled by: *(i)* minimum two directors in case the applicant is a corporate, *(ii)* minimum two parties in case of partnership firm, and *(iii)* the individual in case of individual or sole proprietary concerns.
	(d) The applicant must be engaged solely in the business of securities and must not be engaged in any fund based activities.
	(e) The minimum paid-up capital of a corporate body should be Rs. 30 lakh.
3. Option Writer	*(a)* The applicant must be engaged solely in the business of securities and must not be engaged in any fund based activities
	(b) Minimum net worth of Rs. 5 crores.

from Trading members, public and the management . Besides, the NSE operates various committees are to advice it on areas such as good market practices, settlement procedures, risk containment systems etc. The committees manned by industry professionals, Trading Members, and Exchange Staff. The day-to-day management of the Exchange is delegated to the Managing Director who is supported by a team of professional staff.

Membership

The admission standards laid down by the NSE stress on factors such as capital adequacy, corporate structure, track record, education, experience etc. Admission of members is a two stage process with applicants requiring to go through a written examination followed by an interview. Candidates are interviewed by a committee consisting of experienced people from the industry to assess the applicant's capability to operate as an exchange member. The capital accuracy requirements stipulated by the NSE are substantially in excess of the minimum statutory requirements as also in comparison to those stipulated by other exchanges. This reflects a conscious effort by the Exchange to strengthen the membership standards so as to build confidence in the Exchange Operations. The NSE admits members separately to different segments such as the whole sale Debt Market Segment and capital market segment. Only corporate members are admitted on the debt market segment whereas individuals and firms are also eligible on the capital market segment. Membership for the Futures and Options segment is open to members with a minimum net worth of Rs. 3 crores. In addition, for any member who wishes to act as an option writer is proposed a minimum net worth of Rs. 5 crores due to higher level of risk involved in this area. Thus composition of trading members in regard to capital market segment consists of 84 per cent corporate bodies, 8 per cent individuals and 8 per cent registered figures.

WDM	=	Wholesale Debt Market
CM	=	Capital Market
NSCCL	=	National Securities Clearing Corporation
DVP	=	Delivery Versus Payment.

Trading System

The NSE provides a facility for screen based trading with automated order matching. The system is order driven and conceals the identity of parties to an order or a trade. The trading system operates on a price time priority. All orders received on the system are sorted with the best price order getting the first-priority for matching, i.e., the best buy order matches the best sell order within similar priced orders, they are sorted or time i.e., the one that came in early gets priority over the later one. Orders are matched automatically by the computers keeping the systems transparent, objective and fair. Where an order does not find a match it remains in the system and is displayed to the whole market, till a fresh order comes in or the earlier order is cancelled or modified. The trading system provides a tremendous flexibility to the users in terms of the kind of orders that can be placed on the system—several time related, price related or volume related conditions can easily be placed on an order. Besides, it provides complete information on line through various inquiry facilities. The market screens at any point of time give the member complete information on the total order depth in a security, the best buys and sells available in the market, the quantity traded in that security, the high price, the low price, last traded price etc. This information is updated on-live real time enabling the member to make better decisions.

Operations

The NSEIL runs two market segments, namely:

- *(i)* Capital Market (CM), and
- *(ii)* Wholesale Debt Market (WDM).

Capital Market Segment (CM) Commenced trading on November 3, 1994. This segment covers trading in equities, convertible debentures etc. As of the end February 1992 number of securities traded exceeded 1600. If a security is listed on any exchange , it may be permitted to trade.

NSE started trading in the Depositors segment in December, 1996. Another additional market segment that has been set up for the institutional investors is Trade for Trade (TT) segment which is meant to cater to institution who prefer bilateral settlement as a means of minimising exposure risks.

CM clearing and settlement operations of the **exchange** is managed by its wholly owned subsidiary the National Securities Clearing Corporation Limited (NSCCL) which is a key factor in the growth of exchange. The NSE operates a well defined settlement cycle. The weekly settlement cycle starts every Wednesday and ends on Thursday with the pay in of securities on the next Monday, pay in of funds on the next Tuesday and pay out of funds and securities on the next Wednesday. The settlement is completed within 8 days of last day of the trading cycle. All settlements are through the Clearing House and fund movements through a clearing bank. The settlement in the depository market is conducted on a DVP basis on the following Tuesday.

NSC-50 index (NIFTY) was introduced on April 22, 1996 with the explicit objective of *(i)* liquidity, *(ii)* Hedging Effectiveness, and *(iii)* High market capitalisation. Another index titled NSE - Mid cap Index (Junior NIFTY) comprises of companies which are of a reasonable size offering high risk with high returns. This index reflects the movement in the market prices of equities of medium capitalised stocks to measure the performance of stocks in the midcap range.

Wholesale Debt Market Segment (WDM) or the Money Market is operation on June 30, 1994 dealing in pure debt instrument such as Government securities, Treasures bills, Public Sector Bonds, Corporate debentures, commercial paper, Institutional bonds, Bank bonds, certificates of deposit etc., are traded. The investor on this market are the banks, institutions, corporates and mutual funds. There are two types of entities on the segment. First is *Trading Members* who place orders and execute trades on the system on their own or on behalf of the clients. Second is *Participants* who take direct settlement responsibility for the trades executed on the exchange on their behalf by NSE trading member.

Trades on the wholesale Debt Market are settled gross on a trade for trade (TT) basis. Each transaction is settled individually and cumulation of transactions is disallowed. Each trade has a unique settlement date specified up front at the time of order entry and used as a matching parameter. It is mandatory for trades to be settled on the predefined settlement date . The NSE currently allows settlement periods ranging from same day (T+0) settlement to maximum of (T+5) six days.

TT = Trade for Trade

Inventors Grievances cell operated by the NSEIL. Usual investors grievances are:

(i) Non-receipt of shares sent for transfer,

(ii) Non-receipt of corporate benefits,

(iii) Non-rectification of bad delivery by the broker

(iv) Non-receipt of funds/securities on sales/purchase,

(v) Introduction of fake, forged and stolen securities,

(vi) Non-rectification of company objections,

(vii) Contract notes not issued by the broker, etc.

On receipt of investor's letter of complaint, NSE will forward such letter to the company concerned and consistent follow-up is done. NSE gives suggestion to settle the long-pending matters by recruiting a special officer. In some cases, it takes actions like suspension of trading of the securities by the member corporate body. In regard to brokers, after they are intimated about complaint, a reply is expected within 21 days of intimation. Amicable settlement is requested. If not possible, the matter will be referred for arbitration. Arbitration is a quasi-judicial process that is faster and is an inexpensive way of resolving a dispute. The NSE facilitates the process of arbitration between the brokers and their clients. Arbitrator is appointed by the both parties and amicable settlement is made within three to four months. The arbitrators are panel of 20 eminent professionals approved by SEBI.

Concluding Remarks

National Stock Exchange is incorporated at Mumbai. It is a leading stock exchange covering more than 160 cities and towns across the country providing a modern fully computerised trading system. It introduced automated screen based trading. NSE is eligible to trade in equities, preference shares, debentures, Deep Discount Bonds, warrants units of mutual Funds etc. NIFTY is a market capitalisation weighted index comprising 50 scientifically selected stocks having highest liquidity and largest market capitalisation. NSE has an excellent Investor Grievance Cell, Arbitration facilities, and Depository system.

Appendix 1

List of Recognised Stock Exchange in India

1. The Stock Exchange, Phiroze Jeejeebhoy Towers, Dalal Street, Bombay - 400 001.
2. The Stock Exchange, Market Chowk, Ahmedabad - 380 001.
3. The Calcutta Stock Exchange Association Ltd., 7, Lyons Range, Calcutta - 700 001.
4. Madras Stock Exchange Ltd., Exchange Building, Post Box No. 183, 11, Second Line Beach, Madras - 600 001.
5. The Delhi Stock Exchange Association Ltd., West Plaza, I.G. Stadium, Indra Prasta Estate, New Delhi - 110 002. 384/4B, Asaf Ali Road, New Delhi - 110 002.
6. The Hyderabad Stock Exchange Ltd., Kautilya Complex, 4th Floor, Next to Syndicate Bank, Somajiguda, Hyderabad - 500 482, A.P.
7. Madhya Pradesh Stock Exchange Ltd., Rajani Bhavan, 3rd Floor, M.G. Road, Opp. High Court, Indore - 452 001.
8. Bangalore Stock Exchange Ltd., UNI Building, Millers Tank, Vasanthnagar, Bangalore - 560 052.
9. Cochin Stock Exchange Ltd., Veekshanam Road, Ernakulam, P.B. 3529, Cochin - 682 035.
10. The Uttar Pradesh Stock Exchange Association Ltd., Padam Towers, 14/113, Civil Lines, Kanpur - 208 001.
11. Pune Stock Exchange Ltd., Shivleela Chambers 752, Sadashiv Peth, R.B. Mumthekar Marg, Pune - 411 030.
12. The Ludhiana Stock Exchange Association Ltd., Lajpat Rai Market, Clock Tower, Ludhiana - 141 008.
13. The Gauhati Stock Exchange Ltd., Saraf Building Annexe, A.T. Road, Guwahati - 781 001.
14. Mangalore Stock Exchange Ltd., 4th Floor,

Rambhawan Complex,
Kodiabail,
Mangalore - 575 003.

15. The Magadh Stock Exchange Ltd., 9th Floor, Ashina Plaza, Budh Marg, Patna - 800 001.
16. Jaipur Stock Exchange Ltd., Rajastan Chamber Bhawan, M.I. Road, Jaipur - 302 001.
17. Bhubaneswar Stock Exchange Association Ltd., 217, Budharaja Building Jharpoda, Cuttack Road, Bhubaneswar - 751 006.
18. Sanrashtra Kritch Stock Exchange Ltd., 21, New Janpath, Dr. Yagnik Road, Rajkot - 360 001.
19. The Vadodara Stock Exchange Ltd., 101, Paradise Complex, Tilak Road, Sayajiganj, Baroda - 390 005.
20. The Coimbatore Stock Exchange Ltd., Chamber Towers, 8/732 Avanashi Road, Coimbatore - 641 018
21. OTC Exchange of India, 92-93 Maker Towers - F, Cuffe Parade, Bombay - 400 005.
22. National Stock Exchange of India Ltd., Mahindra Towers, 1st Floor, A - Wing R.B.C., Worli Bombay - 400 018.

CREDIT RATING

Capital is one of the important factors of production for the growth and development of a unit at micro and macro level in a market economy. It is a scare factor of production and hence due caution is taken to raise and allocate over different avenues to achieve maximum possible benefits. The role of financial markets in a market economy is that of an efficient intermediator, mediating between savers and investors, mobilising capital on one hand and efficiently allocating them between competing uses on the other. Such allocative role hinges crucially on the availability of reliable information and data. The principle of "efficient market allocation" indeed has its bedrock, what economists label "perfect information". A prudent investor in search of investment avenues has recourse to different sources of information :

(i) offer documents of the issuer (s),
(ii) research reports of market intermediaries,

(iii) media reports,
(iv) financial dailies,
(v) journals
(vi) publications, and
(vii) consultancy usage, etc. In addition to these sources, credit rating agencies have come to occupy an important role as information providers

Historical View on Credit Rating

The origin of credit rating can be traced back to the 1840's. A great financial crisis of 1837 in USA, Louis Tappan established the first mercantile bank credit agency in New York in 1841 which rated the ability of merchants and traders to pay their financial obligations. The mercantile agency was subsequently acquired by Robert Dun. This had published its first rating guide in 1959. John Brad street established another credit rating agency in 1849 who published a rating book in 1857. In 1933, these two rating agencies merged together to form Dun and Bradstreet, which became the owner of Moody's Investors Service in 1962. The history of Moody's itself goes back about a 100 years. In 1900 John Moody founded Moody's Investors Service . In 1909 it published his 'Mannual of Railroad Securities'. It was followed by the rating of utility and industrial bonds in 1914. Rating of bonds issued by U.S. cities and other municipalities in the early 1920's. Yet another credit rating industry has taken place in 1916 when the Poor's Publishing Company published its first ratings, followed by the standard statistics company in 1922 and Fitch Publishing Company in 1924. The Standard Statistics company and the Poor's Publishing company merged in 1941 to form Standard and Poor's which was subsequently taken over by McGraw Hill in 1966. Till 1972 from 1924, almost around 50 years, since setting up of Fitch publishing company in 1924, there were no major new entrants in the area of credit rating. During 1970's numerous credit rating agencies started operations all over the world. In 1972, Canadian Bond Rating Service was incorporated. In 1974, Thomson Bank watch was established. It was based in Toronto, Canada. It was a subsidiary of Thomson Corporation. It is a rating agency exclusively following Financial Institutions including banks, securities firms and finance companies. In 1975, Japanese Bard Rating Institute was incorporated, Mc Carthy Crisanti and Maffei (1975 acquired by Duff and Phelfs in 1991). In 1977, Dominican Bond Rating Service was established. IBCA Limited was incorporated in 1978. Duff and Phelfs Credit Rating company in 1980. It is a major source of credit information internationally which rates all major types of Fixed-Income Securities, Long-Term and Short-Term debt of corporations, Sovereign nations and financial institutions. Besides, it rates structured financing, mortgage backed securities and insurance companies. Beginning in 1992, it has established Joint Venturers largely in Latin American countries and also in Asian countries viz., Pakistan and India. IBCA Limited is an independent and privately owned international credit agency based in London. It was established with the objective of offering credit analysis of banks in different countries. It was the first rating agency to issue credit reports on bank. In 1988 it expanded its coverage to include industrial and commercial corporates and presently provides credit analysis of banks and financial institutions in more than 25 countries and a large number of corporates in Europe. There are credit rating agencies in Malaysia, Phillipines, Mexico, Indonesia, Israel, Pakistan, Cyprus, Korea, Thailand, and Australia. In Thailand, Thai Rating and Information Services; in Japan, Bond Research Institute; in Israel, Israel Securities Rating company; etc., are leading international rating agencies.

Indian Scenario

The credit rating started in India in recent years. In India, the Credit Rating and Information Services of India Ltd. (CRISIL), ICRA Ltd., (Formerly known as Investment Information and Credit Rating Agency of India Ltd.), Credit Analysis and Research Limited ; and Duff and Phelps has tied up with Indian NBFCs to set up Duff and Phelps Credit Rating India (P.) Ltd.

CRISIL (Credit Rating and Information Services of India Limited) was established in 1987. It was promoted by ICICI, nationalised and foreign banks and insurance companies. It went public in 1992. It is the only listed credit rating agency in India. In 1995 it entered into a strategic alliance with Standard and Poor's to extend its credit rating services to borrowers from the overseas market. The services offered are broadly classified as Rating, Information Services, Infrastructure Services and Consultancy. Rating services cover rating of debt instruments. Debt instruments include long, medium and short-term securities. Information services include corporate research reports and CRISIL 500 index. Infrastructure and consultancy services include assistance on specific sectors such as power, telecom and infrastructure financing.

The Investment Research Division (IRD)

Provides analysed and value added information on the Indian economy, capital markets, industry and companies, through various products and services. In addition, CRISIL undertakes customized studies. This division has a large base of subscribers and clients such as institutional investors, merchant bankers, commercial banks, financial institutions, finance companies, brokers, mutual funds and asset management companies. The products IRD are:

(i) CRISIL ECOSCAN which provides detailed macroeconomic statistics with regular updates.

(ii) CRISIL RATING SCAN is a quarterly publication which disseminates all information on CRISIL Ratings.

(iii) CRISIL VIEW is CRISIL's opinion on the credit quality of a company based on which investors and medium term lenders can take investment and lending decisions: It provides an in-depth analysis of a company based on published information and CRISIL's understanding of the relevant qualitative and quantitative factors affecting the credit quality of the company.

(iv) CRISIL BANCARD provides analysed information on select Indian banks. In addition to the information on the background and management of the bank, it contains analysed financial information for accounting periods including financial and productivity ratios and an analysis of the funding and lending profiles.

(v) CRISIL-IDBI Bond Yield Tables are reference tables for calculating yield to maturity on bonds in the Indian debt market.

The Credit Rating Information Services of India Limited (CRISIL) is the premier rating agency in India. It is promoted by leading financial institutions like the Industrial Credit and Investment Corporation of India Limited (ICICI), Unit Trust of India (UTI), Housing Development Finance Corporation Limited (HDFC). It was established in 1987. Among the other initial shareholders are the Asian Development Bank, Life Insurance Corporation (LIC) General Insurance Corporation of India (GIC) and its subsidiaries and nationalised and foreign banks. In November 1993, CRISIL made its initial public offer of equity, making it one of rare rating agencies in the world to be listed on a stock exchange. CRISIL has three divisions, viz. Credit Rating, Investment Research and Advisory Services group.

Objectives

1. To assist both individual and institutional investors in making investment decisions in fixed income bearing securities;
2. To enable companies to mobilise funds from a wider investor base, in larger amounts and at a fair cost;
3. To enable intermediaries in placing debt instruments with investor's by providing them with an effective marketing tool;
4. To provide regulations with a market-driven system for bringing about discipline and healthy growth of capital markets.

Credit Rating Division

CRISIL rates all rupee dominated debt obligations. These include long-term instruments such as bonds and debenture; medium term instruments such as fixed deposit programmes and short-term instruments such as commercial papers programmes and certificate of deposit. CRISIL also rates preference shares, and other new and innovative instruments like structured obligations including asset-backed securities.

Advisory Services Group (ASG)

This group provides its clients with a range of financial advisory services which aim at identifying, mitigating risks and formulating and executing strategies. It gives service on restructuring operations, privatisation services, financial evaluation, credit management, risk management, resource mobilisation, infrastructure advice, and credit assessment. It offers restructuring services through diagnostic studies, redefinition of business, corporate organisational strategies which aim at viable and efficient operations. This group provides advice on policy guidelines and strategy for disinvestment. Based on in-depth understanding of business and industry conditions, privatisation and disinvestment services comprises shortlisting of public sector units for disinvestment on the basis of their current operations. Their strategic importance; and potential for disinvestment and resource generation. The ASG group conducts evaluation of bids for projects, especially for the states and Central governments, development agencies, and financial institutions. This capability also extends to evaluate bidders for prospective joint ventures. This group offers detailed studies of credit management functions of banks and financial institutions offer the banks comprehensive and effective approaches to adopt in a changing, competitive environment. This offers studies to bank and financial institutions in providing specialised port folio studies which aim at providing strategies for optimising risks related returns. It provides to its clients financial engineering solutions and options to enable resource mobilisation in the context of the Indian capital markets. It offers active services to the infrastructure sectors such as roadways, ports, power, telecommunication and other. Credit assessment to Indian states assesses the credit quality of the various state governments. It reflects ASG opinion as to the credit issues associated with the state governments, especially with respect to guarantees provided for power and other infrastructure projects. Credit assessment of utilities, particularly State Electricity Boards (SEBs) analyses credit risks based on their fundamental strengthens in terms of operating and financial efficiency. This group undertakes customized studies for Indian and International consultants, project advisors, financiers and experts who value the CRISIL reputation for quality and responsiveness.

Investment Information and Credit Rating Agency of India Limited (ICRA) is promoted by IFCI and 21 other shareholders comprising of nationalised and foreign banks and insurance companies. It was established in 1991. It is the second rating agency in India. The services offered by ICRA can be broadly categorised into:

(i) Rating Services,
(ii) Advisory Services, and
(iii) Investment Information Services.

Rating services include rating of debt instruments and credit assessment. Advisory services are comprising of strategic counselling, general assessment such as restructuring exercise and sector specific service such as for power, telecom, ports, municipal rating etc. Investment Information services include reports on specific industries, sectors and corporates; Equity related services like equity rating, Equity Assessment etc. In 1996 , ICRA entered into a strategic alliance with Financial Proforma Inc., a Moody's subsidiary to offer services on Risk Management Training and software. These, both, entered into a memorandum of understanding (MOU) to support these efforts.

Credit Analysis and Research (CARE)

Was incorporated in 1992. It is promoted by IDBI and several other banks and insurance companies and investment institutions. Its headquarter is located at Mumbai having four regional offices. Services offered are:

(i) Credit rating,
(ii) Information Services,
(iii) Equity Research, and
(iv) Rating of parallel markets of LPG and kerosene.

Credit rating of all types of debt instruments, both short-term and long-term. Information Services include information on any company, local body, industry or sector required by business enterprise. CARE also prepares 'Credit reports" on companies for the benefit of banks and other business counter parties. Equity Research of CARE comprises of an extensive study of the shares listed in the major stock exchanges and identification of potential winners and losers among them on the basis of the fundamentals effecting the industry, economy, market share, management capabilities, international competitiveness and other relevant factors. Rating services as a useful tool for different constituents of the capital market. The beneficiaries of the services offered by CARE are:

(a) Investors,
(b) Issuers of debt instruments,
(c) Financial intermediaries,
(d) Business counter parties, and
(e) Regulators.

Conceptual View on Credit Rating

Credit rating is an opinion on the relative ability and willingness of an issuer to make timely payments on specific debtor related obligations over the life of the instrument. Credit rating thus provides a relative ranking of the credit quality of debt instruments. In a developing market which is shedding its strict regulatory frame work, as in India, credit rating agencies have a significant role to play. In such a market, the rating agency forms an integral part of a broader programme of disintermediation, broadering and deepening of the market and removal of barriers.[9] Ratings are usually expressed either in alphabetical or alphanumerical symbols. They are a simple and easily understood tool enabling the investor to differentiate between debt instruments on the basis of their credit quality. Thus, the credit rating is a symbolic indicator of the current opinion of the relative capability the issuer to service its debt obligation in a timely fashion, with specific reference to the instrument being rated.[10] Credit rating is focused on communicating to the investors, the relative ranking of the default, loss probability, etc., for a given fixed income investment, in comparison with other rated instruments. A rating is specific to a debt instrument. Credit rating is intended as a grade. It is an analysis of the credit risk associated with the particular instrument. Credit rating is based upon the relative capability and willingness of the issuer of the instrument to service the debt obligations, both principal and interest as per the terms of the contract.

Objectives of Credit Rating

To provide guidance to investors/creditors in determining a credit risk associated with a debt instrument/credit obligation. "In determining a rating both quantitative and qualitative analysis are employed. The judgment is qualitative in nature and the role of the quantitative analysis is to help make the best possible over all qualitative judgment because ultimately, a rating is an opinion."[11] Credit rating helps investors by providing an easily recognisable, simple tool that occupies a possible unknown issuer with a infomative a meaningful symbol of credit quality. It is an opinion given by credit rating agencies about the worthfulness and capability of organisation to repay both principal and interest over the tenure of debt obligation. The rating process is based on certain 'givers'. The credit rating agency is recommending the issuers capabilities only. It is not auditing. It is only assessing and giving opinion for a specific purpose. It is not giving guarantee the completeness or accuracy of the information on which the rating is based.

Features

1. Credit rating is basically aiming at guiding the lay investors about corporate entities. It exerts a very powerful influence in the domestic capital and money markets.
2. Ratings are chalked out exclusively for the purpose of grading debentures, loan bonds, bonds, Government bonds, Municipality bonds, public deposits, commercial paper etc., according to their investment qualities.
3. Rating is a current assessment of the credit worthiness of an obligator (issuer of securities) with respect to specific obligations.
4. Credit rating provides lenders with a simple system of gradation by which the relative capabilities of companies to make timely payment of interest and principal on a particular type of debt can be noted.
5. Credit rating is an opinion of credit rating agencies indicating relative safety of timely payment of interest and principal on a debenture, preference share, fixed deposit or short-term instrument.
6. Credit rating is exhibited either alphabetical manner or alphanumerical way for quick understanding of lay investors and prospective investors.
7. Credit rating is not a general evaluation of issuing organisation but a specific disclosure reflecting the opinion on repayment. Capacity of issuer body in regard to principal and interest over the tenure of the obligation.
8. Rating is not based on audit.
9. Rating can be revised, either upward or downward assessing various conditions and factors of an entity. Thus, credit rating is flexible in nature.
10. Rating helps in investment decision-making of the investors.

11. Rating is based on current information about issuer of obligations and securities.

Classification of Credit Rating

Bond Rating : Rating the bonds and debt securities by issuer corporate bodies, governments or quasi-governments like municipalities, corporations etc. Bond rating is the primary and major business of credit rating agencies.

Equity Rating : The rating of equity shares of companies of the capital market is titled as equity rating.

Commercial Paper Rating : Commercial papers are issued by reputed and high sound corporate bodies to public and financial institutions to raise short-term finance. It is mandatory on the part of a corporate body to obtain the rating of approved credit rating agency to issue commercial paper.

Rating the Borrowers : Borrower is business entity who is raising loans or credit facilities. The borrower's capabilities are assessed and grading is fixed by the credit rating agencies.

Sovereign Rating : Sovereign Rating includes rating a country as to its credit worthiness, probability to risk etc.

Customer Rating : Customer Rating includes rating a customer (debtor) in regarded to his paying capacity in due time.

Rating Process : Rating is an interactive process with prospective approach involving a services of steps. They are:

1. Rating Request,
2. Rating Team,
3. Information Needs,
4. Secondary Information,
5. Management meetings and plant visits,
6. Prereview meetings,
7. Rating committee meetings,
8. Rating communication, and
9. Surveillance. These are, more or less adopted by to all credit rating agencies. A chart showing rating process is exhibited elsewhere.

Rating Request is initiated by the issuer in writing requesting to make rating of a specific issue of the company. On such as request, the rating agency make out a detailed agreement inscribing terms and conditions of such assignment. This includes rating of an issue and subsequent surveillance. Such is called mandate.

Rating Team is usually comprising of two members which is based on the expertise and skills required for evaluating the business of the issuer.

Information Requirements are provided by issuers which is containing a detailed list of information and broad framework for discussions. Issuer is to supply all requirements, data and information.

Secondary Information is drawn by the credit rating agency from its own research division. The agency has a panel of industry experts who provide guidance on specific issuer to the rating team. The secondary sources usually provide data and trends including policies about the industry.

Management Meetings and Plant Visits is necessary for assessment of number of qualitative factors with a view to estimate future earnings of the issuer. A thorough discussion on various matters like management of plants and units, future outlook, competitive position and funding positions etc. Plant visits facilitate understanding of the production process, assess the state of equipment, quality of technical personnel, quality of goods, cost of production etc.

Preview Meeting is convened after completing the analysis. Findings are discussed at length in the internal committee. Internal committee is consisting of senior analysts. In this stage all issues relating to rating are discussed and opinions are formed.

Rating Committee Meeting is convened by rating agency. It is the final authority for assigning ratings. Basing on discussions, views of internal committee, data, etc. Rating is assigned.

Rating Communication is made by the agency to the issuer in detail. If the rating is not acceptable by the issuer, he has a right to appeal for a review of the rating. These reviews are taking place provided the issuer puts some fresh inputs on the issue. Again rating process is reviewed considering fresh inputs and additional information.

Surveillance is a monitoring of credit rating agency over the tenure of the rate instrument. Ratings are reviewed, generally, every year. In such review, initial rating may be upgraded or downgraded or kept unchanged considering various factors by the rating agency.

Methodology of Credit Rating

The credit ratings are based on the current information provided by the client organisation to the rating agency. Sometimes, credit rating agency gathers information from sources it considers reliable. In determining credit ratings, a credit rating agency will analyse various aspects concerning the borrowing company. The aspects are, namely :

1. Business analysis,
2. Financial Analysis,
3. Management Evaluation,
4. Geographical analysis,
5. Regulatory and competitive environment, and
6. Fundamental Analysis.

Business Analysis includes an analysis of industry risk, market position of the company within the industry, operating efficiency of the company and legal position of the company. Financial analysis includes an analysis of accounting quality, earnings protection, adequacy of cash flows and financial flexibility. Management Evaluation includes track record of the management, planning and control system; depth of managerial talent; succession plants; Evaluation capacity to overcome adverse situations; goals, philosophy and strategies. Geographical Analysis consists of locational advantages and demerits; and Backward area benefits, subsidies to the company. Regulatory and Competitive Environment is consisting of structure and regulatory framework and their impact on the company. The different trends in regulations and deregulation and their infact on the company. Fundamental Analysis includes an analysis of liquidity management, asset quality, profitability, financial positing, historic profits, spreads on funds deployment; revenue on non-fund based services, accretion to reserves, etc., Interest and tax sensitivity, exposure to interest rate changes, hedge against interest rate and tax law changes, etc. Considering all these factors, the evaluation is carried out by a team of professionally qualified persons and includes data collection, analysis and meeting with the key persons in the company to discuss strategies, plans and other issues relevant to the credit rating. Such process of evaluation of credit rating taken place four to six weeks time.

Significance of Credit Rating

A rating is an opinion on the future ability and legal obligation of the issuer company to make timely payments of dues, i.e., principal and interest on a specific fixed income security, that is, debt security. Since credit rating has a lot of advantages than demerits, at this stage, we are inclined to study the significance on different fronts such as:

- *(i)* Investors view point,
- *(ii)* Issuers point of view,
- *(iii)* Intermediaries point of view, and
- *(iv)* Regulator point of view.

For investor, credit rating is an information service. It is communicating the relative ranking of default and loss probability for a given fixed income investment in comparison with other rated instruments. Since professional credit rating agencies are equipped with the requisite skills, the competence and credibility, well research activities scientifical analysis process, quality analysis and professional-knowledge, their ratings are presumed to be dependable, indeed helpful to investors to take decisions. For a small and marginal investor, the rating provided by credit rating agencies are low cost but high quality for their decision-making aids. Investing community, in generate, benefits from the allied services of credit rating agencies such as research in the form of industry reports, corporate reports, seminars and open access to the analysis of the agencies for discussion.

For issuers (client companies who issue debt securities and instruments), credit rating agencies serve by providing rating services. Basing on rating ranks, issuers can make issues of debt securities instilling public confident in their issuer. The issuers of rated securities are likely to have access to a much wider investor base as compared to unrated securities. The opinion of a rating agency enjoying investor confidence could enable the issuers to raise funds from the investing lot.

For intermediaries, rating is a useful tool for merchant bankers and other intermediaries in the process of planning, pricing, underwriting and placement of issuers. The intermediaries could use rating as input for their monitoring of risk exposures.

For regulators, they have promoted and permitted to promote credit rating agencies by according permission due to many

Chart 7.2

Rating Processon Overview

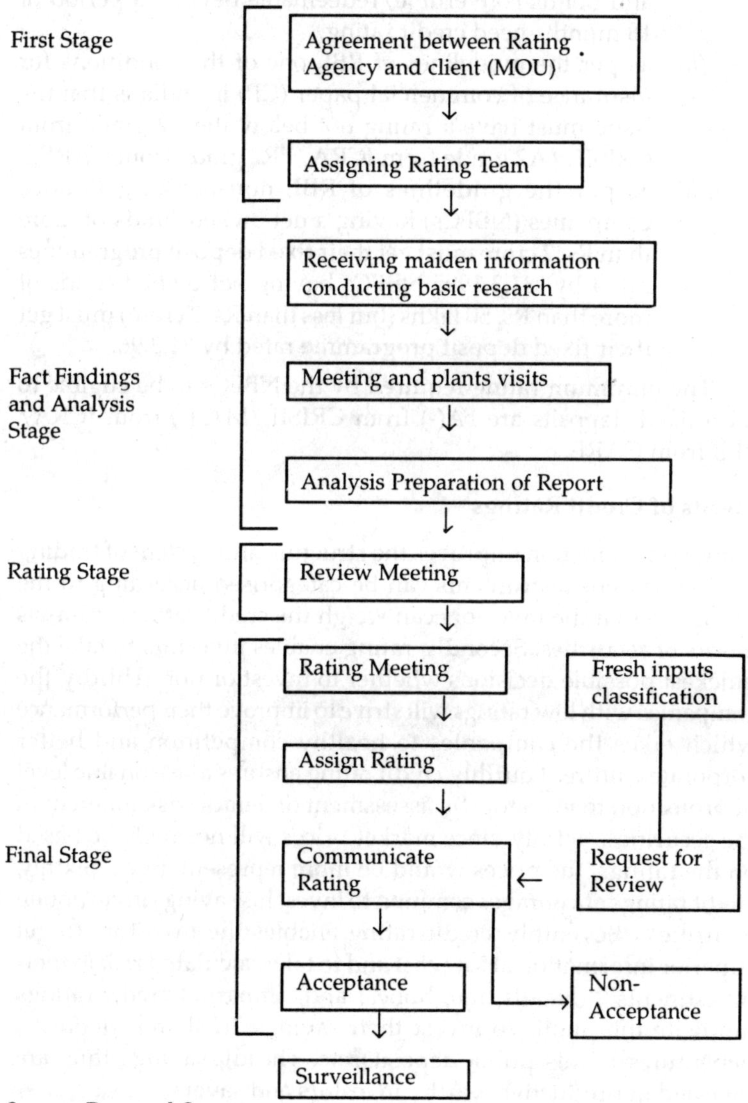

Source : Personal Survey.

advantages to investing public, improvement in capital market activities, boost in industrial activities etc. Regulators can put some checks and measures like:

(i) SEBI is putting a check on public issue of debentures and bonds convertible/redeemable beyond a period of 18 months need credit rating,

(ii) as per the guidelines of RBI, one of the conditions for insurance of commercial paper (CP) in India is that the issue must have a rating not below the P2 grade from CRISIL /A2 grade from ICRA/PR2 grade from CARE,

(iii) as per the guidelines of RBI, non-banking finance companies (NBFCs) having a net owned funds of more than Rs. 2 crore must get their fixed deposit programmes rated by 31.3.1995 NBFCs having net owned funds of more than Rs. 50 lakhs (but less than Rs. 2 crore) must get their fixed deposit programme rated by 31.3.96.

The minimum rating required by the NBFCs to be eligible to raise fixed deposits are FA(-) from CRISIL/MA (-) from ICRA/ BBB from CARE.

Merits of Credit Ratings

Rating phenomenon improves the structure and system of trading market as debt instruments can be categorised according to the ratings so that the investors can weigh the credit ratings vis-a-vis merits of securities. Secondly, rating enables investors to take the quickest possible decisions whether to invest or not. Thirdly, the companies with low ratings will strive to improve their performance which takes the companies to healthy competition and better corporate culture. Fourthly, credit rating ensures a seasonable level of protection to investors by assessment of default risk inherent in the securities. Fifthly, since market prices will normally be based on the ratings, the prices would be more representative . Sixthly, credit ratings encourages common to invest his savings in corporate securities. Seventhly, credit rating enables the investors to get superior information at low cost and to take calculated risk in their investments . Finally, fair, honest and impartial credit ratings motivate the public to invest their savings, in shares, deposits, debentures, bonds, public deposits, etc. The idle savings, thus, are invested in productive way by investors and savers.

Conclusion

Ratings are opinion of the rating agencies on a specific issue and aspect of corporate entity. Ratings are 'guiding posts' to lay investors. Credit rating inspires encouragement to investors to inflow their savings into capital market activities which results in productive use of the funds. Credit rating creates confidence in the minds of investors and public. Credit rating activities are slowly entering into equity rating from debt instruments, rating of primary marketing, a sectors of capital market. It has not touched the secondary market segment of capital market keeping in view of significance of credit rating both for joint stock companies and investing public, government should instill a law to mandate and popularise credit rating every Indian public and corporate sector. Making mandatory in respect of new issues as well as listed company's issues by the Government is essential at this situation. Credit rating agencies are to be accorded an autonomy in evaluation process on their rating process which causes significant confidence among the lay investors and public so that household savings be channelled to corporate investment enhancing production.

CUSTODIAL SERVICES IN INDIA

Consequent upon economic liberalisation, capital market of India showed new vistas and openings for further development in all and sundry aspects of economy. It resulted into incoming of Foreign Institutional Investors (FIIs) to pipe out their funds into industries and business. Many countries, including USA have flowed their funds into Indian economy in terms investments. This caused a lot of improvement in foreign reserves. For instance, according to SEBI's press release dated September 15, 1995, the net cumulative investment amounted to 3846.5 million US dollars. Another organisational trustee groups called "Mutual Funds" entered into national economy as catalysts to increase investment position of our country by pooling funds of investing Indian vast public to common pool under the Trustee Management system. The Mutual Funds have become a major vehicle for mobilisation of savings, particularly from the small and household sectors for investment in the stock market. Although there is Unit Trust of India doing business since 1964, the Mutual Funds business took momentum only after the liberalisation policy of the country emerged during late nineties. Both public sector and private sector Mutual Funds registered with SEBI to do mutual funds business in our country. This business could gather and pool a lot of funds. Both FIIs and MFs use to drain out their funds in investing in securities of various types covering short-term money market instruments, medium term securities, and long-term securities and Government notes and bonds. Since these institutions are pouring a lot of funds in acquiring shares and securities from the existing market, i.e., stock market, their interest should be protected. Once their interest is protected, indirectly, investors (i.e., public) interest is protected, for the moneys invested are belonging to the investing public. These two are pooling moneys from the public investors and doling out into various shares and securities. In the very process of purchasing securities, these two organisations are collecting a lot of papers and documents and certificates of investment which are very vital and important. These documents should be safely kept and managed.

The documents which these two institutions are acquiring should be properly well protected. These should be free from any type of risk. Safe custody of these instruments is very necessary. The dictionary meaning of "custody" is "duty of caring for, guarding." It means, the valuable documents and papers should be carefully guarded by keeping in proper place under tight security. Custodian is a person who has custody of something; caretaker of a public building and property. These securities and valuable documents, which should be kept under a custodian. Custodian is a caretaker of these securities and in return he gets some benefit for his services called "Custodial Charges." Custodial charges are revenue to the custodian whereas an expenditure/ expense to the person who entrusted the work. Since, the work of custodian is risky, costly, and cumbersome in nature, only entities can do such work of custodian services which involves a lot of money, space requirement, fully safety measures, etc. Institutions can do it successfully.

Custodian services are also called as "custodial services." Custodian is a caretaker of a public property or securities. Custodians are intermediaries between companies and clients (Security-holders) and Institutions (FIIs and MFs). In legal and financial parlance, custodial services are essential where wealth is subject to mobile in its condition. Custodians are intermediaries who are a link between real owners and entities. There is an arrangement and agreement between custodians and real owners to act as custodians of those who handover it. Custodial services are a capital intensive and technology driven business. Custodial service is specialised service in which custodians (Corporate bodies of Banks) act as intermediaries to protect the customers and reduces the potential for systemic risk. There are at present 10 firms, who have been approved by SEBI, to provide custody services to Mutual Funds and Foreign Institutional Investors. Of these, seven are Banks and 3 (three) have been set-up by non-banking institutions. These two types of firms providing custodian services, viz., one, which provides custody services as a separate business to FIIs and MFs etc.; second, which provides services holding securities in custody, often temporarily, in the course of management of investments of their clients, such as brokers portfolio manager, financial institutions, insurance companies, NBFCs.

For the first category of custodial services, regulation and control is inevitable since it is exclusively done by specialised institutions. This category needs proper control and, therefore, provisions and regulations suiting the needs of custodian services to FIIs, MFs, etc., should be framed. SEBI has powers to frame regulations on the subject. According to SEBI, 'Custodian' means 'custodian of securities' and 'custodian of securities' means any body corporate who at least provides 'Custodial service.' Custodial services means and includes post trade service such as safe keeping of securities, documents of title on behalf of clients. Safe keeping of securities includes physical custody of securities controlling of securities, arranging for registration of securities, receiving securities, accounting securities, issuing securities on authority of the clients, administration of securities, settlement functions and cash management functions for and on behalf of clients. Thus, custodial services include, safekeeping of assets, accounting treatment and recording, issuing, administration, clearing function, cash management, etc. Proper control measures viz., safe-keeping and custody, recording and issuing is made by custodian on behalf of clients.

Registration of Custodian

Custodian services are very important, SEBI puts some sort of registration of custodians as a matter of mandate. An application has to be made for registration fulfilling the legal formalities as prescribed by the SEBI. The conditions to be fulfilled are, viz., capital adequacy requirement, infrastructural facilities such as office space, vault space for safe custody of securities, adequate insurance cover, computer systems, effective managerial manpower, expert management. The partner of director of the applicant should be free from any moral guilty, applicants should not involve in any litigation connected with the securities market, the partner or director of an applicant or principal officer has not at any time been convicted for any moral turpitude or at any time has been found guilty of economic offence.

Grant of Registration

SEBI grants a registration certificate if satisfies all the conditions and formalities, fees, capital adequacy norm, necessary infrastructural facilities, organisation structure of the client applicant, etc.

Duties and Responsibilities of Custodians

The general obligation, duties and responsibilities of the custodians, both national and global custodians, are laid down by the SEBI regulations should be taken into base for performing their respective duties. These are :

1. Custodians must exercise due care in safe-keeping and administration of the assets, *i.e.*, securities of the clients. He should act like 'bailee.'
2. Separate custody account must be opened by the custodian in the name of each client.
3. A separate deposit account may be opened in the name of each client.
4. Recording of assets should be made by the Custodians.
5. Manner of receiving, recording, delivery, receiving rights, cash, interest warrants, dividend warrants, etc.
6. Registration of securities.
7. Physical segregation of all securities and cash belonging to each client from those of other person including custodian's own.
8. Where a custodian business is a part of a firm's large business, separation of back office and front office functions so that the activities of safe-keeping and

administration could be kept separate from dealing, arranging deals, managing investments.

9. The separation of personnel should be made for this.
10. Adequate insurance of risks would be made with the general insurance companies.
11. Records must be maintained either manually or in a machine readable form.
12. The manner and method and system of receiving proper instruction from client regarding to collection, receipt, reporting, release, delivery, etc., should be clearly stated.
13. Conduct of physical verification of securities and control mechanism should be stated and followed.
14. Annual Audit should be made.
15. Conditions for indemnification are laid in custodial agreements.
16. Manner of accessing records.
17. Circumstances for termination of contract and manner of appointing a successor custodian.
18. Fees charged should be specifically specified in the agreement.

Concluding Remarks

Custodial services is a new method of services provided to FIIs and MFs to protect their assets i.e., security certificates and documents of ownership. A custodian is essentially a service provider. Every custodian should have adequate facilities and enough of capital and financial strength to manage the custodial services since it is a capital intensive and technology driven business. He keeps clients' assets under a safe custody. He keeps, records, maintains, takes physical stock verification, collects the cash on behalf of client the dividend cheques, interest warrants, etc. A custodian settles the accounts of client with others. Under agreement, custodian fixes his fees, settlement process, maintenance of records, etc.

BOOK BUILDING—A GLIMPSE

There are innumerable inefficiencies and pitfalls in the existing Indian Capital market such as, high cost of raising funds, unrealistic pricing of issues on account of a wide gap of 45 days between date of final pricing and the date on which the issue opens, procedural delays in availability of funds, immaturity in the money market, infancy of mutual funds excepting the Unit Trust of India, developing status of merchant banking etc. To overcome, at least one or many, inefficiencies, a novel concept titled 'Book Building' brought to India with new shapes to suit Indian conditions and it is a new and budding concept in India.

Concept

Book-building is a novel and budding concept to India. Under book-building process, the issuer (or issuing company) is required to tie up the issue amount by way of private placement. The issue price is not priced in advance. It is determined by offer of potential investors about price which they may be willing to pay for the issue. To tie up the issue amount, the company organises road shows and various advertisement campaigns. In course of exercise, the book-runner notes the amounts offered by various investors such as institutional investors, Mutual Funds, Underwriters, Foreign Institutional Investors, etc. The price of instrument (i.e., equity, debenture of bonds) is weighted average at which the majority of investors are willing to buy the instrument.

$$\text{Weighted Average } (\overline{X}_w) = \frac{W_1X_1 + W_2X_2 + W_3X_3 .... + W_nX_n}{EW} \text{ or } \frac{EWX}{EW}$$

where, $(\overline{X}_w)$ = Weighted arithmetic average, W = Weights, X= the variable.

Illustration

Starline limited issued bonds of Rs. 100 each amounting to Rs. 1,000 crores. The company appointed Mr. Investor as Book-Runner who collected information from various investors to his book building purposes. The quoted prices of various investors are :

X_1 Quoted price for each bond @ Rs. 95 for Rs. 100 crores
X_2 Quoted price for each bond @ Rs. 98 for Rs. 500 crores
X_3 Quoted price for each bond @ Rs. 101 for Rs. 100 crores
X_4 Quoted price for each bond @ Rs. 100 for Rs. 200 crores
X_5 Quoted price for each bond @ Rs. 99 for Rs. 100 crores

Based on the said information and data, the computation is

made hereunder :

Work-sheet of computations made by Mr. investor is given in Table 7.1.

Table 7.1
Computations Regarding Book-Building

Variables (X)	*Weights* (W)	*Product of Variables and Weights* (WX)
Rs. 95	Rs. 100 crores	Rs. 9,500 crores
Rs. 98	Rs. 500 crores	Rs. 49,000 crores
Rs. 101	Rs. 100 crores	Rs. 1,100 crores
Rs. 100	Rs. 200 crores	Rs. 29,000 crores
Rs. 99	Rs. 100 crores	Rs. 9,900 crores
	EW = Rs.1,000 crores	EWX = Rs. 97,500 crores

$$\text{Weighted Average} = \frac{\text{EWX}}{\text{EW}} = \frac{97,500}{1,000} = 97.50\text{ps.}$$

Rs. 97.50 is the price arrived at by computations under weighted average formula. This price is derived and recorded by the issue manager (i.e., Book Runner Lead Manager of Book Runner). Thus, the issue price is detèrmined and finalised. The Book-Runner builds up his book atleast to the size of the issue and syndicate members. On the strength of their commitment, he enters into a procurement or underwriting agreement with the issuer. The syndicate members agree to the securities at an issue price and specify the payment date.

Objectives

Book-building is a process of price discovery. Book-building is a pricing mechanism whereby new shares and securities are valued on the basis of a demand feedback following a period of marketing. Book-building is a transparent and flexible system based on real time feedback of investors and is a variable alternative to the rigidity of the existing system of fixed pricing.

The objectives of book-building are :

(*i*) Under book-building process, highest market-clearing price for the securities can be determined; and

(ii) Demand level from high-quality long-term investors in order to adjust pricing and allocation decisions.

Book-Building Process

The process of book-building is a novel and innovative concept introduced in India in 1995 which is a fair pricing of the issue and is supposed to emerge out of offers given by various institutional investors. The issue price determined at a date very close to the date of opening of the issue and hence it could be realistic to a particular market. Due to its relative merits, the book-building is attractive. The steps involved in the process of book-building are as under :

Book-Runner or Book-Running Lead Manager files a draft prospectus with SEBI. Draft prospectus is submitted to SEBI without a price or price-band. The draft prospectus is circulated to eligible investors with a price-band. Price-band is arrived at by the Book-Runner in consultation with the issuer.

Chart 7.3
Book Building Process

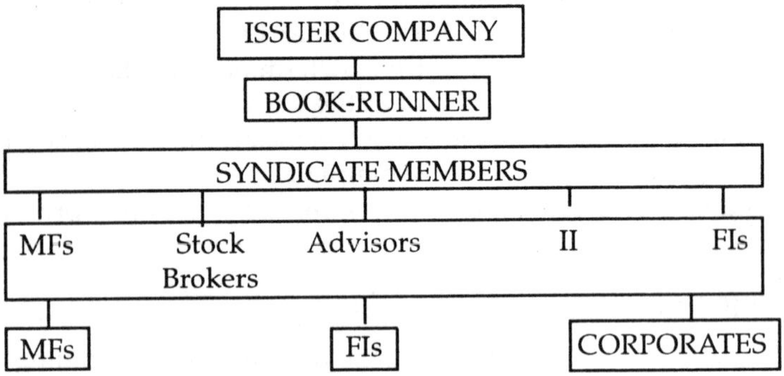

Two

Book-Runner forms a syndicate of about 100 to 130 members along with Joint Lead Managers. The syndicate consists of Book-Running Lead Managers, Joint Lead Managers, Advisors, Co-managers and other members. The syndicate memebrs would procure subscription from the investors including members of the public. These members collect orders from their clients on the amount of securities required by them. The book-runner obtains orders from these members and builds up its book to the size of the placement portion.

Three

Book-Runner conducts awareness campaigns which include advertising, road shows and holding conferences.

Four

Syndicate members create demand and feedback to the Book-Runner.

Five

Book-Runner builds up "Book" after receiving the orders from the members of the syndicate. Book-Runner is required to maintain a record of the same in details.

Six

Book-Runner is required to close the "Book" in consultation with the issuing company and determine the size of the placement portion. The issue comprises two parts *(a)* placement portion and *(b)* public issue portion. Placement portion is that portion of the issue which is offered to public through the syndicate by way of book-building process.

Seven

Book-Runner finalises the allocation to syndicate members and enters into a procurement agreement with them. Procurement agreement is signed between the issuer and syndicate members for the "placement portion." The agreement will broadly provide for :

(i) aggregate amount of subscription to be produced by the syndicate members,

(ii) payment of investor application money by the syndicate member by a certain date, i.e., one-day before public issue opens, and

(iii) procurement and selling commissions payable.

Eight

Final prospectus is filed with Registrar of Companies (ROC) along with procurement agreements within two-days of the determination of the offer price and receipt of acknowledge card from SEBI.

Nine

Placement portion opens for subscription after the filing of final prospectus with the ROC.

Ten

The placement portion closes a day before the opening of the public portion. Book-Runner is required to collect application moneys one day prior to opening of the issue from the subscribers to the placement portion.

Eleven

Allotment and listing of issues (shares, debentures or bonds) under placement portion.

Twelve

Public portion opens.

Thirteen

Allotment and listing of public portion is made on the 11th day from closure of issue. Allotment of Net Offer to public is made as per the existing statutory requirements which is 30 days.

Statutory Requirements

Book-Building is a novel concept and is in infancy stage in India. The concept has assumed significance in India as the SEBI has approved w.e.f. 01.11.1995, the book-building process in pricing new issues. Part B of clarification XIII of SEBI Guidelines for Disclosure and Investor Protection relates to the book-building process. The requirements are outlined as :

(i) The issue should exceed Rs. 100 crores;
(ii) One of the Lead Managers to the issue should be

appointed as the Book-Runner to the issue;

(iii) The issue should be bifurcated into two parts, *viz., (a)* "Placement portion" and *(b)* "Net offer to public." Underwriting for 'net offer to public' is mandatory. Such Runner can also retain the option of requiring underwriters to the 'net offer to public' to pay in advance all moneys in respect of their underwriting commitment by the 11th day of issue closure;

(iv) A Draft Prospectus is to be submitted to SEBI without a price or price-band. Such draft prospectus is to be circulated to eligible investors with a price-band arrived at by the Book-Runner in consultation with the issuer;

(v) The participants in the book-building process are :

(a) Institutional investors and institutional buyers eligible for "firm allotment;" and

(b) SEBI registered intermediaries eligible to act as underwriters;

(vi) Syndicate members should forward orders to the Book-Runner, who is required to maintain a record called "BOOK" of the same;

(vii) Issue price is determined by the Book-Runner in consultation with the issuer company. Issue price for 'placement portion' and 'net offer to public' should be the same.

(viii) The final prospectus should be filed with Registrar of Companies (ROC) within two days for determination of the offer price and receipt of acknowledgement card from SEBI;

(ix) The Book-Runner is required to collect application moneys for the placement portion one day prior to opening of the issue. It is collected from the subscribers. Collection of advance application moneys by the eleventh day from colsure of the issue from the underwriters to the net offer to public in case of under-subscription;

(x) Allotment is made on the 2nd day of closure of issue with regard to net offer to public is made as per the existing statutory requirements;

(xi) Listing of placement portion is done with the Stock Exchanges on the 11th day from closure of issue. Listing

of net offer to public issue as the existing statutory requirement which is now reduced to 30 days.

Principal Documentation

The principal documentation required for the book-building process is:

(a) Mandate Letter

It is a letter issued by the issuer company to the Book-Running Lead Manager (Book-Runner) and authorising the Book-Runner to form syndicate and co-ordinate syndicate for procuring subscription for the 'placement portion.'

(b) Prospectus

Prospectus is also referred to as the offering circular or information memorandum, prepared as per statutory requirements under the Companies Act, 1956 and Securities and Exchange Board of India (SEBI) Guidelines for Disclosure and Investor Protection. As part of the marketing exercise, a "red herring" or preliminary prospectus with a price band is required to be circulated to syndicate members and investors. Based on the "red herring," investors give "Indications of Interest" (IOIs).

(c) Procurement Agreement

Procurement is signed between the issuer and the syndicate members for the "placement portion." Procurement agreement will broadly provide for :

(i) aggregate amount of subscription to be produced by the syndicate member;
(ii) payment of investor application money by the syndicate member by a certain date *i.e.,* one-day before public issue opens;
(iii) procurement and selling commissions payable.

(d) Underwriting Agreement

It is entered into between the issuer-company and underwriters to the "net offer to public." The format follows the model underwriting agreement prescribed by SEBI.

(e) Standard Bidding Form

It is the indication of interest : Syndicate members will be required to submit all indications of interest (IOIs) on a standard form to ensure uniformity in bidding and accuracy. The standard bidding form indicates the :

(i) identity of the investor;
(ii) desired number of shares and;
(iii) price sensitivity/range.

Benefits of Book-Building

1. Book-building helps in evaluating the intrinsic worth of the instrument being offered and the company's credibility in the eyes of public. The entire exercise is done on a wholesale basis.
2. Price of instrument is determined in a more realistic way on the commitments made by the prospective investors to the issue.
3. The prime objective of book-building process is to determine the highest market price for shares and securities and demand level from highest quality investors in order to adjust pricing and allocation decision.
4. Book-building is a process of fixing price for an issue on feedback from potential investors on how they are willing to bid to pick-up issues and instruments.
5. The process of book-building is advantageous to the issuer-company as the pricing of issue would be more realistic as the final price is decided about 11 to 12 days before the opening of the issue. Book building also offers access to capital more quickly than the public issue.
6. As the issue is pre-sold, there would be no uncertainties relating to the fate of the issue involved.
7. The issuer-company saves advertising and brokerage commissions.
8. Issuers can choose investors by quality.
9. Investors have a voice in the pricing of issues. They have a greater certainty of being allotted what they

demand. Investors need not lock up huge amount of capital with the issuer as they pay at the end of the process.

10. The issue price is market-determined. As it is market-determined, it is a distant possibility that the market price of the shares would fall lower than the issue price. Hence the investor is less likely to suffer from erosion of his investment on listing.
11. Optimal demand-based pricing is possible.
12. Efficient capital raising with improved issue procedures, leading to a reduction in *(a)* issue costs, *(b)* paper work, and *(c)* lead times.
13. Flexibility to increase/decrease price and/or size of offering the issues is possible.
14. Transparency of allocations is made.
15. Upgraded information flow of issues, lead managers, syndicate members and investors is made possible.
16. Book-building process inspires 'investors confidence' leading to a larger investor universe.
17. Book-building process creates a liquid and buoyant after-market.
18. As the syndicate members will get firm allocation, the investors to that extent are assured of allotment.
19. Immediate allotment and listing of placement portion of securities.

Dangers

The concept and process of book-building is very much new to Indian Capital Market. It is in infancy stage. The concept of book-building *prima facie* appears to be very beneficial. However, it would not be admissible to apprehend that it might take some time to bring about the results expected of it. A huge portion of the issue is free to be reserved on firm allotment basis to the categories of investors who can offer bids to price the issues under the book-building procedure. The book-building, thus, carries an element of *Bought out Deal.* Most Bought Out Deals by Indian corporates have run into rough weather as their scrips after having been subsequently offered by the sponsors to the public, are not faring well on the Stock Exchanges. Fairly large number of sponsors are yet to offer their holdings to the public for the simple reason that the market is not in a position to give them the returns they expected at the time of conclusion of such transaction with the issuer companies. Secondly, book-building process in the Indian capital market is still far from that in the international arena. It runs very much efficiently in the matured market conditions where the investors are in a position to keep themselves abreast of various parameters affecting the market price of securities. On the other hand, in India, it has been constantly observed that the fluctuations in the market prices do not have desired relation with the financial soundness or otherwise of the company. External forces influence the prices to a large extent and general investors act from contagious impulse which leads to paranormal fluctuations in the market prices. Third, there are fears of a few institutional investors forming a cartel and cornering the placement portion by quoting a lower bid to the issues of the issuer company. Fourth, our capital market is not yet ready to accept *in toto* an international concept titled 'bookbuilding.' In the West, the number of investors addressed is far less. Whereas, in India, lakhs of applications would be received and, therefore, it is very difficult to arrive at a price with so many players.

Concluding Remarks

For the project financing and working capital financing, a joint stock company requires huge and large amount of capital. Such a large amount of capital is required to acquire fixed assets, working capital, etc. It is accumulated through the issue to the public. A new and budding concept is introduced in India is titled 'Book Building' by the SEBI w.e.f. Ist November, 1995 to give more emphasis because of its benefits to the investors and the issuer-company. Book-building focuses on the prospect of fair pricing of an issue being determined by the offers of various investors.

Further, book-building aims to have the issue pre-sold reduces the threat of development or undersubscription. With the aid of book building, collection of funds is much faster and the cost of doing so is relatively lower than that in the conventional method. It focuses on fair pricing of the issue which is supposed to emerge out of offers given by various investors such as institutional investors, foreign financial institutions, mutual funds and underwriters. The fair price is determined at a date very close to the date of opening of the issue and hence could be realistic to a particular market. The concept is appearing to be very much beneficial and advantageous to both the issuer-company and investors. To achieve a successful result on using the concept, many a person/institution/governmental body should shower helping hand.

VENTURE CAPITAL FINANCING—AN AGGREGATE VIEW

Venture Capital (VC) is a pivotal financial innovation in the 20th Century which is considered as a synonym of high risk capital. Often it is thought of as 'the early stage financing of new and young entries in business families seeking to grow rapidly.' It usually implies an involvement by the venture capitalist in the management of the client enterprises. Venture capitalists, thus, finance only highly risky new technologies. Besides, they participate in the management of client enterprises. They take all risks by supplying long-term as well as working capital finance. They recover their capital after 3 to 5 years. They gain profits in the name of 'Capital Gains'. In broad terms, venture capital is the investment of long-term equity finance where the venture capitalist acts as 'partner.' Venture Capital is confined to high technology as well as risky idea which is usually confined to small scale enterprises specialising new ideas and new technologies.

Features

1. There are two parties in venture capital ideology, namely Venture Capital Firm (VCF) and Assisted Firm (AF). Venture Capital Firm supplies funds. Assisted firm gets funds to do business.
2. The Venture Capital Firm is inclined to assume a high degree of risk in the expectation of earning a high rate of return.
3. The Venture Capital Firm is providing funds to assisted firm for the commencement, development and growth of the venture.
4. The Venture Capital Firm takes an active role and interest in guiding the assisted firm.
5. The financial burden for the assisted firm tends to be

negligible in the first few years of the newly ventured concern.

6. The Venture Capital Firm usually plans to liquidate its investment in assisted firm after 3 to 5 years span.
7. Venture Capital Firm potentially participates in the direct acquisition of shares, options or convertible securities. The objective is to make capital gains by selling off the investment once the enterprise becomes profitable.
8. Venture capital financing is a long-term illiquid investment. It is not repayable on demand. It requires long-term investment attitude that requires the venture capital firm to wait for a long period, say 5 to 10 years. To make large profits, venture capital firm endeavours to finance its funds through equity participation.
9. Continuing participation of the venture capitalist in the management of the assisted firms is available. This hands on management approach helps him to protect and enhance his investment by actively involving and supporting the entrepreneur. More than finance, venture capitalist gives his marketing, technology, planning and management skills on the new venture.

Evolution of Venture Capital Activities Developed Countries

Venture Capital represents financial investment in a highly risky new proposition in the hope of earning a high rate of profits and returns. Although it is an old concept in the field of business, it has gained momentum during the past five decades or so.

United States of America

The origin of venture capital, in its present form, may be traced to General Doriot (the United States of America) established the American Research and Development Fund at the Massachuttes Institute of Technology (MIT) in 1946 in Boston. It was formed to finance the commercial exploitation of new technologies developed in the U.S. Universities. Secondly, small Business Investment Company (SBIC) Act in 1958 was formed in the U.S.A. which permitted the small business administration to licence. Besides, it supported the small business financially. It acted as a vehicle of small business financing giving a real impetus to the development of venture capital industry, which proved to be very effective VCFs during the sixties and seventies. Today, SBICs in their newly modified form, are the major sources of its growth. Thirdly, US Government used to provide substantial tax incentives to investors investing their funds in VCFs. VCFs use to provide finance to new firms to boost industries in the USA. Fourthly, the venture capital industry in USA has been growing ever since its inception. Its growth was accentuated after 1978 when the capital Gains Tax was reduced from 49 per cent to 28 per cent. The rate was again brought down to 20 per cent for individuals in 1981. These reductions resulted into substantial return to investors, and the venture capital industry was able to attract capital as their securities were readily acceptable in the stock market and accepted by the investors through trading facilities in the Stock Exchanges.

Europe

Venture Capital activities started in Europe in eighties. A number of European countries now have venture capital firms which are members of the European Venture Capital Association (EVCA) founded in 1983. In spite of these developments, about three-fourths of venture capital investment in Europe is confined to three countries, namely, the United Kingdom (U.K.), France and Netherlands.

United Kingdom

Historically, the small firms in the U.K. have received equity finance from the investment trusts. In the post-war periods, investment trusts started investing in large quoted companies at the cost of small risky companies. The most important source of equity finance for new firms during 1960s and early 1970s. A large number of factors, such as tax incentives, establishment of unlisted securities market (USM), encouragement of investment trusts, etc., contributed to this venture capital concept.

France

In 1972, Societies Financiers d' Innovation (SFI) were established. They were not successful. French Government provided more and more tax incentives to revitalise the Venture Capital industry recently. Fonds Commun de placement a Risque in 1983 was established. Investors receive tax exemption capital gains at the end of 5 years. Venture Capital Funds are established and supported by banks. They encourage and supply funds to small firms. The creation of the Second Marche' and Development of financial instruments such warrants and options have helped to the growth and development of venture capital industry in France.

Netherlands

In Netherlands, venture capital industry is very fast growing. Twenty-five private VCs have been established. Twenty Small Risk Finance Funds have been established. A number of the funds are owned or supported by banks. Government provides a lot of encouragement to the VCF industry. A special measure was introduced by the Government in 1981 to help provide risk capital for small business sector. A scheme titled 'Particularly participate Martschappijen' (PPM scheme) was started. PPMs are small—business companies. Funds upto 50 of the risk is indemnified by the Government under this scheme.

West Germany

Mostly, companies in West Germany are private owned, of which three-fourths are family owned. Family owned companies are uninterested to raise equity capital. Significance of equity in the financial sector is very limited. Company resources are generally come in the form of loans. But such an attitude is changing recently. Because enough loans are available due to recession, many companies incline towards equity finance. A number of public issues increased recently. Recently a number of public companies and venture capital funds have been established.

Japan

Japan is a developed country outside the Western countries. It has some sort of venture capital activity. Japan has not adopted the US model of VC. It has its own model of Venture Capital. In 1974, the Ministry of International Trade and Industry (MIT) of Japan founded a Venture Enterprise Centre (VEC) which also collects information about venture business.

Evolution of Venture Capital Industry in Developing Countries

Venture capital industry is not wide spread in developing countries. VCFs have been generally set up by development banks as subsidiaries or separately managed funds. Developing countries have established VCFs through commercial banks. Private Sector VCFs are generally absent in the developing countries. However, they have come up in countries with the support of International Finance Corporation (IFC) since 1978. Private Sector VCFs have come up in countries such as Korea, Taiwan and Malaysia at their own initiative. Foreign venture capital funds are not existing in developing countries. The development of VCFs in developing countries suffer from a number of factors:

- *(i)* Paucity of Funds,
- *(ii)* Lack of entrepreneurship approach by banks since banks are mainly concentrated on commercial banking activities.
- *(iii)* Lack of incentives,
- *(iv)* Lack of encouragement from Governments,
- *(v)* Equity aversion by VCFs,
- *(vi)* Lack of specialised VCFs,
- *(vii)* Lack of Stock Exchange and stock market activities, etc.

Evolution of Venture Capital Funds Industry in India

The development of Venture Capital concept current is a phenomanon in India which is still in an infant stage. It needs promotional efforts as well as policy initiatives for a quick and rapid growth. In India, the growth of small scale enterprises (SSEs) has been one of the significant features of its industrial economy. A number of institutional sources of finance for SSEs have been developed in India since independence in 1949 which include banks and specialised financial institutions. Until 1981, the Reserve Bank of India (RBI) had been supporting lending to SSEs through a *Credit Guarantee Scheme.* Currently a similar scheme, the small loans guarantee scheme, is being operated by a Deposit Insurance and Credit Guarantee Corporation (DICGC), a fully owned subsidiary of Reserve Bank of India.

Regarding to risk finance to SSEs, the various financial institutions finance equity capital. These are :

- *(a)* Risk Capital Foundation of the IFCI;

(*b*) Seed Capital Scheme and National Equity Scheme of IDBI; and

(*c*) Programme for Advancement of Commercial Technology (PACT) of the ICICI.

These schemes provide for the development of the SSEs by direct equity participation or loan to bridge the equity gap.

The concept of Venture Capital is catching up in India only after 1986-87 budget. The venture capital companies can be categorised in India as :

(*i*) promoted by All-India development finance institutions;

(*ii*) state level financial institutions;

(*iii*) promoted by public sector financial and commercial banks;

(*iv*) Foreign banks and private sector financial institutions (Chart 7.4).

The promotion of Venture Capital appears to be instrumental in inducing technological development, stimulating creativity and innovation and nurturing entrepreneurship. To encourage the VCF activities in India, a concerted effort by the Government, financial institutions, commercial banks, private sector companies, and other agencies is very much essential. Favourable and regulatory frame is to be made to boost the VCF industry.

Methods of Financing Venture Capital Industry

Venture capital is a risk-finance. Since it is risk finance in nature, it should be available in the form of equity share capital. Any other form of capital is not suitable for formation and development of venture capital firms. Initially, venture capital firms would neither get funds from the public nor it is incapable to invest from its own sources due to heavy size investment. Venture Capital Firms should come forward to supply funds which are supplied either in form of equity or quasi-equity. Quasi-equity indicates the funds are conditional or convertible loans. Convertible loans are primarily loans in nature for a certain initial period and on expiry of the tenure, these will be converted in equity. Venture Capital is typically available in three forms in India, viz. Equity, Conditional loans and income notes.

Equity

All VCFs in India provide equity capital to the concerns. But their contribution does not exceed 49 per cent of the total equity capital of the concern. Thus the effective control and management and majority of shares remain with the entrepreneur. When a venture capitalist contributes equity capital, he acquires the ownership in the business. He is entitled to share the profits and dividends in the enterprises. The venture capitalist buys the equity share capital with an intention to ultimately sell them off to make capital gains.

Conditional Loan

Venture Capitalist provides conditional loans to the concern. A conditional loan is repayable in the form of royalty after the venture is able to generate sales. No interest is paid on such loans. VCFs charge royalty on such schemes. The royalty is ranging between 2 per cent to 15 per cent.

Income Note

Income note is an hybrid security which combines the features of both conventional and conditional loan. The entrepreneur has to pay both interest and royalty on sales, but substantially of low rates.

Venture Capital Schemes in India

Assuming venture capital industry is vital and very important for the industrial development of Indian industry especially, small and medium scale industries, various financial institutions at national and State level come forward to fund the new, risk and high technologies. In the fray of the venture capital, many have joined such as commercial banks, foreign banks, private sector financial organisations and funds, etc.

All-India Development and Financial Institutions

1. Industrial Development Bank of India (IDBI)
2. Industrial Credit and Investment Corporation of India (ICICI)
3. Industrial Finance Corporation of India (IFCI).

State Level Finance Corporations

State Finance Corporations (SFCs)
State Industrial Promotion and Investment Corporations.

Venture Capital Funds of Commercial Banks

1. State Bank of India set up SBI Capital Markets (SBI Cap) a venture capital fund for "bought out deals." SBI cap invests in the equity shares of new and unknown companies.
2. Canara Bank has set up a venture capital fund as its subsidiary, Canbank Financial Services (Canfina).
3. Grindlays' Bank has set up India Investment Fund to provide venture capital assistance to high risk projects.

Others

1. Credit Capital Finance Corporation set the first Indian private venture capital fund.
2. 20th Centure Finance
3. Indus Technology Ventures
4. Infrastructure Leasing and Financial Services.
5. International Finance Corporation, Washington D.C.

Fiscal Incentives

Financial incentives have been found to play a very vital role in the growth of venture capital industry. Besides, tax concessions cause a great deal in developing the venture capital industry. In this connection some suggestions are worth consideration for the full development of VC activities in India. These are :

1. Section 80CC should be restored. A separate deduction should be extended to investment in VCFs. The benefits could be extended to shares through private placements. A maximum percentage of share holding could be prescribed so that the facility is not abused.
2. The dividends paid to the investors of VCFs should be exempted from income tax.
3. Long-term capital gains should be taxed at lowest percentage.
4. The benefits of Section 80 HHC of the Income Tax Act

Chart 7.4
Classification of VCFs

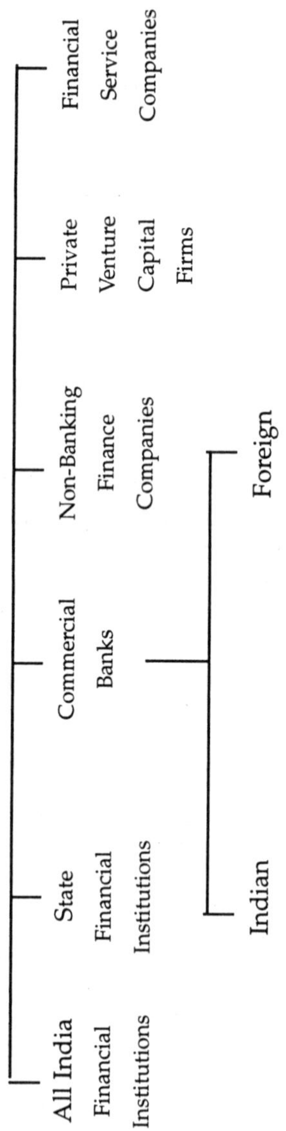

Source : Personal Survey.

should be extended for 50 per cent of the profits earned on venture capital investment which would encourage private sector companies to establish venture capital funds.

5. Venture capital joint stock companies should be given tax benefits available for companies in which the public are substantially interested, as defined in Section 2(18) of the Income Tax Act, 1961.
6. Foreign venture capital investment should be further encouraged.
7. Listing guidelines for VCFs should further be liberalised.
8. The formation of limited partnership should be introduced in India, in case of venture capital firms and concerns.
9. Non-voting shares should be introduced by amending the Indian Companies Act of 1956 which would eliminate the fear of the entrepreneur's apprehension of being owned and controlled by VCFs.

Concluding Remarks

For the quick and fast development of the Venture Capital Industrial activities in India, a lot of regulatory and fiscal measures are to be adopted and sanctioned by the Central and State Governments and suitably related Acts should be amended. The activities of venture capital can boost the industries if proper amendment in the various sections of relevant Acts is made. The various Acts like Indian Partnership Act, Indian Companies Act, Income Tax Act, etc., are to be amended. The VCFs can rehabilitate the sick industrial units of the country. Capital pumping by the investors and venture capital firm is essential to boost the new risk and highly technological ventures which would lead to industrial development of the country. VCFs provide adequate capital in the equity, conditional notes, and Income notes to the venture capital firms and clients. VCFs also provide enough managerial support to the concerns. To encourage the venture capital business activities in India, many a financial concerns like all India Financial Institutions, State Financial Corporations, Commercial Banks of India, Commercial Banks of Foreign countries located in India, private sector financing companies come forward. Government is also encouraging the VCF activity by suitably amending the various laws of the country. Regulatory bodies like SEBI is taking active part in amending the related rules and regulations.

ANNEXURE

RATING SYMBOLS OF VARIOUS CREDIT RATING AGENCIES

ICRA (Investment Information and Credit Rating Agency of India Limited)

Long-term Debt—Debentures, Bonds and Preference Shares

LAAA Highest safety. Indicates fundamentally strong position. Risk factors are negligible. There may be circumstances adversely affecting the degree of safety but such circumstances, as may be visualised, are not likely to affect the timely payment of principal and interest as per terms.

LAA+
LAA
LAA— High Safety. Risk factors are modest and may vary slightly.The protective factors are strong and the prospect of timely payment of principal and interest as per terms under adverse circumstances, as may be visualised, differs from LAAA only marginally.

LA+
LA
LA— Adequate safety. The risk factors are more variable and greater in periods of economic stress. The protective factors are average and any adverse change in circumstances, as may be visualised, may alter the fundamental strength and affect the timely payment of principal and interest as per terms.

LBBB+
LBBB
LBBB— Moderate safety. Considerable variability in risk factors. The protective factors are below average. Adverse changes in business/economic circumstances are likely to affect the timely payment of principal and interest as per terms.

LBB+
LBB
LBB— Inadequate safety. The timely payment of interest and principal are more likely to be affected by present or prospective changes in business/economic circumstances. The protective factors fluctuate in case of changes in economy/business conditions.

LB+
LB Risk prone. Risk factors indicate that the obligations may not be met when due. The protective factors are

LB—	narrow. Adverse changes in business/ economic conditions could result in inability/unwillingness to service debts on time as per terms.
LC+ LC LC—	Substantial risk. There are inherent elements of risk and timely servicing of debts/obligations could be possible only in case of continued existence of favourable circumstances.
LD	Default. Extremely speculative. Either already in default in payment of interest and or/principal as per terms or expected to default. Recovery is likely only on liquidation or re-organisation.

Medium-term Debt—including Fixed Deposit Programmes

MAAA	Highest safety. The prospect of timely servicing of interest and principal as per terms is the best.
MAA+ MAA MAA—	High safety. The prospect of timely servicing of the interest and principal as per terms is high, but not as high as in MAAA rating.
MA+ MA MA—	Adequate safety. The prospect of timely servicing of the interest and principal is adequate. However, debt servicing may be affected by adverse changes in the business/ economic conditions.
MB+ MB MB—	Inadequate safety. The timely payment of interest and principal are more likely to be affected by future uncertainties.
MC+ MC MC—	Risk prone. Susceptibility to default high. Adverse changes in business/economic conditions could result in inability/unwillingness to service debts on time and as per terms.
MD	Default. Either already in default or expected to default.

Short-term Debt—including Commercial Paper

A1+ A1	Highest safety. The prospect of timely payment of debt/obligation is the best.
A2+ A2	High safety. The relative safety is marginally lower than A1 rating.
A3+ A3	Adequate safety. The prospect of timely payment of interest and instalment is adequate, but any adverse change in business/economic conditions may affect the fundamental strength.

A4+ **A4**	Risk prone. The degree of safety is low. Likely to default in case of adverse changes in business/ economic conditions.
A5	Default. Either already in default or expected to default.

CRISIL (Credit Rating and Information Services of India Ltd.)

Debenture Rating Symbols

High Investment Grades

AAA (Triple A) Highest Safety	Debentures rated 'AAA' are judged to offer highest safety of timely payment of interest and principal. Though the circumstances providing this degree of safety are likely to change, such changes as can be envisaged are most unlikely to affect adversely the fundamentally strong position of such issues.
AA (Double A) High Safety	Debenture rated 'AA' are judged to offer adequate safety of timely payment of interest and principal. They differ in safety from 'AAA' issues only marginally.

Investment Grades

A Adequate Safety	Debentures rated 'A' are judged to offer adequate safety of timely payment of interest and principal. However, changes in circumstances can adversely affect such issues more than those in the higher rated categories.
BBB (Triple B) Moderate Safety	Debentures rated 'BBB' are judged to offer sufficient safety of timely payment of interest and principal for the present, however, changing circumstances are more likely to lead to a weekend capacity to pay interest and repay principal than for debentures in higher categories.

Speculative Grades

BB (Double B) Inadequate Safety	Debentures rated 'BB' are judged to carry inadequate safety of timely payment of interest and principal, while they are less susceptible to default than other speculative grade debentures in the immediate future, the uncertainties that the issuer faces could lead to inadequate capacity to make

	timely interest and principal repayments.
B High risk	Debenture rated 'B' are judged to have greater susceptibility to default; while currently interest and principal repayments are met, adverse business or economic conditions would lead to lack of ability or willingness to pay interest or principal.
C Substantial Risk	Debentures rated 'C' are judged to have factors present that make them vulnerable to default, timely payment of interest and principal is possible only if favourable circumstances continue.
D Default	Debentures rated "D' are in default and in arrears of interest or principal payments are expected to default in maturity. Such debentures are extremely speculative and returns from these debentures may be realised only on reorganization or liquidation.

Note :

1. CRISIL may apply '+' (plus) or '—' (minus) signs for ratings from AA to C to reflect comparative standing within the category.
2. The contents within parenthesis are a guide to the pronunciation of the rating symbols.
3. Preference share rating symbols are identical to debenture rating symbols except that the letter 'pf' are prefixed to the rating symbols, e.g., 'pfAAA'.

CRISIL Fixed Deposit Rating Symbols

Investment Grades

FAAA (F Triple A) Highest Safety	This rating indicates that the degree of safety regarding timely payment of interest and principal is very strong.
FAA (F Double A) High Safety	This rating indicates that the degree of safety regarding timely payment of interest and principal is strong. However, the relative degree of safety is not as high as for Fixed Deposits 'FAAA' rating.
FA Adequate Safety	This rating indicates that the degree of safety regarding timely payment of interest and principal is satisfactory. Changes in circumstances can affect

such issues more than those in the higher rated categories.

Speculative Grades

FB Inadequate Safety	This rating indicates inadequate safety of timely payment of interest and principal. Such issues are less susceptible to default than fixed deposits rated below this category, but the uncertainties that the issuer faces could lead to inadequate capacity to make timely interest and principal payments.
FC High Risk	This rating indicates that the degree of safety regarding timely payment of interest and principal is doubtful. Such issues have factors at present that make them vulnerable to default, adverse business or economic conditions would lead to lack of ability or willingness to pay interest or principal.
FD **Default**	This rating indicates that the issue is either in default or is expected to be in default upon maturity.

Note:

1. CRISIL may apply '+' (plus) or '—' (minus) signs for ratings from FAA to FC to indicate the relative position within the rating category.
2. The contents within parenthesis are a guide to the pronunciation of the rating symbols.

CRISIL Rating for Short-Term Instruments

P-1	This rating indicates that the degree of safety regarding timely payment on the instruments is very strong.
P-2	This rating indicates that the degree of safety regarding timely payment on the instruments is strong; however, the relative degree of safety is lower than that for instruments 'P-1'.
P-3	This rating indicates that the degree of safety regarding timely payment on the instrument is adequate; however, the instrument is more vulnerable to the adverse effects of changing circumstances than an instruments rated in the two higher categories.
P-4	This rating indicates that the degree of safety regarding timely payment on the instrument is minimal and it is likely to be adversely affected by

short-term adversity or less favourable conditions.

P-5 This rating indicates that the instrument is expected to be in default on maturity or is in default.

Note : 1. CRISIL may apply '+' (plus) or '—' (minus) signs for ratings from P-1 to P-3 to reflect comparative standing within the category.

CARE (Credit Analysis and Research Ltd.)

Rating Symbols for Long-Term and Medium-Term Instruments

CARE AAA (FD)/(CD)/(SO) Instruments carrying this rating are considered to be of the best quality, carrying negligible investment risk. Debt service payment are protected by stable cash flows with good margin. While the underlying assumptions may change, such changes as can be visualized are most unlikely to impair the strong position of such instruments.

CARE AA (FD)/(CD)/(SO) Instruments carrying this rating are judged to be of high quality by all standards. They are also classified as high investment grade. They are rated lower than CARE AAA securities because of somewhat lower margins of protection. Changes in assumption may have a greater impact or the long-term risks may be somewhat larger. Overall, the difference with CARE AAA rated securities is marginal.

CARE A (FD)/(CD)/(SO) Instruments with this rating are considered upper medium grade instruments and have many favourable investment attributes. Safety for principal and interest are considered adequate. Assumptions that do not materialize may have a greater impact as compared to the instruments rated higher.

CARE BBB (FD)/(CD)/(SO) Such instruments are considered to be of investment grade. They indicate sufficient safety for payment of interest and principal, at the time of rating. However, adverse changes in assumptions are most likely to weaken the debt servicing capability compared to higher rated instruments.

CARE BB (FD)/(CD)/(SO) Such instruments are considered to be speculative, with inadequate protection for interest and principal payments.

CARE B (FD)/(CD)/ (SO)	Instruments with such rating are generally classified susceptible to default. While interest and principal payments are being met, adverse changes in business conditions are likely to lead to default.
CARE C (FD)/(CD)/ (SO)	Such instruments carry high investment risk with the likelihood of default in the payment of interest and principal.
CARE D (FD)/(CD)/ (SO)	Such instruments are of the lowest category. They are either in default or are likely to be in default soon.

Rating Symbols for Short-Term Instruments

PR-1	Instruments would have superior capacity for repayment of short-term promissory obligations. Issuers of such instruments will normally be characterised by leading market position in established industries, high rates of return on funds employed, etc.
PR-2	Instruments would have strong capacity for repayment of short-term promissory obligations. Issuers would have most of the characteristics as for those with PR-1 instruments.
PR-3	Instruments have an adequate capacity for repament of short-term promissory obligations. The effect of industry characteristics and market composition may be more pronounced. Variability in earnings and profitability may result in changes in the level of debt protection.
PR-4	Instruments have minimal degree of safety regarding timely payment of short-term promissory obligations and the safety is likely to be adversely affected by short-term adversity or less favourable conditions.
PR-5	The instrument is in default or is likely to be in default on maturity.

OVER THE COUNTER EXCHANGE OF INDIA (OTCEI)

Indian capital market has witnessed a gigantic change with the mushroom growth of new instruments like convertible debentures and bonds, partly convertible debentures, fully convertible debentures, zero interest bonds and debentures, public sector bonds, etc., and new institutions floated like capital market companies and institutions, financial services companies, leasing and hire purchase business companies, mutual funds companies both in public sector and private sector, financial markets institutions etc., over the last few years. These instruments have quite enticed a vast cross-section of Indian society from the extremely wealthy to the laborious jacks and from blue-collared executives to peons and panwallahs. The exponential rise of both in terms of number of investors and market capitalisation has led to severe pressure on infrastructure. Alongside, problems cumulated rapidly since the stock exchanges have negligible infrastructure, brokers and dealers are losing interest in the individual investors, and they prefer to do business with the Institutions owing to large volumes and bulk operations and the small investor is left high and dry. In this light, the Pherwani Committee has boldly criticised the poor liquidity of the scrips on the Indian sources, as out of the 3,000 odd companies listed not the Indian stock exchanges, day-to-day transactions are carried out in only 250 of them and the remaining of the listed companies hardly have any liquidity. Brokers and dealers usually have a tendency to pursue a handful of blue chip securities which are most profitable. Consequently, the investors who need cash desperately for domestic or other purposes have to plead before brokers and dealers to sell off their holdings and in many number of occasions they just can- not get their shares encashed. Besides, small and marginal investors have been suffering from delays in settlements and transfers, and are blind to the actual price at which their transactions took place on their behalf. Indeed the investors for long have lamented that when they buy stock they get it at the highest price of the day and when they sell the scrips, they are caught up getting lowest price of the day which drugs them to a mournful state causing serious loss of interest in the scrips. There is no transparency in the transactions. The investors could not understand at what prices their shares are sold or bought since there is no clear-cut display of the quotations. Unscrupulous brokers often have a field day taking gullible investors for a ride. Small and newly incorporated and freshly started companies have a problem of raising capital through a public issue at exorbitant costs and delays involved in realisation of proceeds. In order to overcome the pitfalls and loop-holes of the Indian capital market phenomenon, to face the sweeping changes in the Indian financial sector and corporate sector, money market operations, stock exchange operations and workings, to follow-up the liberalisation process and measures in the economy, to enter into the international market, a radical change in the stock exchange operations in the last one/two years, witnessed the ecstatic brain child is 'OTCEI' which is 'Over the counter' Exchange of India.

Over the Counter Exchange of India (OTCEI) is a company incorporated under Section 25 of the Indian Companies Act, 1956 whose objective is setting up and operating an 'over the counter' exchange (the OTC exchange) of India the first of its kind in our country which is a recognised stock exchange under Section 4 of the Securities Contract (Regulations) Act, 1956 and therefore, companies listed on this exchange in the country as regards the taxes and interest rate on borrowings. It has picked up the model from the National Association of Securities Dealers Automated Quotations (NASDAQ) system, prevalent in USA with modifications suiting the Indian conditions. It has been incorporated as company under the provisions of the Indian Companies Act as well as the Indian Securities Contract (Regulations) Act, 1956 with an authorised capital of Rs. 10 crores and paid-up capital of Rs. 5 crores and has been promoted by eight financial institutions, viz., ICICI, UTI, IDBI, IFCI, LIC, GIC and its subsidiaries, Canbank Financial Services Limited and SBI Capital Markets Ltd., and it got formal clearance from the Controller of Capital Issues (CCI) in February, 1992. Thus, on July 28th, 1992 the Indian Stock Exchanges added another chapter to their history, as on that day, the maiden issue of Vasundara Rasayans Limited opened for public subscription for listing on OTCEI. It commenced its operations from October 6, 1992. By the end of March, 1993, 7 scripts were listed with OTCEI. As the monthly turnover of it moved up to Rs. 106 lakhs during June 1993 from Rs. 17 lakhs in October, 1992, OTCEI has decided to offer benefits of their trading to investors for shares currently listed with OTCEI. It is expected that trading on 25 permitted securities will commence very shortly. OTCEI has started trading in debt instruments, beginning May, 1993, with Infrastructure Leasing and Financial Services (IL & FS) as the compulsory market maker, OTCEI is in the process of opening regional windows, beginning with Delhi and Madras, to be followed by Calcutta and other metropolitan areas.

Features

OTCE has been proclaimed as a different stock exchanges and a novel model dedicated to the national interest and vigorously functioning recently which has set up as an electronic screen based stock exchange. All the activities of it are computerised which enables speedier transactions. The investors get the feel of a computerised and computer based trading system—the Automated Security Trading Over the Counter System (ASTOCS). Apart from the investors, the market constituents are counters of members and dealers, registrars and companies. The trading mechanism is easier and is different from the trading outcry method.

Advanced communication network system is adopted to have a nationwide reach enabling widely disbursed trading across the cities. It operates on two main communication networks, viz., Remote Area Business Message Network (RABMN) which is linked to INSAT IB and Interr.. tional Network (INET) which is 20 times faster than RABMN,

OTCEI is a screen based trading system of exchange. All dealers will transact business through the computers from their respective offices or counters. The system is more peep-through in the sense that the investors can have a full ideal about the price their scrips are traded and they can have quotations of their scrips.

OTCEI is a 'Ringless Trading' in the sense that all dealers of it will transact business through the computers' screens by sitting at their counters/offices.

OTCEI is a national exchanges as it has been designed in the lines of NASDAQ system of the USA which is the largest screen based exchanges of that country and the fourth largest exchange in the world.

OTCEI is to list only the small-sized companies of the country. As a core fixed that companies with a paid-up equity share capital of up to Rs. 25 crores (at the time of public issues) will be allowed listing on OTCEI, and which would easily cover all small sized companies.

The unique feature is that it will not list and trade in companies listed on any other exchanges and it will list entirely new set of companies, sponsored by members of the OTCEI.

The market of OTCEI consists of companies, investors, members, licensed dealers. Companies with equity capital of less than Rs. 10 crores closely-held companies, and companies assisted by venture capitalists.

Sponsor

Members on the OTCEI would only be financial institutions, scheduled banks, and banking subsidiaries, Mutual funds, Venture Capital Funds, and SEBI approved Merchant bankers and non-banking financial companies. Members are essentially high net worth entities with a minimum of net worth of Rs. 2.5 crores and are authorised to act as brokers for securities, make market in scrips, and act as sponsors to companies. A sponsor is very important person on OTC stage who is solely responsible for all activities i.e., from appraising to listing and then to trading by giving a certificate to OTC recommending the viability of the project. He has to give 100 per cent financial commitment that in the event of under subscription he will put in the money. Under the sponsorship functions, a member is required to :

(i) appraise the company's management capability;
(ii) appraise the financial and technological viability of the company's project;
(iii) sponsor the scrips to other members/ dealers;
(iv) value the scrips and determine the price;
(v) hold the scrips and later offer it to the public;
(vi) arrange for additional market-maker;
(vii) perform all pre-issue, post-issue functions for listing the company on the OTC; and
(viii) do compulsory market making in the issued scrips for at least 3 years from the date of trading commencement.

Primary Market Operations

The OTCEI will list all categories of securities including equity stock, convertible debentures, partly convertible debentures, redeemable preference shares, cumulative convertible preference shares, bonds, warrants etc., of the companies. The face value of equity shares will be Rs. 10 and that of the company preference shares and debentures will of Rs. 100 and the face value of all of other securities could be of any value decided by the company but usually, it is Rs. 10. The standard lot of securities for trading will be 100. But sometimes, the OTC may permit for non-standard lots for trading purposes giving the option to quote the price to the brokers/dealers for the non-standard lots.

A public new issue on the OTCEI is more or less identical to a public issue on regular stock exchanges and allotment procedures is also same barring a few alternations. The basic change is that companies listed on the OTC prohibited to be listed on any other stock exchange. The provisions of the Companies Act prescribes that allotment or refunds of issues has to be done by companies within 10 weeks from the date of closing of the subscription lists. However, under the guidelines issued by OTCEI, allotment and refunds have to be finalised within 28 days from the date of closure of subscription list. The Share Certificate is not a mercantile documents, it will be kept with the Registrar cum Custodian and as against this, one copy of the Counter Receipt (CR) would be issued to the allottee along with the allotment advice. If the investor so desires, he can obtain Share Certificate in exchange for the CRs at any of the counters of the OTCEI. The CR is a tradable document and shall contain :

(i) Name of the investor, company, number of shares, name and address of the registrars,

(ii) Price, commissions, date and time of the transaction,

(iii) Investor' signature, investors' bank's name and account number; and

(iv) Name and signature of issuing counter.

Four copies of CR will be prepared and sent to Investor Counter, OTCEI and Registrar and to the Investor. The CR will work as document for trading purposes but for other purposes, for instance, to raise loans, share certificate is essential.

Trading at OTCEI Secondary Market Operations

OTCEI promotes companies with a maximum equity capital of Rs. 25 crores. The sponsor ensures underwriting of the issue completely. The sponsor ensures the liquidity of the issue for ensuing three years. Members and dealers on OTCEI conduct market operations during the working hours from 9.30 a.m. to 11.30 a.m. from Monday to Friday. Only registered investors can trade on OTC exchange. On registration the investor will be given a Registration Code which will have to be quoted in all subsequent transactions. The share prices displayed on the PTI-OTC scan are relayed by the PTI computer which disseminates prices received from the OTC Central Computer. The OTC Central Computer will be linked through modems with other network of computers of the different counters. The trading documents of OTC are totally different and have been formulated in a manner so as to facilitate faster movement of papers. And the documentation is also such that a continuous monitoring of transactions is possible. The trading documents are:

(i) Temporary Counter Receipt (TCR);
(ii) Permanent Counter Receipt (PCR);
(iii) Sale Confirmation Slip (SCS);
(iv) Application Acknowledgement Slip (AAS); and
(v) Transfer Deed (TD).

The Mechanism of Purchase : Investor visualises the price on OTC scan placed in the office of every dealer. Investor conveys decision of purchase to the Dealer. The dealer confirms the deal and blocks the scrip on OTC computer. Investor makes a cheque for the amount. Temporary Counter Receipt (TCR) is given to investor. After cheque clearance, Permanent Counter Receipt (PCR) is issued in place of TCR.

Mechanism for Sale : Investor watches price on OTC scan. And conveys the decision to sell to the dealer. Sales Confirmation Slip (SCS) is given by the dealer to investor. Investor gives his PCR and Transfer Deed to the dealer. PCR and TD are validated by the Registrar and a cheque is issued to investor in exchange for SCS.

Benefits

Though the OTC exchange concept is very popular abroad, it is a recent phenomenon and is in the infant stage in our country and is often described as the stock market of tomorrow. It is in the process of renovation and change can be foreseen in stock market along with other components of economic liberalisation in our country. It can be very popular by the very system which is expected to remove certain stigma of the regular stock exchanges created and experienced by the stock exchanges and investing public. It can remove the agonies of small and marginal investors, decrease the high cost public issues. Small companies can easily approach the public through their fresh issue since it is created basically to cater the needs of small companies having paid-up capital of 10 lakhs to 1000 lakhs of rupees.

The benefits are enjoyed by varied parties from the new system of OTCEI, namely, these are enjoyed by :

(i) companies listed on OTCEI;
(ii) benefits are enjoyed by investors; and
(iii) Benefits are enjoyed by general public and the Government.

The benefits which the OTCEI will offer are :

(a) Providing a method of raising funds through capital market instruments which are priced fairly. The company will be able to negotiate the issue price with the sponsors who will market the issue;
(b) Issue costs will be substantially lowered. Issue costs on OTCEI are approximately 5-8 per cent of the issue amount as compared to 13-15 per cent on the regular stock exchanges;
(c) OTCEI saves unnecessary issue expenses on raising funds from capital markets. The method of sponsors placing the scrips with members of OTCEI now will in turn off-load the scrips to public obviating the need for a public issue. Therefore, almost all associated costs will be eliminated;
(d) It is ideal for the companies with issued Capital upto Rs. 25 crores;
(e) National listing is possible in this since it is a single stock exchange having network of exchanges covered by the chain of computers;
(f) It provides greater degree of management stability by listing scrips even with 40 per cent of the capital made available for public trading;
(g) This provides greater accessibility. It will create a nationwide network where investors will be serviced who will form the captive investor base for companies.

Benefits to the Investors : OTCEI's wide network will bring the stock exchanges to every layman. OTCEI provides greater confidence and fidelity of trade. Investor can look at the prices displayed at each OTC counter. The investor knows the price he is trading at the right market price. Investor is happy to settle his transaction more quickly across the OTC counter and return home happily. OTC will provide definite liquidity to investors. The market making system proposed to be introduced in the OTC will have two way prices which are quoted regularly to provide sufficient opportunity for investors to exit. Display of prices and market information at every dealers' counter will allow the investor to make good decision on the very floor of the OTC counter. The investor has wider choice since he gets information. In that manner he feels more secured.

Benefits to the General Business Climate and Government : OTCEI will help spreading the stock exchange operations geographically and link up the various places with the help of national network satellite technique to every place of the country which results into a national forum. OTC encourages closely-held companies to go public. Venture capital activities in our country are expected to get a boost with the avenues for small companies opening up in a big way. By allowing a large number of corporate and financial institutions as members of stock exchanges and also bring about healthy structural changes in the capital market and stock market operation.

Concluding Remarks

OTCEI concept is a great innovation in the India stock market and is a recognised stock exchange under the Securities Contract (Regulations) Act as well as the Indian Companies Act. OTCEI is a computer based screen system exhibiting the quotations of the scrips of the companies of different industries of the nation. It has a national network and there is not geographical barrier for listing. Dealers and investors can decide on the spot and make a deal on the spot more quickly than on the regular stock exchanges. It is a great boon to the small and marginal investors who are greatly neglected till today.

Notes

1. Bhole, L.M., 1994, *Financial Institution and Markets—Structure, Growth and Innovation,* Tata McGraw-Hill Publishing Company Ltd., New Delhi, Second Edition, p. 1.
2. Sadhak, H., 1997, *Mutual Funds in India—Marketing Strategies and Investment Practices,* Response Books, Sage Publications, New Delhi, p. 1.

3. Guerley, J.G and Shaw, E.S., 1955, "Financial Aspects of Development", *American Economic Review*, Vol. 45, pp. 515-538.
4. Kaizuka, K., 1987, "A Comparative Study on Financial Development" in Ryuzo Sato (ed.), "Development in Japanese Economics," Academic Press, TOKYO.
5. Kaufman, K., 1986, *Interest Rates, Markets and New Financial Instruments*, Times Book, New York.
6. Husband, W.H., and Dockerbay, J.C., 1962, "Modern Corporation Finance," R.D. Irwing Inc. Illingis, USA, p. 314.
7. Livingston, F., 1929, "The English Capital Market," Methwen, London.
8. Arun K. Datta, Gupta, 1963, "Government Finance and Capital Market," The Post-Graduate Book Mart, Calcutta, p. 17.
9. CARE, 1996, *Care View—Quarterly-corporate Rating Bulletin*, Mumbai, Vol. 96/3 July-September, p. 3.
10. ICAI, New Delhi, 1997, *Credit Rating*, p. 3.
11. Standard and Poor's.

References

Jerome B. Choen, Edward D. Zinbarg and Arthur Zelkel, 1982, *Investment Analysis and Portfolio Management*, R.D. Irwin, Howewood, Illinois, 4th Edition.

Standard and Poor's Rating Guide, 1979, McGraw-Hill , New York, USA.

Jack Clark Francis, 1986, *Investment Analysis and Management*, McGraw Hill, International Editions, 4th Edition.

Mohansule, 1991, "The Importance of being CRISIL"; *Economic Times*, March.

Economic Survey 1991-92, 1992, "A Special Supplement of Economic Problems and Prospectus"; *Saturday*, February 29.

Ojha, P.D. , 1988, "Capital Market-Emerging Trends", *RBI Bulletin*, January.

Sarkar, A.K., 1994, "Credit Rating in India: A New Feather in the Capital Markets Cap", *The Management Accountant*. ICWAI, Calcutta, July, 496-500.

Mohd. Akbar Alikhan, 1993, "Crisil Rating in India—A New Financial Service in Capital Market", *The Management Accountant*, Calcutta, January, 22-28.

Reserve Bank of India, 1987, "Report of the Working Group on Many Market", Bombay.

Sankar, T.L., Mishra. R.K. and R. Nand Gopal, "Credit Rating—A New Concept in Security Analysis in India", *New Financial Instruments Working Group*, IPE, Osmania University Campus, Hyderbad- 500 007.

CRISIL, 1991, *Monthly Report of CRISIL—Ratings Cal*; Bombay, August.

ICAI, 1997, Credit Rating, Continuing Professional Education Directorate,

The Institute of Chartered Accountants of India, New Delhi.

Dwivedi, J.K., "Book-building : Emerging Scenario in the Indian Capital Market" *Chartered Secretary,* March 1996, Vol. XXVI, No. 3, pp. 266-267.

Parthasarathy, N., "Book-building—An Effective Alternative to High Premium Blue", *The Hindu,* February 11, 1996 (Wednesday), p. 25.

"Guidelines Relating to Book-building Process", *SEBI Guidelines, Taxman's Corporate Laws,* 1996, Taxman Publications, pp. 9, 53-9.65.

Goenka Anurag, "Building Blocks of Book Building", *The Chartered Accountant,* August, 1996, pp. 20-22.

Anupama Reddy, C., "Book Building Battling to Build-up", *Analyst,* September, 1996, pp. 76-68.

CHAPTER EIGHT

Conclusions

Introduction

Mutual Funds of intermediaries between investing public and stock markets who pool vast resources of investors and venture to invest in acquiring shares and securities on behalf of investors. The income so arrived would be distributed among unit holders. Thus, they act as intermediaries. They are created by law, perpetual entities, registered under the existing laws of the country. There are three parties to any mutual fund : trustee company, management company and unit holders. Unit holders are beneficial holders of trust funds. Many mutual funds offer a number of schemes such as, regular income scheme, growth schemes, income and growth schemes, tax planning schemes, etc. In India, mutual funds have come into existence very recently although UTI was incorporated in 1963 as a financial institution. Till 1986, UTI has monopoly in the country. In order to pool resources and saving of household and middle income class of Indian society, Central Government allowed public sector banks and Insurance Sector to enter in mutual fund industry. Later, Government permitted the private sector to take part in mutual fund business. Now, there are eight public sector mutual funds and about 15 private sector funds operating in India.

The *First Chapter* is devoted to a panoramic view on mutual funds touching meaning, concept and definitions of various authorities. Features are highlighted. The regulations of SEBI regarding to mutual funds are explained. Evolution and development of mutual funds in India through different phases has been narrated. Guidelines of Reserve Bank of India and Ministry of Finance are briefed. Role of SEBI in connection with Mutual Funds has been briefed. Role of private sector in the development of mutual fund industry has been emphasized. Various types of mutual funds operating in India are depicted through chart. Regulatory frame of mutual funds in India has been revealed. Different mutual fund schemes are offered to suit the requirements, choices and tastes of investing public. A chart has been developed explaining various funds with their objectives. Distinction between open-ended and close-ended funds has been narrated. Structure of a mutual fund organisation has been explained through chart. The work, role, aims and functions of AMC, Trustees, Sponsor Organisation and Custodian have been explained. A total view on mutual fund industry, Indian financial system, growth of mutual funds has been narrated. Significance of mutual fund has been explained.

The *Second Chapter* highlights on methodology on working of mutual fund organisations in India which covers objectives, hypothesis, design, simple unit, source list, size of sample, non-probability sample, statistical design, period of study and collection of data. The limitation in the present study is that the study has not considered private sector mutual funds. Only Big-Eight mutual fund organisations have been considered for study. In the content, a few terms used have been shown. The present position of all the eight mutual fund organisations have been charted. A comprehensive analysis in form of tables has been summarised.

The *Third Chapter* is devoted to working of mutual funds. It covers all the Big-Eight mutual funds, viz., SBI MF, Canbank MF, BOI MF, PNB MF, Indbank MF, LIC MF, GIC MF and Unit Trust of India. For a detailed study, the public sector mutual funds have been undertaken. The reason is that all these mutual funds offered as many as 133 schemes to the investing public to suit their needs, choices, tastes, time period, risk, growth, liquidity etc. It is understood that Unit Trust of India offered 54 schemes to the public. The second position has been taken by LIC MF offering 18 schemes. SBI MF is sponsored by the State Bank of India. It has been constituted as a trust with the State Bank of India as the principal trustee. An Assets Management Company (AMC) has been formed.

The day-to-day operations are looked after by experienced and qualified professionals consisting of series officials from the State Bank Group as well as directly recruited officials of the AMC. It offered different types of schemes such as Regular Income Schemes, Monthly income schemes, 80 CC Scheme, 80 CCB Schemes, Growth Schemes and Cumulative Income Schemes. A detailed classification and tabulation has been picturised for quick glance and understanding. Canara Bank MF is sponsored by Canara Bank. The basic objective of the Fund is to channelise the savings from a wide cross-section of the people and to provide them attractive returns by way of annual income distribution/capital appreciation by investment in capital market and to provide security and liquidity. The Board of Trustees created Asset Management Company (AMC) to look after management of fund. It has offered different schemes to the investing public. Indian Bank sponsored Indbank MF to pool the savings of lower and middle income groups of India by offering suitable schemes. It has offered different schemes to the investing public. Bank of India sponsored BOI Mutual Fund. BOI Asset Management company limited has been created to operate the fund. The design of various schemes is done by a joint management team. It has issued different types of schemes to attract investing masses.

Punjab National Bank has set-up PNB Mutual Fund in 1990 it has offered different schemes. Life Insurance Corporation of India (LIC) a public sector insurance company has entered into mutual fund industry by creating LIC Mutual Fund. It also set up an Asset Management Company to entrust MF operations and day-to-day management of it. It offered a variety of schemes to suit the choice of investors. General Insurance Corporation of India and its four subsidiaries sponsored GIC MF. It offered different schemes to the investing public. Unit Trust of India was founded in 1963 to start mutual fund business as well as allied services to the vast Indian public. Being a premier organisation in mutual fund industry, it has offered a variety of schemes keeping in view of all categories of Indian citizens. It has successfully offered as many as 54 schemes to the public. The organisation structure, management style, schemes, portfolio management and investment pattern is quite different as that of other Mutual Funds due to its constitution and nature.

Fourth Chapter devotes on 'investment procedure of Mutual

Funds in India variety securities and instruments are available in India to choose. Mutual Funds can chalk out a portfolio by selecting suitable securities for their befitting needs of various schemes. A host of securities are enlisted in Chart 4 A. Types of investments, investment choice and risk are explained'. SEBI guidelines on investment pattern of mutual funds' restrictions, revised and investment norms have been highlighted. Investment mix is analysed. Investment port folio is explained. Aggregate investments of all Mutual Funds, investment pattern of Mutual Funds, investment pattern of individual Mutual Fund have been interpreted and analysed.

Fifth Chapter is devoted to Accounting and Reporting practices in Mutual Funds in India. It covered (1) Legal Aspect, (2) Accounting Aspect, (3) Analysis of Income and Expenses, and (4) Reporting Practices and Disclosure Practices. Various rules and provisions of SEBI, Ministry of Finance, etc. have been adhered to in preparing final accounts of Mutual Funds. Revenue Account and Balance Sheet are the final accounts. Revenue account is comprising of incomes on credit side and expenses on debit side. If credit balance is higher, revenue account indicates net income. Income of a mutual fund comprised of current income, short-term capital gains and long-term capital gains. Mutual Funds disclose all the actual facts and figures in detail and communicate these through periodical reports, annually through audited financial statements and auditor's report, half-yearly unaudited financial statements through dailies, a quarterly statement of movements in net assets for each of the schemes of the mutual fund, a quarterly portfolio statement, including charges from the previous period, for each scheme. For preparation, finalisation, reporting and auditing of mutual fund schemes, the Generally Accepted Accounting Principles of the country are adhered to. Analysis of incomes and expenses are made elaborately. Proformal Balance Sheet and Revenue Account are exhibited. Various schedules have been published. Different types of expenses and their implications have been explained.

The *Sixth Chapter* deals with perceptions. The present study has been undertaken with the object of examining analysing and inferring the perceptions of the investors on mutual funds on different aspects. For the purpose a suitable questionnaire has framed and served to different cross-section of Indian society. On an analysis of the perceptions, the top most popular MF is Unit Trust of India, followed by SBI Mutual Funds. The most popluar financial asset preferred are the products of UTI. The last preferred financial asset is Government bonds. Around 67 per cent concentration of respondents were found in the income class of Rs. 600 per month. A vast majority of respondents chooses close-ended funds as rank Number one followed by Quarterly Regular Income Schemes. Majority of the respondents agreed that Mutual Funds are desirable and necessary for growth of Indian Capital and money market. Majority of respondents showed their willingness to invest their savings on private sector mutual funds. Majority of respondent strongly agree that Mutual Funds should disclose full information in their annual reports. Seventh chapter deals financial system and institutional services.

Scope of Future Research

1. Private Sector Mutual Funds can be undertaken for study.
2. Scheme-wise indebt study can be undertaken.
3. Portfolio analysis on Private Sector Mutual Funds can be made.
4. A comprehensive study on off-shore mutual funds should be made.

Suggestions

1. Uniform accounting period should be adopted, i.e., financial year ended 31st March.
2. Uniform financial statements should be prepared.
3. Uniform schedules should be prepared.
4. Full and standardised disclosure policies should be followed as per the provisions laid by ICAI, New Delhi.
5. Scheme-wise final accounts on uniform basis should be prepared and presented.
6. Consolidated final statement combining all schemes should be made.
7. Investor's services should be improved.
8. Uniformity in methods of valuing investments should be done.
9. Uniform accounting principles for treatment of expenses, provisions, etc., should be made.
10. Full and comprehensive disclosures should be made to

satisfy investing public, government and regulating bodies.

11. An indepth study on UTI can be undertaken.
12. An indepth research may be undertaken on each of the public sector Mutual Fund.
13. A detailed study on Money Market Mutual Funds can be made.
14. An independent study on open-ended schemes of mutual funds can be undertaken.
15. An exclusive study on close-ended schemes of mutual funds can be studied.

Questionnaire

INVESTMENT PATTERN OF HOUSEHOLD SURPLUSES
(With Special Reference to Mutual Funds)

1. Name of the Investor
2. Address
3. Occupation
4. You fall in the annual income group:

Upto 36,000 p.a.	36,000 to 48,000	48,000 to 60,000	60,000 to 75,000	75,000 to 1,00,000	1,00,000 to above

5. Your Household Surplus is:

Less than 5,000	5,000 to 10,000	10,000 to 25,000	25,000 to 50,000	Above 50,000

6. Your Investments:

Less than 5,000	5,000 to 10,000	10,000 to 25,000	25,000 to 50,000	Above 50,000

7. Your Preference for investment:
   (i) Term Deposits
   (ii) Primary Capital Market Investment
   (iii) Secondary Capital Market Investment
   (iv) Mutual Fund
   (v) Life Insurance Scheme
   (vi) Post Office Savings Certificates
   (vii) Private Banking/Financial Institutions
8. What is proportion of investment under different investment avenues, if more than one of them are opted.

9. Which Mutual Fund you prefer:

   (*i*) Sponsored by Financial Institutions
   (*ii*) Sponsored by Commercial Banks
   (*iii*) Sponsored by Private Institutions.

10. What would be your preference for these mutual funds:

   (*a*) (*i*) U.T.I.
   (*ii*) L.I.C.
   (*iii*) G.I.C.
   (*iv*) Others
   (*b*) (*i*) S.B.I.
   (*ii*) P.N.B.
   (*iii*) Indian Bank
   (*iv*) Bank of Baroda
   (*v*) Canara Bank
   (*c*) Private Mutual Funds

11. What is proportion if investment among above Mutual Funds, if you invest in more than one:
12. Which form of mutual fund you will prefer:

   (*i*) Open ended
   (*ii*) Closed ended

13. What is your preference for the following mutual fund scheme:

   (*i*) Income Scheme
   (*ii*) Growth Oriented Scheme
   (*iii*) Income and Growth Scheme
   (*iv*) Balance Scheme
   (*v*) Tax Saving Scheme

14. What is your source of information regarding mutual funds:

   (*i*) Daily Newspaper
   (*ii*) Magazines
   (*iii*) Professional Magazines
   (*iv*) T.V.
   (*v*) Agents
   (*vi*) Friends and Relatives

15. What is your risk resistance:

(i) High risk
(ii) Balanced risk
(iii) Low risk

16. How you would assess the performance of Mutual Fund:

(i) Past performance
(ii) Group Image
(iii) Safety

17. Do you understand the following term generally used with respect to mutual funds :

(i) Net assets value
(ii) Capital appreciations
(iii) Price earning ratio
(iv) Investment Portfolio
(v) Earning per share
(vi) Right Issue
(vii) Bonus Issue

18. What is your preference for investment in following schemes:

(i) Three year closed ended scheme
(ii) Four year closed ended scheme
(iii) Five year closed ended scheme
(iv) Seven year closed ended scheme
(v) Ten year closed ended scheme

19. What would be your preference for the following:

(i) Constant regular income
(ii) Regular income with opportunity of capital appreciation
(iii) Pure capital appreciation'
(iv) Safety of investment

20. What would be your preference for the following facilities offered by the mutual fund:

(i) Repurchase facility
(ii) Loan availing facility
(iii) Easy transferability
(iv) Tax saving
(v) Act these

21. What would be your suggestions preference-wise to improve the working of mutual funds:
    - *(i)* Quick mailing of certificate
    - *(ii)* Transparency and disclosure of accounts
    - *(iii)* Easy and prompt transferability
    - *(iv)* Quick payment of re-purchase price
    - *(v)* Timely payment of annual payments

Bibliography

Ansari, M.N.A., "Mutual Funds in India"—Emerging Trends", *The Chartered Accountant,* August 1993, pp. 88-89, 93.

Agharkar, Ajit and Nadkarni, Shirish, "Mutual Funds on the Move", *Sunday Observer,* July 19, 1987, p. 16.

Arnald, A.A., *Investment Trust Explained,* Association of Investment Trust Companies, II edition, 1983.

Alexander, G.J. and Sharpe, William F., *Fundamentals of Investments,* Prentice Hall Inc., USA, 1989.

Association of Investment Trust Companies., *How to Make It,* Woodhead, 1988.

Agrawal, G.D., "Mutual Funds and Investors Interest", *Chartered Secretary,* January 1992, pp. 23-24.

Agrawal, H.N, "India Capital Market: Present Scenario", *IJC,* June, pp. 1̈4-125.

Ananthakrishnan, E.P., *Mutual Funds,* (CBIEB) *Central Bank of India Economic Bulletin,* 9 (10) October, 1989, pp. 5-7.

Ananil Kumar, Sinha, "Growth of Mutual Funds: An Appraisal", *Management Accountant,* Vol. 26, No. 3, March, 1991, pp. 186-188.

Bansal, L.K., *Mutual Funds: Management and Working,* Deep & Deep Publications, New Delhi, 1996.

Bakshi Vishal, "SEBI Crackdown Soon on Erring Mutual Funds", *The Economic Times,* August 3, 1991.

Bhagat Mukaram, "Mutual Funds: Need for Greater Regulation", *The Economic Times,* November 7, 1989, p. 12.

Bhaskaran, T.S., *Can Times Quarterly News Letter,* from Can bank Mutual Fund, Vol. 1, No. 2, October-December, 1991.

Basu, Debashis, "The New Money Game", *Business Today,* February 22, March 6, 1992, pp. 59-62.

Bhandare Sunil, "Private Sector to Bring in the Competitive Edge", *The Economic Times,* February 27, 1992, p. 12.

Blake, David, *Financial Market Analysis* Mc Graw-Hill Editions, Financial Services, 1992.

Bhatt, R.S., *Financial System for Economic Development*, Indian Investment Centre, (N.M. Tripathi).

Barua, S.K., V. Raghunathan and J.R. Varma, *Port Folio Management*, Tata McGraw Hill, New Delhi. 1996, p. 256.

Bolte E. Steven, *Security Analysis and Portfolio Management*, Holt, Rinehart and Winston Inc., 1972.

Boroson, Warren, *Keys to Investing in Mutual Funds*, Borrons, 1989.

Brouwerkurt, *Mutual Funds—How to Invest with the PROS*, John Wiley & Sons, Inc., USA, 1988.

Boroson, W., *Ultimate Mutual Fund Guide*, Probus Publishing Company, 1993.

Bogle, J.C., Bogle on Mutual Funds, *Business One*, 1994.

Chander Subhash and Mukesh Mahajan, "Perceptions of Investors Towards Mutual Funds: An Empirical Investigation", *IJC*, June, 1992, pp. 117-119.

Cover Story, "Mutual Funds Makers of Future", *Fortune India*, August, 1989, p. 14.

Cooke, T.E., Mat J. and Stoofferd D.C., *Risk, Portfolio Management and Capital Markets*, (Ed.) Perrius Andrew.

CIB Study Test, *Investment*, BPP Publishing House Ltd., London, 1990.

Corner, D.C. and Staffard, D.C., *Open-end Investment Funds in the EEC and Switzerland*, McMillan Press, U.K., 1977.

Christensen, D., *Surviving the Growth Mutual Funds*, Little Brown, 1994.

DAVE, K.J., "Mutual Fund will Dominate the 90s-Towards a Robust Galloping Capital Market", *Money Opportunities*, A Weekly, January 1-7, 1990.

Das Mohapatra, A.K., and R.K. Jena., "Growth and Performance of Mutual Funds in India", *The Utkal Business Review*, Vol. XI, 1992-93, pp. 69-76.

Damayanty, "Mutual Funds", *PNBMR*, 11(7) July, 1989, pp. 378-380.

Dass, Basuder, "Mutual Funds: Promissiong Show", (131), *Business India*, April 3, 1989, pp. 76-82.

Dave, S.A., "Mutual Funds and Offshare Funds in India", *The A.D. Shroff Memorial Trust Publication*, Mumbai, 1991.

Fowler, J.F., American Trusts, Arno Press, 1975.

Fama, E., "Components of Investment Performance", *Journal of Finance*, No. 27, 1972, pp. 551-567.

Fabozzi, Frank J., *Portfolio and Investment Management* (Ed.), Probus Publishing Company, USA, 1989.

Gupta, A.P., "Mutual Funds in India", *IJC*, June, pp. 132-134.

Gangadhar, V., "The Changing Pattern of Mutual Funds in India", *IJC*, March, 1992, pp. 125-133.

Ghosh, Sudeep, "Our Mutual Funds", *Business Standard*, 7th February, 1988, pp. 4-7.

Garodia, Sunil, "Mutual Funds will they Perform", *Facts for You*, March, 1991.

Gopal Madan, "Mutual Funds in India: The Future is Bright", *The Banker*, December, 1990.

Gupta Sen, A.K., "Mutual Funds—Scenario and Strategic Issues", *Banking Finance*, May 1991.

Goyal Madan, "Offshore Country Funds", *The Indian Experience*, State Bank of India Bulletin.

Garodia Sunil, "Mutual Funds: Will they Perform", *Facts for You*, March 1991, p. 27-28.

GIC Mutual Fund Advertisement, *The Economic Times*, 14th October, 1992.

Gupta, L.C., *Mutual Funds Asset Preference*, Society for Capital Markets and Development, New Delhi, 1994.

Grayson, T.J., *Investment*, Wiley, 1978.

Gardner, D.C., "Savings Plans in Unit Trusts", D.C. Gardner, 1992.

Grind Blatt, M., and Titman, S., "A Study of Monthly Mutual Fund Returns and Performance Evaluation Techniques", *Journal of Financial and Quantitative Analysis*, Vol. 18, No. 4, September 1994, pp. 621-32.

Griffeth, B., *The Mutual Fund Masters*, Vision Books, 1997.

Halin, John, *Investors Guide to Mutual Funds*, Prentice Hall, UK, 1988.

Haslem, John A.; *Investors Guide to Mutual Funds*, Prentice Hall, USA, 1988.

Harris, Robert S. and Pringle, John J., *Introducing Corporate Finance*, Scoll, Foresman & Co., USA and UK, 1989.

Haugen, Robert A., *Modern Investment Theory*, Prentice Hall Inc., USA, 1990.

ICI, Money Managers, McGraw-Hill, 1967.

ICI, 1974, Mutual Fund Fact book, ICI, 1974.

ICI, 1994 Mutual Fund Fact book, ICI, 1994.

Jayashree Bose, "Mutual Fund News: The Right Spirit", *Dalal Street Journal*, December 2-5, 1991.

Jham, Mahendra, "Mutual Fund Dominate Capital Market", *Yojana*, July 15, 1991, p. 11.

Joshi, Navin Chandra, "Mutual Funds: Limited Investment Options", *Business Standard,* May 28, 1988, p. 5.

__________, "Mutual Fund and Public", *Financial Express,* November, 29, 1990.

Jyot, Offshore Mutual Funds: Potential Not Fully Explored", *The Economic Times,* Calcutta, 27 February, 1992.

Jensen, M., "Risks, The Pricing of Capital Assets, and The Evaluation of Investment Performance", *Journal of Business,* April, 1969, p. 658.

Joshi, K.B., *Hand Book on Foreign Mutual Funds,* Everest, 1993.

Jacobb, B., *All about Mutual Funds,* Probus Publishing Company, 1994.

Jensen, M.C., "The Performance of Mutual Funds in the Period 1945-1964", *Journal of Finance,* 23, No. 2, 1968, pp. 389-416.

Kasturi Rangachari "Mutual Funds and Investor", *ALIVE,* July 1994, pp. 88-87, (Available in S.K.C.G. College Library).

Kulshreshta, C.M., *Mastering Mutual Funds,* Vision Books, New Delhi, 1994.

Lal, C. and Sharma, Seema, "Mutual Funds—A Buoyant Financial Instrument", *Finance India,* December, 1992, pp. 811-817.

"LIC Mutual Fund: Banking Finance", January, 1990.

"LIC Mutual Fund: Banking Finance", January, 1991

"LIC Mutual Fund: A Rural Thought", *Business India,* July 10-23, 1989.

Lal, C. and Seema, Sharma, "Performance of Indian Offshore Mutual Funds—An Appraisal", *Banking Finance,* April 1992; pp. 5-6.

Laderman, J.M., *Business Week's Mutual Guide to Mutual Funds,* McGraw-Hill, 1991.

__________, "Guide to Mutual Funds", McGraw-Hill.

Lavine, Alam, *50 Ways of Mutual Fund Profits,* Vision Books, New Delhi, 1997.

Mannar, A.G., "Mutual Fund Scheme and Banks: An Overview", *CBIER,* 8 (7) , July, 1988, pp. 5-8.

Mishra, Loknath, "Mutual Funds and Banks", *IOBMNR* (India Over-seas Bank Monthly News Review), 2 (2), February, 1988, pp. 3-11.

Mishra, Prakash Chand and G. P. Acharya, "Mutual Funds—Implications and Issues", *The Journal of Business Studies,* Vol. 2, 1993, P.G. Dept. of Commerce, Revenshah College, Cuttack, pp. 54-59.

Mutual Fund Income and Investor Taxation, *E.T.,* 24 February 1992, p. 22.

"Mutual Funds and Units: Uniform Legislation Needed", *E.T.,* December, 1987, p. 5.

"Mutual Funds: More Pros than Cons?" *ABABJ*, 79 (4), April, 1987, pp. 33-38.

Murphy, J.J., *Inter Market Technician—A Technical Approach to Inter Market Trading—Analysis and Port Folio Management*, New York Institute of Finance, 1989.

Meyers, Thomas A., *The Technical Analysis Course*, Probus Publishing Co., USA, 1994.

Nabhi Kumar Jain, *Manual of SEBI Guidelines on Capital Issues*, Merchant Banking and Mutual Funds, 1993 Edition.

Narayanan, S., "Mutual Funds and Insurance Covers", *Investment Week*, Vol. 4, No. 3, January, 1994, pp. 17-23.

"A Big Help for Small Investors", *Dalal Street Journal*, August 13-26, 1990.

"PNB Mutual Fund Floats Two New Investor Schemes", *E.T.*, November 30, 1991.

"Private Mutual Funds May be Delayed", *Economic Times*, 25 May, 1992, pp. 1-4.

Piramal, Gita, "Offshore Mutual Funds: The Discovery of India", *The Economic Times*, December 8, 1989, p. 3.

Perritt, Gerald W., *The Mutual Fund Enclopaedia*, 1992-93, Dearbarn, Financial Publishing Inc., 1993.

Quintin, P., *Warrants, Options in Convertibles*, IFR Publishing Ltd., UK, 1990.

Raghavan, R., "Mutual Funds—Global Marketing and Distribution", *Fortune India*, October 1, 1990, p. 7.

Rajshekar B. Hema, "Mutual Funds: Stirring in the Market", *The Economic Times*, January 16, p. 6.

Ananthakrishnan, E.P., "Mutual Funds", *(CBIEB) Central Bank of India Economic Bulletin*, 9 (10) October 1989, pp. 5-7.

Raj, Mulk and Vij, Rajiv., "Household Savings and the Mastershare", *F.E.*, November. 26, 1986, pp. 5, 6.

Rao, K.V., "Mutual Fund: An Instrument Full of Promise", B.S., December 25, 1987, p. 5.

Ross, Joel, *Mutual Funds: Taking the Worry Out of Investing*, Prentice Hall, 1988.

Robert Harris and John J. Pringle, *Introductory Corporate Finance, Scott*, Foresman & Co., USA, 1989.

Ritchie, John G. Jr., *Fundamental Analysis*, Probus Publishing Co., USA, 1989.

Richard B. Toolson, "Strategies for Buying and Selling Mutual Funds", *Journal of Accountancy*, October 1992, pp. 37-48.

Renberg, Werner and Blitzel Jeremiah, *Making Money with Mutual Funds—Investment Strategies to Beat the Market*, Wiley, New York, 1988.

Richard, Dorf, *The New Mutual Fund Investment Advisor: A Guide for the Serious Investor*, Probus Publishing Co., Chicago, 1988.

Sinha, Anil Kumar, "Growth of Mutual Funds: An Appraisal", *The Management Accountant*, March, 1991, pp. 186-188.

Sarkar, A.K., "Mutual Funds in India—Emerging Trends", *The Management Accountant*, March, 1991, pp. 171-174.

Sahu, M. and R.K. Jena, "Emerging Scenario of Mutual Funds and Investors Perception in India," *IJC*, December, 1992, pp. 77-85.

________, "New Financial Instruments in Mobilising Household Savings —A Study of Mutual Fund", *A Project Report*, IIM, Ahmedabad.

Straley, John A., *What about Mutual Fund,* Harper and Row Publishing House, New York, 1969.

Sahu, M., and P.K. Pradhan, "Role of Mutual Funds in Mobilising House Hold Savings", *The Utkal Business Review*", Vols. V– VII, 1988-89, pp. 24-29.

Sen Gupta, A.K., "Mutual Funds—Scenario and Strategic Issues."

Sanjiv Agrawal, *A Manual of Indian Capital Market;* Agrawal Infin Consultants Pvt. Ltd., Jaipur; 1993 Edition.

Sadak, H., "Investment Practices of Mutual Funds Abroad", *Financial Express*, January, 15, 1994, p. 5.

Sadak, H., *Mutual Funds in India*, Sage Publications, New Delhi, 1997.

Shukla, Sharad, "Mutual Funds: Past Performance is No Indicator of the Future", *The Economic Times*, June 1, 1992.

Sabnavis, Madan, "Baning on Mutual Funds", *F.E*, August, 31, 1989, p. 7.

Satyajit Dhar, "Mutual Funds in India—A Close Look", *Finance India*, September, 1994, Vol. VIII, No. 3, pp. 674-679.

Sood, G.S., "Mutual Funds to Boost Capital Markets", *F.E.*, October 5, 1987, pp. 7, 9.

Sundaram, S.M. and D. Ramesh, "Mutual Funds in Private Sector", *E.T.*, April 23, 1987., p. 9.

Sharpe, William F., "Mutual Fund Performance", *Journal of Business*, 39, No. 1, (January 1966), pp. 119-138.

Treynor, J.L., "How to Rate Management of Investment Funds", *Harvard Business Review*, 43, No. 1, 1965, pp. 63-75.

Treynor, J.L., and Kay K. Mazny, "Can Mutual Funds Outguess the Market"? *Harvard Business Review*, 44, No. 4 (July-August) 1966, pp. 131-136.

UTI Capital Markets, Bombay, Introduction to Technical Analysis, December 26-30, 1994.

Vyas, B.A., "Mutual Funds-Boom to the Common Investors, *Fortune India*, July 16, 1990, p. 29.

Vachratith, Viraphong, "Mutual Funds in Thailand", *BBMR* (Bangkok Bank Monthly Review", 29(8), August, 1988, pp. 330-336.

Warner, U.A., "Aggregate Mutual Fund Flows and Security Returns", *Journal of Financial Economics*, Vol. 39, Nos. 2-3, October 1995, pp.209-35.

Index

Accounting
____Cycle 122
____Cycle of Mutual Fund 122
____for the Mutual Fund Schemes 120
____Principle of the Country 242
____Policies of a Concern 144
____Year 121
Accounts of Mutual Fund 145
Advanced Communication Network System 231
Aggregate Investment of All Mutual Fund 110
All India Development and Financial Institutions 218-19, 221
AMC-Objectives 17
Annual Report of Big-Eight Mutual Fund 132
Annual Report of Mutual Fund 121
ASG 186-87
Asian Development Bank 186
Assessment Management Company (AMC) 9, 15-17, 23, 46-47, 58, 60, 78-79, 82-83, 105-06, 121, 240-41
Asset Value of Shares 41
ASTOCS 231
Automatic Reinvestment of Income 39
Average Weighted Scores 150, 153-54, 159

Balance Sheet and Revenue Account 144
Bank of India Mutual Fund 71-73
____Investment Pattern 114
____Schemes 74-76
Banking System in India 162
Bholey, L.M. 161
Big-Eight
____Break-up of 38, 44
____Break-up Capital 39
____Public Sector Mutual Fund 33
Board of SBI Management 46
Bombay Stock Exchange 139
Book-Building 201-03, 205, 211
____Benefits of 209-10
____Process of 204
____Runner 205-08
Brokers and Dealers 229
Budding Concept to India 202
Business Analysis 193

Canara Bank Mutual Fund 59-60, 113
Capital
____Gains Scheme 67
____Gains Unit 86
Capital Market
____Constituents 166
____and Financial Market in India 146
____Segment 177
____Structure 171
CARE 188
Catalyst for Economic and Industrial Growth of India 33
Category of Financial Institutions 163
Characteristics of Mutual Fund of

USA and UK 85
Commercial Banks 163, 221
Companies Act 121-22, 208
Compound Annual Growth Rate (CAGR) 40, 53, 58
Concept of Accounting Policy 122
Controller of Capital Issue 7
Credit Rating
____Agencies 184, 190, 194
____Classification 191-92
____Conceptual View 189
____Features of 190
____in India 184
____Information Services in India (CRISIL) 184-87
____Merits 196
____Methodology 193
____Significance 194
____Symbols 222-28
Custodial Services in India 197-98
Custodian 23

Dave, Panel Recommendation 110
____S.A. 8-9, 85
Debt Market Segment 177
Debt Market Segment (Wholesale) 179
Deep Discount Bond 180
Deferred Revenue Expenditure 141-42
Definition of Mutual Fund 31
Designated Branches of Nationalised Banks 83
Development of Venture Capital Concept 216
DICGC 216
Doriot, General 213
Dun, Robert 183
Dynamic Financial Intemediaries 164

Eight Mutual Fund Organisation 86
Equity Shares 102, 109
European Venture Capital Association 214

Factors Affecting Investors Choice of Mutual Fund Organisation 151-52
Features of Mutual Fund 4
Financial Advisory Services 186
____Institutions 161, 163, 183
____Institutions (Sectoral) 164
____Intemediaries 33, 103
____System in India 163, 168
____System of any Nation 161
Foreign Institutional Investors 197-200
Functions of Mutual Fund 3

General Insurance Corporation of India (GIC) 6
Generally Accepted Accounting Principle 144
Geographic Spread of Individual Household 149
GIC Investment Pattern 117
____Mutual Fund 82, 117
____Portfolio 117
Government of India and Companies Act 122
Growth of Indian Money Market 156
Guerley and Show 162
Guidelines for Mutual Funds 119

Household Classification Income Basis 150
Household Sector 101
Husband and Dockerbay 165

ICICI 184-85
Idea of Mutual Fund 5
Imperial Bank of India 44
Important Factors of Production 182
Income Generated by All Mutual Funds 103-31
Indian
____Bank Mutual Fund 64-65
____Capital Market 28, 156, 201, 210
____Capital and Money Market 160
____Companies Act 221
____Growth Fund 8
____Household Sector 101

Indian Mutual Fund Industry 146, 153
____Stock Exchange 139
____Trust Act (1882) 6, 71
Individual Performance of Mutual Fund 130-31
Initial Issue of Units 142
International Finance Corporation 216
Investible Funds 27, 29
Investment
____Advisor 35
____Companies 2
____in Debentures and Bonds 109
____in Govt. Securities 115-16
____Pattern of UTI Mutual Fund 108
____Policy of Mutual Fund 108
____Scarce Resources 101
____in Security Transactions 47
____Trust 5
Inventors Grievances Cell 180
Investors in a Mutual Fund Schemes 4
Items of Indirect Expenses 144

Judicious Investment Pattern of Mutual Fund 105

Kaizuka 163
Kaufman 163
Krishnamachari T.T. 5, 24-25

LIC and GIC 27
LIC Investment Policy 115
____Mutual Fund 44, 78-79
____Portfolios 115
____Scheme 80-81
Livingstone 165

Magnum Regular Income Scheme (MRIS) 47, 53, 58, 87
Major Assets in UTI Portfolios 117
Management Information System 7
Meaning of Mutual Fund 4
Money Market Instruments 106-07, 111
Monopoly of Big-Eight 8-9
Moody, John 183
Most Bought out Deals by Indian Corporate 210
Mutual Fund
____Growth 27-28, 30-31
____Industry 24-25, 130
____Scheme 12-13
____Various Sources of Income 124
Mutual Funds in India 5

NASDAQ System 230
NAV (Net Asset Value) 120, 145
National Characteristics 172
____Market System 167, 171
____Objectives 172
____Three Tier Structure 172
National Stock Exchange 139, 167, 171, 173, 177-78, 180
National Stock Exchange of India Limited (NSEIL) 173, 178, 181
NBFCS 199
NBFCSIs 162
Nehru, Pandit Jawaharlal 84
NIFTY 179-80
Non-Banking Financial Institutions 162
Non-Intermediary Institutions 162

Objectives of Mutual Fund 18
____Portfolio Management 105
Opinion of Investors Towards Mutual Funds 157-58
Origin of Venture Capital 213
OTC Exchange 233-34
OTCEI 167, 171, 228, 230-33
____Concept 236
____New System of 235

PACT of ICICI 217
Pattern of All Mutual Funds 110
Performal Balance-Sheet and Revenue Account 242
Pherwani Committee 171, 229
PNBMF 76-78, 114
____Scheme 76
Primary Market Fund Manager 93-94

Principal Stock Exchanges 172
Private Sector Mutual Fund 154
Products of SBIMFs 47
Promotion and Regulation of Capital Markets 8, 25
Promotion of Venture Capital 217
Public Sector Banks 6
Public Sector and Private Sector 229

RABMN 231
RBI 5-6, 44, 71, 85, 108
____Guidelines 7, 240
Redemption Prices 39
Registrar of Companies (ROC) 206-07
Regular Income Scheme 153
Reilly, K. Frank 2, 102
Revenue Account 132-33, 139-40, 142
Revenue Account, Usual Contents 132
Ross, Joel 3

Sadhak, K. 161
SBI 6, 44, 46-47, 58, 219, 243
SBIMF at a Glance 50-57
Schemes of Can Bank MF 60-63
Schemes of Mutual Fund 12-15, 44
SEBI
____Act 165
____Guidelines 106-07, 207-08
____Objective 164
____Regulation'93 16, 78, 106, 120, 123, 144, 200, 239
Security Contracts Regulation Act 167
____Market of India 169
Security and Exchange Board of India (SEBI) 6-9, 21, 25, 71-72, 106, 120-21, 142, 165, 196, 198-99, 211
Significance of Mutual Fund 27-28, 30
Singh, Man Mohan (Dr.) 8
Societies, Financirs d' Innovation (SFI) 214
Soro Fund Management USA (SFM) 83
Structure of Mutual Fund 22
Suppliers of Indirect Financing 162

Tappan, Louis 183
Trade for Trade 178-79
Trading Documents 234
Trust Deed 23
Trustee Management System 197
Types of Investments 103-04
Types of Mutual Fund 10

ULIP 71 27, 86, 94
Unit Scheme-1964 5, 24
Unit Trust of India 5-6, 8-9, 24-26, 35, 40, 49, 85-86, 94, 108, 110, 124, 146-48, 197, 239, 241
Unit Trust Prices 40
Unlisted Securities Market 24
UTI Act 63 85, 93
____Investment Fund 97
____Mutual Fund 84
____MF Schemes 95-96
____Policy 118
Useful Tool for Management Bankers 194

Variable Risk 104
Variety of Financial Instruments 105
VCF 212 17, 19, 21
____Classification 220
Venture Capital 212-13, 215
Venture Capital-Activities 213-14
Venture Capital Companies 217
Venture Capital Feature 212
Venture Capital-Industrial Activities 221
Venture Capital-Industry, 215-17
Venture Capital-Promotion of 217
Venture Capitalist 218

Wholesale Debt Market 179